Social and Cognitive Approaches to Interpersonal Communication

Social and Cognitive Approaches to Interpersonal Communication

Edited by

Susan R. Fussell
Carnegie Mellon University

Roger J. Kreuz
The University of Memphis

LEA   LAWRENCE ERLBAUM ASSOCIATES, PUBLISHERS
1998   Mahwah, New Jersey   London

Lawrence Erlbaum Associates, Inc., Publishers
10 Industrial Avenue
Mahwah, NJ 07430

Cover design by Kathryn Houghtaling Lacey

Library of Congress Cataloging-in-Publication Data

Social and cognitive approaches to interpersonal communication /
edited by Susan R. Fussell and Roger J. Kreuz.
p. cm.
Includes bibliographical references and indexes.
ISBN 0–8058–2269–0 (cloth : alk. paper). —
ISBN 0–8058–2270–4 (pbk. : alk. paper)
1. Interpersonal communication. 2. Cognition. 3. Psycholinguistics. I. Fussell, Susan R. II. Kreuz, Roger J.
BF637.C45S63 1997
302.2—dc21 97–21638
CIP

Books published by Lawrence Erlbaum Associates are printed
on acid-free paper, and their bindings are chosen for strength
and durability.

The final camera copy for this work was prepared by the
author, and therefore the publisher takes no responsibility for
consistency or correctness of typographical style.

Printed in the United States of America
10 9 8 7 6 5 4 3 2 1

To Bob Krauss, friend and mentor, for stimulating my interest in the interplay between social and cognitive processes in interpersonal communication, and to Nick, for his support throughout this and all my other projects.

SRF

To James K. Larson, for his encouragement and support.

RJK

Contents

PART III: PERSPECTIVE–TAKING AND CONVERSATIONAL COLLABORATION

PART IV: COGNITION, LANGUAGE AND SOCIAL INTERACTION

Contributors

Susan E. Brennan
Department of Psychology
SUNY—Stony Brook
Stony Brook, NY 11794.

Chi-yue Chiu
Department of Psychology
The University of Hong Kong
Pokfulam Road, Hong Kong.

Lori Coppenrath
Department of Psychology
The University of Memphis
Memphis, TN 38152.

Susan R. Fussell
Human-Computer Interaction Inst.
Carnegie Mellon University
5000 Forbes Avenue,
Pittsburgh, PA 15213.

Raymond W. Gibbs, Jr.
Department of Psychology
Clark Kerr Hall
University of California
Santa Cruz, CA 95064.

Thomas M. Holtgraves
Department of Psychological Science
Ball State University
Muncie, IN 47306.

Max A. Kassler
Bell Communications Research
33 Knightsbridge Road
Piscataway, NJ 08854.

Boaz Keysar
Department of Psychology
University of Chicago
5848 South University Avenue
Chicago, IL 60637.

Robert M. Krauss
Department of Psychology
Columbia University
116th Street and Broadway
New York, NY 10027.

Roger J. Kreuz
Department of Psychology
The University of Memphis
Memphis, TN 38152.

Ivy C-M. Lau
Department of Psychology
The University of Hong Kong
Pokfulam Road, Hong Kong.

Mallie M. Moss
Department of Psychology
University of Nebraska-Lincoln
P.O. Box 880308
Lincoln NE 68588-0308.

Michael F. Schober
Department of Psychology
New School for Social Research
65 5th Avenue
New York, NY 10003.

Norbert Schwarz
Institute for Social Research
University of Michigan
Ann Arbor, MI 48106.

Gün R. Semin
Social Psychology Department
and Kurt Lewin Graduate School
Free University of Amsterdam
van der Boechorststraat 1
1081 BT Amsterdam.
The Netherlands.

PART I

Introduction and Background

— 1 —

Social and Cognitive Approaches to Interpersonal Communication: Introduction and Overview

Susan R. Fussell **Roger J. Kreuz**

Carnegie Mellon University *The University of Memphis*

Any utterance, from a simple "uh huh" to an hour-long lecture, is the complex output of a variety of psychological processes—formulating what to say, selecting the right words, monitoring the effects of the message on the audience, and so forth (Levelt, 1989). Likewise, any act of message interpretation is based on both psycholinguisticprocesses (e.g., lexical retrieval, syntactic processing) and social-interactional factors such as beliefs about what a speaker is trying to achieve by his or her message (Gernsbacher, 1994). Historically, the social aspects of language use have fallen in the domain of social psychology, and the underlying psycholinguistic mechanisms have been the purview of cognitive psychology. In recent years, however, it has become increasingly clear that these components of language use are highly interrelated: Cognitive mechanisms underlying speech production and comprehension interact with social psychological factors—such as beliefs about interlocutors and politeness norms—and with the dynamics of the conversation itself, to produce shared meaning. This realization has led to an exciting body of research examining how social and cognitive aspects of language use interact to affect interpersonal communication and to substantial progress in understanding the content and processes underlying language use.

This volume aims to show that the cross-fertilization of theories and findings from social, and cognitive psychology has proved extremely fruitful for understanding many aspects of human language use. Each of the four sections of the book illustrates this theme as it applies to such topics as people's intentions or goals when using language, the role of language in research settings, indirect and figurative language, perspective-taking and conversational interaction, and the relationship between language and cognition .

In this chapter, we first discuss the scope and aims of the book. Then, we outline some basic themes and historical influences on the work presented in the ensuing chapters. As will be seen, many of these influences arise from fields other than psychology—ordinary language philosophy, conversational analysis, and sociolinguistics—and much research can be viewed as an attempt to empirically test ideas and findings from other fields in an experimentally rigorous fashion. Finally, we provide a brief overview of each chapter with an emphasis on how it embodies the book's goal of integrating social and cognitive approaches to interpersonal communication.

THE SCOPE OF THE BOOK

The field of interpersonal communication is clearly immense, and comprehensive coverage of all approaches to this topic would far exceed the page limitations of this book. The decision to select contributors for such a volume is difficult and necessarily entails a focus on some aspects of communication at the expense of others. In this section we briefly describe the ways in which we have limited the content of this volume and the motivations behind our decisions.

Verbal Communication

Collecting contributions from psychologists whose theories and research focus on the production and comprehension of *verbal* language was our obvious way of limiting the scope of this volume. Although individual chapters discuss the relationship between verbal communication and closely aligned disciplines, such as nonverbal communication, paralinguistics, decision making, memory, and norms of social interaction, all contributions share a primary focus on spoken or written language. It should be emphasized that this limitation is not meant to imply that we consider nonverbal and paralinguistic phenomena to be of lesser importance to interpersonal communication; rather, it reflects our goal of illustrating the many ways a joint social–cognitive approach can be usefully applied to a relatively narrow set of research problems

Experimental Research Paradigms

A second way we limited the scope of this volume was to solicit contributions that discuss *experimental research* on language use and understanding, as opposed to case studies, observational research, or purely theoretical discussions. This decision was motivated by our desire to provide a body of work illustrating the strengths of experimental psychological research for answering key questions regarding human communication. Thus, this volume makes an excellent companion for recent volumes that focus on alternative approaches to communication (e.g., Carter & Presnell, 1994; Coulthard, 1992; Leeds-Hurwitz , 1995; Markova & Foppa, 1990) and fleshes out other volumes that contain a variety of approaches (e.g., Hewes, 1995; Slobin, Gerhardt, Kyratzis & Guo, 1996).

Although all contributors use experimental methods, the topics they address and thus the research paradigms they have developed are by no means identical. An understanding of any complex process, of which interpersonal communication is an example *par excellence*, requires a variety of converging methodologies. The studies described in the chapters of this book differ in their focus on conversational roles (message initiator, recipient, or both), modality of communications (written, spoken, computer-mediated), level of analysis (words, sentences, conversational exchanges), and research strategies (audio- and video-taped conversations, vignette studies, on-line reaction time studies, and so forth). Readers can glean insight into both common and novel experimental approaches to communication by glancing though the methodological descriptions in each chapter.

THEMES AND HISTORICAL INFLUENCES

Krauss and Fussell (1996) identified four basic models or sets of theoretical assumptions that have guided much of the research on interpersonal communication: *Encoder–Decoder* models, *Intentionalist* models, *Perspective-taking* models, and *Dialogic* models . These models differ in their assumptions about how meaning arises from language use: For Encoder–Decoder models, meaning is a property of messages; for Intentionalist models it resides in speakers' intentions; for Perspective-taking models it derives from an addressee's point of view; and for Dialogic models it is an emergent property of the participants' joint activity. Each contribution to this volume, although perhaps more closely aligned to some models than to others, can be viewed as an effort toward a hybrid theory of interpersonal communication that takes into account what has been learned from all these approaches. Although the contributors address different topics from different theoretical angles, it is possible to identify several interrelated themes or assumptions that run through most if not all chapters. We outline these themes briefly in this section.

Communication Involves the Exchange of Communicative Intentions

Most contributions to this volume can each be viewed as stemming, either directly or indirectly, from the view that successful communicationentails the exchange of *communicative intentions* (Grice, 1957, 1969). In this view, words do not have a one-to-one relationship to the ideas a speaker is attempting to express; rather, a single utterance, such as "It's cold in here," can convey a range of meanings (e.g., a statement about weather conditions or a request to close the door), and a single meaning can be expressed in a potentially infinite number of ways. Consequently, listeners must go beyond the literal meaning of a message to derive the speaker's intended meaning. Clarification of when, why and how they do so is a goal of chapters throughout this volume.

Communication is Goal-Directed

Austin (1975) observed that many utterances can be described as *acts* on a speaker's part (e.g., questions, promises, demands). Similarly, Searle's *Speech Act Theory* (Searle, 1969, 1975) distinguished between three rather different types of acts that an utterance can be designed to achieve: a *locutionary* act (the act of uttering a specific sentence with a specific conventional meaning), an *illocutionary* act (the act of demanding, promising, etc. through the use of a specific locution), and a *perlocutionary* act (an attempt to achieve a verbal or behavioral response from the addressee). For example, "It's cold in here" is a locutionary act that is a statement about the weather; but as an illocutionary act, it might be a request to close the door, and as a perlocutionary act, it might be an attempt to get the listener to close the door. Why speakers decide to create one type of speech act versus another and the mechanisms underlying listeners' understanding of these speech acts is a topic of several chapters.

Communication is a Cooperative Endeavor

Grice (1975) proposed that conversation be viewed as a cooperative endeavor. Even when their purpose is to dispute, criticize, or insult, communicators must shape their messages to be meaningful to their addressees. To do so, Grice proposed, they follow a general *Cooperative Principle* comprised of four basic rules. Grice termed these rules *Conversational Maxims*: Messages should be consistent with the maxims of *quality* (be truthful), *quantity* (contain neither more nor less information than is required); *relation* (be relevant to the ongoing discussion); and *manner* (be brief and unambiguous). Grice argued that even in the face of apparent violations, communicators typically assume that the cooperative principle holds and seek to interpret messages in a way that resolves these apparent violations. The various chapters in this volume address such issues as what motivates speakers to create utterances that on the surface violate the Cooperative Principle and how listeners understand these violations in both conversational settings and special circumstances such as laboratory settings and human–computer interaction.

Communication Consists of Ordered Exchanges
Between Speaker and Listener

A fourth major influence on the work presented in this volume stems from *conversational analysis,* a field that focuses on the structure of conversation (e.g., Atkinson & Heritage, 1984; Drew & Heritage, 1992; Jefferson, 1975; Sacks, Schegloff, & Jefferson, 1974; Schegloff, 1982; Schegloff, Jefferson, & Sacks, 1977). Conversational analysts have demonstrated that conversations consist of orderly sequences of utterances (such as question–answer pairs); others have argued that alternative forms of communication, such as writing, follow the same orderly organization (Bakhtin, 1981). Many of the conversation analysts' theoretical ideas have been formulated in psychological terms by Clark and Wilkes-Gibbs (1986, Wilkes-Gibbs & Clark, 1992) in their influential *Collaborative Theory* of communication, which assumes that speakers and hearers work jointly to ensure that a message is understood. The influence of this model on current research and theory in the psychology of interpersonal communication can be seen throughout this volume.

Communication is Socially-Situated

Finally, in keeping with the overall theme of this volume, contributors' chapters illustrate the many ways in which language use is socially-situated. For example, Brown and Levinson's (1987) theory of politeness, which states that the indirectness of a message is a function of the relative status and social distance of communicators, plays a strong role in Holtgraves' contribution (Chap. 4). In addition, the assumption that communicators tailor speech to their addressees (e.g., Bakhtin, 1981; Brown , 1965; Clark & Marshall, 1981; Coupland, Coupland, Giles & Henwood, 1988; Krauss & Fussell, 1991; Mead, 1934; Rommetveit, 1974; Volosinov, 1986) is the subject of an entire section of this book. Many of the contributions can be viewed as attempts to delineate precisely *how* social factors, such as to whom one is speaking, influence language production and comprehension.

OVERVIEW OF CHAPTERS

Although all contributors to this book combine elements of both social and cognitive psychology in their studies and theories of interpersonal communication, the particular ways they do so and the types language phenomena on which they concentrate vary substantially. The grouping of the chapters into four sections is meant to relect these differences in approach; however, it should be noted that there is much overlap between sections and many chapters could have been placed in more than one part of the book. Below, we briefly describe these four sections and the chapters they contain.

Section I, *Introduction and Background*, includes two chapters, in addition to this introductory one, which form a foundation for later sections of the book. Both are sophisticated extensions of Grice's (1957, 1969, 1975) seminal formulations of speaker intentions and the Cooperative Principle, one with respect to the concept of intentionality itself and the other with respect to how speaker intentions and the cooperative principle influence research participants' responses in experimental and survey settings.

In Chapter 2, *The Varieties of Intentions in Interpersonal Communication*, Raymond W. Gibbs, Jr. analyzes in detail the concept of *intention* in communication. As Gibbs points out, intentionality plays an important role in many discussions of interpersonal communication, including those in this volume, and a person's knowledge that he or she is interacting with an intentional agent affects how a message is understood (Gibbs, Kushner & Mills, 1991). Yet, he argues, our present understanding of intentions, especially communicative intentions, is rather limited. Gibbs stresses that speakers can have both different levels and different kinds of intentions when they create a message, and he carefully delineates several types. He also tackles other thorny issues, including the role of intentions in nonverbal communication and in art and cultural and medium differences in identifying speaker intentions. Of particular interest is his discussion of collective intentions, or *we–intentions* (Searle, 1990)—communicative intentions that are created through collaborative interaction between speaker and listener. Gibbs stresses the need for new research paradigms to study these and other issues concerning the role(s) of intentions in communication.

In Chapter 3, *Communication in Standardized Research Situations: A Gricean Perspective,* Norbert Schwarz draws important implications from Grice's (1975) theory of cooperative discourse for laboratory and survey research procedures and for interpretation of results. Schwarz argues that despite the standardization of research procedures, which minimizes the extent to which experimenters and participants can negotiate meaning, subjects rely on the same comprehension and interpretation strategies that they use in ordinary conversation to infer how they should respond. Specifically, participants assume (often erroneously) that experimenters' messages will follow Grice's Cooperative Principle and be informative, relevant, truthful, and succinct. Schwarz then details how subjects' reliance on the Cooperative Principle influences their responses to surveys and experimental materials. Schwarz convincingly demonstrates that Gricean implicatures are at least partially responsible for findings that seemingly reflect human errors in judgment, such as the fundamental attribution error (Ross, 1977) and under-reliance on base-rate information (Tversky & Kahneman, 1974).

The chapters in Section II, *Indirect Speech and Figurative Language,* address how people produce and understand messages in which the actual words uttered do not directly reflect speakers' intentions. The original claim (Grice, 1975; Searle, 1975) that indirect meanings are derived in part from literal meaning has been examined in a number of studies, the results of which clearly indicate that in many circumstances nonliteral language requires no more time or effort to understand than does literal language (Gibbs, 1983, 1986; Glucksberg, Gildea & Bookin, 1982). In recent years, research has focused on social and cognitive factors underlying specific types of indirect speech, such as indirect requests (e.g., Gibbs, 1979, 1983; Holtgraves, 1986, 1994), metaphor (e.g., Gibbs, 1987; Gibbs et al., 1991; Glucksberg, 1989; Glucksberg et al., 1982; Keysar, 1989) and idioms (e.g., Gibbs, 1980, 1986; Gibbs & Gonzales, 1985; Gibbs & O'Brien, 1990; for recent reviews see Cacciari & Glucksberg, 1994; Gibbs, 1994a, 1994b; Kreuz & Roberts, 1993). The focus, however, has typically remained on message comprehension rather than message production; many types of indirect speech have been neglected (e.g., indirect disagreements, exaggeration, understatement); and most research has ignored the ways in which social and contextual factors affect the production and comprehension of nonliteral language. The chapters in this section attempt to redress the previous dearth of research in one or more of these areas.

Chapter 4, *Interpersonal Foundations of Conversational Indirectness,* by Thomas M. Holtgraves, addresses the role of social context and politeness conventions in the production and comprehension of indirect speech (e.g., "It's cold in here" versus "Shut the door"). Holtgraves observes that Grice's (1975) classic discussion on understanding indirect speech in light of the conversational maxims of quantity, quality, relation, and manner is limited in that it neglects the reasons *why* speakers choose to violate these maxims. In the first half of his chapter, Holtgraves discusses how social goals, particularly face management concerns (Brown & Levinson, 1987; Goffman, 1967) determine decisions about when, why, and how to speak indirectly. He then reviews research on two types of indirect speech: requests and disagreements. In the second half of his chapter, Holtgraves explores the intriguing two-sided relationship between social–interpersonal factors and the comprehension of indirect speech acts. On the one hand, knowledge of social and contextual variables such as speaker status influences both the speed at which indirect speech acts are understood (Holtgraves, 1994) and how they are interpreted. On the other hand, listeners draw inferences about others' status, personality, motives, goals, and so forth from indirect messages themselves (Holtgraves & Yang, 1990).

In Chapter 5, *The Use of Exaggeration in Discourse: Cognitive and Social Facets*, Roger J. Kreuz, Max A. Kassler, and Lori Coppenrath discuss how hyperbolic statements in discourse may be constrained by pragmatic influences. As they point out, there has been little or no empirical research on hyperbole despite its frequency in conversation and in written language (Kreuz, Roberts, Johnson, & Bertus, 1996) and its role in the interpretation of other forms of indirect speech such as irony (Roberts & Kreuz, 1994). Kreuz et al. observe that speakers can choose from a wide range of values to complete a hyperbolic statement (e.g., "I've been waiting in line for [hours, days, weeks, months, years]."). They evaluate three hypotheses about the choice of value in an exaggerated statement: the "more is better" hypothesis, in which the more extreme the value, the better the expression; the "optimal level" theory, in which more is better to a point, after which the goodness of the expression declines; and the "threshold" model, in which a certain degree of extremity must be achieved but after that no further improvements in goodness are found. Kreuz et al. describe a series of studies evaluating these three hypotheses by comparing ratings of statement sense, appropriateness, likelihood of use, and other message characteristics as a function of value extremity.

In the last chapter in this section, *Figurative Language in Emotional Communication* (Chap. 6), Susan R. Fussell and Mallie M. Moss examine the production of figurative language, particularly metaphors and idioms, in the communication of emotional states. They first review literature on the use of figurative language in descriptions of autobiographic affective experiences that shows that the production of figurative expressions varies as a function of the intensity and type of emotion. Then, they discuss some limitations of experimental designs in which participants describe their own personal affective experiences and argue that this method may lead researchers to overlook important generalizations about how people use metaphors, idioms, and the like to express emotional states. Fussell and Moss review a series of studies in which speakers described movie characters' emotions to an addressee; studies that demonstrate surprising consistency in the metaphors and idioms people use to describe emotional states. They demonstrate how this research technique can be used to examine the effects of stimulus properties and social-contextual factors such as gender on figurative language use.

Section III, *Perspective-Taking and Conversational Collaboration*, focuses on how speakers and hearers take each other's perspectives into account when formulating and interpreting messages and on how they coordinate their conversational contributions to ensure that messages are mutually understood (Clark & Wilkes-Gibbs, 1986). The idea that communicators tailor speech to their addressees' characteristics (physical vantage point, background knowledge, attitudes, etc.) has been widely expressed (Bakhtin, 1981; Brown, 1965; Clark & Marshall, 1981; Graumann, 1989; Krauss & Fussell, 1991; Mead, 1934; Rommetveit, 1974; Volosinov, 1986), and supported in a growing number of empirical studies (e.g., Clark, Schreuder & Buttrick, 1983; Fussell & Krauss, 1992; Hupet, Chantraine & Neff, 1993; Isaacs & Clark, 1987; Krauss, Weinheimer & Vivekananthan, 1968; Schober, 1993). As Krauss and Fussell

(1996) observe in their review of this literature, however, theoretical development in this area has been hampered by the lack of a clear definition of what constitutes a perspective and by a limited understanding of when and how people assess and use perspective during message production and comprehension. The three chapters in this section attempt to redress this lack of theoretical refinement.

In the first chapter in this section, *Different Kinds of Conversational Perspective-Taking* (Chap. 7), Michael F. Schober analyzes and organizes the diverse ways in which the term *perspective* has been used in the field of human communication. He first presents a classification system that distinguishes among four interrelated types of speaker perspective: (1) time, place, and identity, (2) conceptualizations of the topic of discussion, (3) conversational agenda, and (4) background knowledge, beliefs, attitudes, opinions, and so forth. Then, he discusses the different sources of information or *grounds* people use to infer each kind of speaker perspective—physical context, utterances themselves, conversational history, beliefs about others' social category memberships, and direct knowledge of another person—and points out that these sources of information vary in how direct or observable they are. Schober argues that forms of speaker perspective that rest on indirect evidence, such as conversational agendas, may be more problematic for listeners to identify as well as more difficult to study empirically.

In Chapter 8, *Language Users as Problem Solvers: Just What Ambiguity Problem Do They Solve?,* Boaz Keysar analyzes *how* perspective-taking occurs in message production and comprehension. He focuses on the issue of ambiguity, and asks how, in view of the many possible interpretations for a single message, does a listener identify the speaker's intended meaning? Keysar presents arguments against the traditional view that addressees first compute a literal, perspective-free interpretation of a message and then revise their interpretations in light of conversational principles (Grice, 1975; Searle, 1975). He then describes several studies that support an alternative model, the *Perspectival Adjustment Model,* (Keysar, Barr, Balin, & Paek, 1997) that proposes that listeners first rapidly and perhaps automatically interpret messages from their own perspectives and then perform the more effortful and time-consuming process of adjusting their interpretations to take into account the speakers' perspectives. This adjustment process is sensitive to factors such as cognitive load, and frequently, listeners are unable to fully correct their original interpretations. Keysar argues that speakers perform a similar process: They design their utterances in light of their own perspectives and then monitor and adjust them as necessary to accommodate the listeners' viewpoints.

In Chapter 9, *The Grounding Problem in Conversations With and Through Computers,* Susan E. Brennan discusses how fundamental principles of collaborative theory (Clark & Wilkes-Gibbs, 1986)—communication as coordinated activity, grounding, and so forth—apply to both human–computer interaction (conversations *with* computers) and computer-mediated interpersonal communication (conversations *through* computers). She observes that although grounding occurs in all forms of communication, it takes different forms and requires varying degrees of effort depending on such factors as the amount and timeliness of a partner's feedback. Brennan first provides a brief review of the history of human–computer interaction and then discusses how the grounding process works in different types of human–computer interfaces (e.g., language-based, graphical). She points out how interface design limitations—particularly, the dearth of system feedback—can lead to problems in the grounding process and hence undesirable consequences for a user. Brennan proposes a new model of human–computer interaction in which interactions with a system are viewed as incremental conversational contributions that are grounded through feedback from the system, coordination of knowledge states, and other basic elements of collaborative theory.

Finally, Section IV, *Cognition, Language and Social Interaction*, contains of two chapters that focus on the complicated relationships among cognitive processes, language, and social interaction. As opposed to recent discussions of the Whorfian hypothesis, which focus on the cognitive effects of *specific* native languages (e.g., Hoffman, Lau & Johnson, 1986; Hunt & Agnoli, 1991; Kay & Kempton, 1984), these chapters address the more fundamental relationship between language itself and cognition.

In Chapter 10, *Cognition, Language, and Communication,* Gün R. Semin distinguishes between language and language use by analogy with tools and tool use. According to Semin, words, like tools, have a limited set of invariant properties and a potentially limitless set of *affordances* (Gibson, 1979), purposes to which they lend themselves in communicative contexts. Semin begins by describing the fundamental principles of his *Tool and Tool Use Model* (TATUM) and poses four key questions derived from this model: (a) What are the tools of language use and how can they be classified? (b) What are the properties of these linguistic tools? (c) What are the affordances of linguistic tools (i.e., how are they realized in communicative contexts)? (d) What are the relationships between cognition, tools and tool use in communicative contexts? Next, Semin discusses research he and his colleagues have done on the Linguistic Category Model (Semin & Fiedler, 1991), a model of word and word use within one tool domain—terms for interpersonal relations (descriptive action verbs, interpretative action verbs, state action verbs, state verbs, and adjectives). He demonstrates how TATUM can be used to separate the properties of these terms from their affordances in particular communicative contexts. Semin concludes by discussing how his model helps clarify the relationships among culture, cognition, language, and communication.

Finally, in Chapter 11, *Some Cognitive Consequences of Communication,* Chi-Yue Chiu, Robert M. Krauss, and Ivy Y-M Lau, address the relationship between language and cognition. They argue that although recent research has, for the most part, disproved Whorf's (1956) hypothesis that a person's native language affects how he or she experiences the world, language use *per se* can and does affect cognitive processes. In support of their argument, Chiu et al. review research showing, among other things, that when people formulate a description of a stimulus it affects their memory for that stimulus (e.g., Carmichael, Hogan, & Walter, 1932; Schooler & Engstler-Schooler, 1990; Wilkes-Gibbs & Kim, 1991). Similarly, research indicates that when speakers verbalizing arguments for or against one's beliefs, these verbalizations can create attitude change (e.g., Higgins & Rholes, 1978; McCann, Higgins & Fondacaro, 1991). A noteworthy contribution of this chapter is the authors' integration of these findings with the perspective-taking literature to illustrate their hypothesis that any factor affecting language use, such as adjusting a message to a partner's perspective, can potentially affect basic cognitive processes.

CONCLUSION

Through our cursory description of the themes and content of this book, we hope to have illustrated the potential fruitfulness of approaching human language use from a joint social and cognitive psychological perspective. The remainder of this volume expands in detail on this theme as it applies to such topics as people's intentions or goals when using language, the role of language in research settings, indirect and figurative language, perspective-taking and conversational interaction, and the relationship between language and cognition.

ACKNOWLEDGMENTS

We would like to thank Judi Amsel for her enthusiastic support throughout this project.

REFERENCES

Atkinson, J. M., & Heritage, J. (1984). *Structures of social action: Studies in conversational analysis.* Cambridge, England: Cambridge University Press.

Austin, J. L. (1975). *How to do things with words* (2nd ed.). Cambridge, MA: Harvard University Press.

Bakhtin, M. M. (1981). Discourse in the novel. In M. Holquist (Ed.), *The dialogic imagination: Four essays by M. M. Bakhtin* (pp. 259–422). Austin, TX: University of Texas Press.

Brown, P., & Levinson, S. C. (1987). *Politeness: Some universals in language usage.* Cambridge, England: Cambridge University Press.

Brown, R. (1965). *Social psychology.* New York: Free Press.

Cacciari, C., & Glucksberg, S. (1994). Understanding figurative language. In M. A. Gernsbacher (Ed.), *Handbook of psycholinguistics* (pp. 447–477). San Diego, CA: Academic Press.

Carmichael, L., Hogan, H. P., & Walter, A. A. (1932). An experimental study of the effect of language on the reproduction of visually perceived form. *Journal of Experimental Psychology, 15,* 73–86.

Carter, K., & Presnell, M. (Eds.). (1994). *Interpretive approaches to interpersonal communication.* Albany, NY: SUNY Press.

Clark, H. H., & Marshall, C. E. (1981). Definite reference and mutual knowledge. In A. K. Joshi, B. L. Webber, & I. A. Sag (Eds.), *Elements of discourse understanding* (pp. 10–63). Cambridge, England: Cambridge University Press.

Clark, H. H., Schreuder, R., & Buttrick, S. (1983). Common ground and the understanding of demonstrative reference. *Journal of Verbal Learning and Verbal Behavior, 22,* 245–258.

Clark, H. H., & Wilkes-Gibbs, D. (1986). Referring as a collaborative process. *Cognition, 22,* 1–39.

Coulthard, M. (Ed.). (1992). *Advances in spoken discourse analysis.* London: Routledge.

Coupland, N., Coupland, J., Giles, H., & Henwood, K. (1988). Accommodating the elderly: Invoking and extending a theory. *Language in Society, 17,* 253–262.

Drew, P., & Heritage, J. (Eds.). (1992). *Talk at work: Interaction in institutional settings.* Cambridge, England: Cambridge University Press.

Fussell, S. R., & Krauss, R. M. (1992). Coordination of knowledge in communication: Effects of speakers' assumptions about what others know. *Journal of Personality and Social Psychology, 62,* 378–391.

Gernsbacher, M. A. (Ed.). (1994*). Handbook of psycholinguistics.* San Diego, CA: Academic Press.

Gibbs, R. W., Jr. (1979). Contextual effects in understanding indirect requests. *Discours Processes, 2,* 1–10.

Gibbs, R. W., Jr. (1980). Spilling the beans on understanding and memory for idioms in conversation. *Memory and Cognition, 82,* 149–156.

Gibbs, R. W., Jr. (1983). Do people always process the literal meanings of indirect requests? *Journal of Experimental Psychology: Learning, Memor and Cognition, 9,* 524–533.

Gibbs, R. W., Jr. (1986). Skating on thin ice: Literal meaning and understanding idioms in conversation. *Discourse Processes, 9,* 17–30.

Gibbs, R. W., Jr. (1987). What does it mean to say a metaphor has been understood? In R. E. Haskell (Ed.), *Cognition and symbolic structures: The psychology of metaphoric transformation* (pp. 31–48). Norwood, NJ: Ablex.

Gibbs, R. W., Jr. (1994a). Figurative thought and figurative language. In M. A. Gernsbacher (Ed.), *Handbook of psycholinguistics* (pp. 411–446). San Diego, CA: Academic Press.

Gibbs, R. W., Jr. (1994b). *The poetics of mind: Figurative thought, language, and understanding.* New York: Cambridge University Press.

Gibbs, R. W., Jr., & Gonzales, G. P. (1985). Syntactic frozenness in processing and remembering idioms. *Cognition, 20,* 243–259.

Gibbs, R. W., Jr., Kushner, J., & Mills, R. (1991). Authorial intentions in metaphor comprehension. *Journal of Psycholinguistic Research, 20,* 11–30.

Gibbs, R. W., Jr., & O'Brien, J. E. (1990). Idioms and mental imagery: The metaphorical motivation for idiomatic meaning. *Cognition, 36,* 35–68.

Gibson, J. J. (1979). *The ecological approach to visual perception.* Boston: Mifflin.

Glucksberg, S. (1989). Metaphors in conversation: How are they understood? Why are they used? *Metaphor and Symbolic Activity, 4,* 125–143.

Glucksberg, S., Gildea, P., & Bookin, H. B. (1982). On understanding nonliteral speech: can people ignore metaphors? *Journal of Verbal Learning and Verbal Behavior, 21,* 85–98.

Goffman, E. (1967). *Interaction ritual: Essays on face-to-face behavior.* Garden City, NY: Anchor Books.

Graumann, C. F. (1989). Perspective setting and taking in verbal interaction. In R. Dietrich & C. F. Graumann (Eds.), *Language processing in social context* (pp. 95–122). Amsterdam, Netherlands: North-Holland.

Grice, H. P. (1957). Meaning. *Philosophical Review, 64,* 377–388.

Grice, H. P. (1969). Utterer's meaning and intentions. *Philosophical Review, 78,* 147–177.

Grice, H. P. (1975). Logic and conversation. In P. Cole & J. L. Morgan (Eds.), *Syntax and semantics: Vol. 3, Speech acts* (pp. 41–58). New York: Academic Press.

Hewes, D. E. (Ed.). (1995). *The cognitive bases of interpersonal communication.* Hillsdale, NJ: Lawrence Erlbaum Associates.

Higgins, E. T., & Rholes, W. J. (1978). "Saying is believing": Effects of message modification on memory and liking for the person described. *Journal of Experimental Social Psychology, 14,* 363–378.

Hoffman, C., Lau, I., & Johnson, D. R. (1986). The linguistic relativity of person cognition: An English–Chinese comparison. *Journal of Personality and Social Psychology, 51,* 1097–1105.

Holtgraves, T. (1986). Language structure in social interaction: Perceptions of direct and indirectspeech acts and interactants who use them. *Journal of Personality and Social Psychology, 51,* 305–314.

Holtgraves, T. (1994). Communication in context: Effects of speaker status on the comprehension of indirect requests. *Journal of Experimental Psychology: Learning, Memory, and Cognition, 20,* 1205–1218.

Holtgraves, T., & Yang, J.-N. (1990). Politenessas universal: cross-cultural perceptions of request strategies and inferences based on their use. *Journal of Personality and Social Psychology, 59,* 719–729.

Hunt, E., & Agnoli, F. (1991). The Whorfian hypothesis: A cognitive psychology perspective. *Psychological Review, 98,* 377–389.

Hupet, M., Chantraine, Y., & Neff, F. (1993). References in conversation between young and old normal adults. *Psychology and Aging, 8,* 339–346.

Isaacs, E. A., & Clark, H. H. (1987). References in conversation between experts and novices. *Journal of Experimental Psychology: General, 116,* 26–37.

Jefferson, G. (1975). Side sequences. In D. N. Sudnow (Ed.), *Studies in social interaction* (pp. 294–338). New York: Free Press.

Kay, P., & Kempton, W. (1984). What is the Sapir–Whorf hypothesis? *American Anthropologist, 86,* 65–79.

Keysar, B. (1989). On the functional equivalence of literal and metaphorical interpretations in discourse. *Journal of Memory and Language, 28,* 375–385.

Keysar, B., Barr, D. J., Balin, J. A., & Paek, T., (1997). *Definite reference and mutual knowledge: A processing model of common ground in comprehension.* Manuscript submitted for publication.

Krauss, R. M., & Fussell, S. R. (1991). Perspective-taking in communication: Representations of others' knowledge in reference. *Social Cognition, 9,* 2–24.

Krauss, R. M., & Fussell, S. R. (1996). Social psychological models of interpersonal communication. In E. T. Higgins & A. Kruglanski (Eds.), *Social psychology: Handbook of basic principles* (pp. 655–701). New York: Guilford Press.

Krauss, R. M., Weinheimer, S., & Vivekananthan, P. S. (1968). "Inner speech" and "external speech": Characteristics and communication effectiveness of socially and nonsocially encoded messages. *Journal of Personality and Social Psychology, 9,* 295–300.

Kreuz, R. J., & Roberts, R. M. (1993). The empirical study of figurative language in literature. *Poetics, 22,* 151–169.

Kreuz, R. J., Roberts, R. M., Johnson, B. K., & Bertus, E. L. (1996). Figurative language occurrence and co-occurrence in contemporary literature. In R. J. Kreuz & M. S. MacNealy (Eds.), *Empirical approaches to literature and aesthetics* (pp. 83–97). Norwood, NJ: Ablex.

Leeds-Hurwitz, W. (Ed.). (1995). *Social approaches to communication.* New York: Guilford.

Levelt, W. J. M. (1989). *Speaking: From intention to articulation.* Cambridge, MA: MIT Press.

Markova, I., & Foppa, K. (Eds.). (1990). *The dynamics of dialogue.* New York: Springer-Verlag.

McCann, C. D., Higgins, E. T., & Fondacaro, R. A. (1991). Primacy and recency in communication and self-persuasion: How successive audiences and multiple encodings influence subsequent evaluative judgments. *Social Cognition, 9,* 47–66.

Mead, G. H. (1934). *Mind, self and society.* Chicago, IL: University of Chicago Press.

Roberts, R. M., & Kreuz, R. J. (1994). Why do people use figurative language? *Psychological Science, 5,* 159–163.

Rommetveit, R. (1974). *On message structure: A framework for the study of language and communication.* New York: Wiley.

Ross, L. (1977). The intuitive psychologist and his shortcomings: Distortions in the attribution process. In L. Berkowitz (Ed.), *Advances in experimental social psychology* (Vol. 10, pp. 174–221). New York: Academic Press.

Sacks, H., Schegloff, E. A., & Jefferson, G. (1974). A simplest systematics for the organization of turn-taking for conversation. *Language, 50,* 696–735.

Schegloff, E. A. (1982). Discourse as an interactional achievement: Some uses of "uh huh" and other things that come between sentences. In D. Tannen (Ed.), *Analyzing discourse: Text and talk* (pp. 71–93). Washington, DC: Georgetown University Press.

Schegloff, E. A., Jefferson, G., & Sacks, H. (1977). The preference for self-correction in the organization of repair in conversation. *Language, 53,* 361–382.

Schober, M. F. (1993). Spatial perspective-taking in conversation. *Cognition, 47,* 1–24.

Schooler, J. W., & Engstler-Schooler, T. (1990). Verbal overshadowing of visual memories: Some things are better left unsaid. *Cognitive Psychology, 22,* 36–71.

Searle, J. R. (1969). *Speech acts: An essay in the philosophy of language.* Cambridge, England: Cambridge University Press.

Searle, J. R. (1975). Indirect speech acts. In P. Cole & J. Morgan (Eds.), *Syntax and semantics: Vol. 3, Speech acts* (pp. 59–82). New York: Academic Press.

Searle, J. R. (1990). Collective intentions and actions. In P. Cohen, J. Morgan, & M. Pollack (Eds.), *Intentions in communication* (pp. 401–416). Cambridge, MA: MIT Press.

Semin, G. R., & Fiedler, K. (1991). The linguistic category model, its bases, applications and range. In W. Stroebe & M. Hewstone (Eds.), *European review of social psychology* (Vol. 2, pp. 1–30). Chichester, England: Wiley.

Slobin, D. I., Gerhardt, J., Kyratzis, A., & Guo, J. (Eds.). (1996). *Social interaction, social context, and language.* Mahwah, NJ: Lawrence Erlbaum Associates.

Tversky, A., & Kahneman, D. (1974). Judgment under uncertainty: Heuristics and biases. *Science, 185,* 1124–1131.

Volosinov, V. N. (1986). *Marxism and the philosophy of language* (L. Matejka, I. R. Titunik, Trans.). Cambridge, MA: Harvard University Press.

Whorf, B. L. (1956). *Language, thought, and reality: Selected writings of Benjamin Lee Whorf.* Cambridge, MA: MIT Press.

Wilkes-Gibbs, D., & Clark, H. H. (1992). Coordinating beliefs in conversation. *Journal of Memory and Language, 31,* 183–194.

Wilkes-Gibbs, D., & Kim, P. H. (1991). *Discourse influences on memory for visual forms.* Paper presented at the 1991 meeting of the Psychonomic Society, San Francisco, CA.

— 2 —

The Varieties of Intentions in Interpersonal Communication

Raymond W. Gibbs, Jr.

University of California, Santa Cruz

In ordinary conversation, the recovery of a speaker's communicative intentions appears to play a critical role in the interpretation of what is said. The intentions that speakers express in conversation may be relatively straightforward. Consider the following brief exchange:

Jean:	What time is it?
Dale:	It's half past three.

The goal of Jean's question seems transparent, and Dale responds appropriately by providing Jean with the desired information. Although Jean and Dale must assume a good deal about each other in making and responding to each other (e.g., Jean must have some idea that Dale is able to provide the information, and Dale must assume that Jean needs only the approximate time), their respective abilities to recognize the intentions in what each says appear simple. But consider now the following segments of dialogue between a female patient and her surgeon soon after the woman had undergone a mastectomy. The conversation focused on the patient's concern that her own illness might be treated as her late sister's cancer was several years earlier (Cassell, 1985, pp. 137–139).

Patient:	Well, it's just that I watched this with my sister, and I the idea of chasing it all over my body because she ended up dying anyway.
Surgeon:	Well, June, I don't know whether you're going to end up dying of this "anyway" anyway.
Patient:	Yeah.
Surgeon:	But I do know one thing. Between now and your death, whether it's from cancer or whether it's from an automobile accident, a lot of time's gonna pass. You are not faced with widespread cancer. I'm not in the business here of teaching you how to die. That's not the business

I'm about now. I'm in the business of trying to make you a lot more alive. And, we're not in the business of chasing something. You know, taking pieces off you while we're chasing—no, that's not our business. Whatever it was with your sister, we're not your sister.

Patient: No, but—when you've watched it happen once—You know, there are many times when the reason she didn't herself was because she was so close to my folks. But I thought, "How cruel for her." It would have been so much easier to do it in one lump. I know as a doctor you can't do that.

Surgeon: Well-

Patient: But I can.

(Later)

Patient: That was another thing that was so sad to me when my sister died. My father kept saying, "What did I do to deserve this? Haven't I been a good Jew?" And I said to, "What has it got to do with anything, nobody's doing anything to you. You're not being punished." But it was his baby.

Surgeon: You remember that too, though.

Patient: What?

Surgeon: Nobody's doing anything to you.

Patient: No, nobody's doing anything to me . . . But I shouldn't be forced to stick around and just . . . just be kept, put together with spit for the rest of my life.

Surgeon: Please! Please! I'm looking at you right now, you don't look like you're put together with spit. Now . . .

This doctor–patient conversation suggests many levels of complex intentions that each speaker was trying to communicate. Among the meanings expressed by the patient are the comparison of her illness with that of her sister's, the feelings of jealousy and envy in the face of her sister's achievements, and the desire to uphold the family's honor in the face of her illness. The surgeon faced the task of recognizing this complex set of intentions. Failure to understand what the patient intended to communicate could negatively affect her recovery. Believing that her sister died of the same disease and desperately wishing to avoid the course of her sister's horrible illness, the patient might go to extremes to avoid chemotherapy, radiation, and other types of therapy. Clearly, the surgeon's understanding and appropriate response to the patient's intended meanings is critical to her well-being.

Many chapters in this volume describe empirical evidence of a variety of ways that people actively coordinate their beliefs, knowledge, and attitudes to attain successful communication. Implicit in most of this research is the idea that expressing and understanding speaker meaning depends on, and is limited by, the recognition of communicative intentions. Following the work of Grice (1957, 1969), most conversational analysts have assumed that interpersonal communication consists of a sender's intending to cause a receiver to think or do something just by getting the receiver to recognize that the sender is trying to cause the thought or action. Thus, "Communication is a complex kind of intention that is achieved or satisfied just by being recognized," (Levinson, 1983, p. 16).

In this chapter, I explore the importance of communicative intentions for how people express and understand meaning in interpersonal situations. What exactly does it mean to say that a speaker or author has communicative intentions? Does the recognition of intentions completely capture all aspects of how meaning is understood?

VARIETIES OF INTENTIONS

Intentions are traditionally conceived of in individual and singular terms (Anscombe, 1963; Bratman, 1987). Philosophers, psychologists, and others have thought of intentions as mental acts that operate before the performance of behavioral acts. Intentions are psychological states, and people assume that the content of an intention must be mentally represented. In particular, a speaker or writer must have in mind a representation of the set of assumptions that he or she intends to make manifest or more manifest to an audience. For instance, in the first brief conversation above, Jean's question, "What time is it?" is apparently preceded by a private mental act from which an intention to perform some behavior arises, namely to ask Dale a question about the time.

Yet any individual speech event actually reflects a hierarchy of intentions with each level having a different relationship to consciousness (Dipert, 1993). *High-level intentions* refer to beliefs, emotions, behavior and so on that a person wishes to cause in someone else. For example, I utter the expression, "Winter is the best season to go surfing in Santa Cruz," with the high-level intention of getting someone to adopt my belief about the best season to surf in Santa Cruz.

Middle-level intentions are directed toward goals that are the planned means to achieve high-level intentions. In the case of my statement about surfing in Santa Cruz, my middle-level intention is for someone to have a certain perceptual experience in which he or she recognizes my statement as spoken in the English language. Middle-level intentions, therefore, are directed toward chosen sense-experienceable features of the physical object of phenomena.

Finally, a person must make decisions about how to produce certain sense experiences for others. These *low-level intentions* are directed toward the means of bringing about the middle-level intentions and the high-level intentions in turn. Thus, I must make certain audible sounds that are recognized as English to get another person to adopt my beliefs about the best season to surf in Santa Cruz. Of course, I may accomplish my high-level intention via other middle- and low-level intentions. For example, I might have chosen to get someone to have a certain belief about surfing in Santa Cruz (a high-level intention) by choosing a means, such as expressing a certain pattern of light and dark on a page that is called writing (a middle-level intention), and then choosing a typewriter to produce an instance of this pattern (a low-level intention).

These three types of intentions together reflect a hierarchy of different relations between means and ends. Understanding what any speaker or writer has intended to communicate depends on the ability to infer high-level intentions from low- and middle-level) intentions. Determining what high-level intentions to attribute to an action can, however, be tricky. To start with a simple case (Dipert, 1993), when I put a sign in my yard that says, "New Grass," there is little doubt that I intend others to recognize that the sign is an artifact and not a natural object, and that my purpose is to convince people that there is new grass. But in this case I surely also intend for others to come to believe that there is new grass. Getting people to believe that there is new grass may be a means to a future end, such as getting them to not step on it, or still higher in the means–ends hierarchy, allowing the new grass to grow. There are other means to keep people's feet off my grass, many of which do not necessarily involve consideration of others as a cognitive agents who have beliefs (e.g., enclosing the area with a screened roof and walls keeps people, rabbits, and even hail off my grass). So the sign is a communicative artifact, because it is one means among several that usually serve the overall purpose of letting my grass grow that was specifically selected to produce a belief in another person.

Consider now a different type of intention (Dipert, 1993). Imagine that I am sitting on a beautifully crafted wooden chair. The craftsperson who created this chair might well have intended me to believe that the chair was good, not just an to sit on. How does this belief differ from the belief that I want to instill in others with my sign about the grass? The difference is that in the case of the chair, the intended belief is about the chair, the artifact itself. In the case of the sign, the belief is about the grass, a different entity altogether. For something to be a communicative artifact, it must have been made with a purpose to cause a belief about an entity other than the artifact itself.

Another type of intention that is not strictly communicative includes cases in which an artifact is intended to produce a belief about its creator. For example, a good chair is intended to produce the belief that its maker is a good craftsperson. In this situation, the craftsperson's intended belief is not about the artifact itself or about the entity to which the artifact refers (as in the case of the grass sign). Instead, the artifact has been created with the intention of producing a belief about its maker. The intention in this case is expressive not communicative.

Expressive intentions differ from communicative ones because their recognition does not imply their fulfillment. For example, my intention to make someone think of the concept of justice is an intention in which recognition implies fulfillment. That is, a person's recognition of my intention to get him or her to think of justice logically implies that the person thinks of justice and hence my intention is fulfilled by its recognition. On the other hand, my intention to get a person to believe that winter is the best season for surfing in Santa Cruz is not an intention in which recognition implies fulfillment. Recognition of the intention does not itself bring about another's believing that winter is the best season for surfing in Santa Cruz. A person might may understand my utterance, "Winter is the best season for surfing in Santa Cruz," to express a particular proposition (itself a recognition–implies–fulfillment intention), but recognition of the contents of the proposition does not itself necessarily lead the person to adopt my belief about Santa Cruz surfing.

In many interpersonal situations, the mere fact that an intention is recognized may lead to its fulfillment. Sperber and Wilson (1986) provide a nice illustration of this with the following example. Suppose that Mary intends to inform Peter of the fact that she has a sore throat. Merely letting him hear her hoarse voice provides salient and conclusive evidence of her sore throat. Mary's intention can be fulfilled whether or not Peter is aware of it: He might realize that she has a sore throat without also realizing that she intends him to realize this fact.

Suppose now that Mary intends to inform Peter on July 1 that she had a sore throat on the previous Christmas Eve. Now, she could not produce direct evidence of her past sore throat, but she could give Peter direct evidence, not of her past sore throat but of her present intention to inform him of it. How would she do this, and what good would it do? She might utter the expression, "I had a sore throat on Christmas Eve." Doing so gives Peter indirect but nonetheless strong evidence that she had a sore throat on the previous Christmas Eve. If Peter assumes that Mary is sincere and if he is likely to know whether or not she had a sore throat on the previous Christmas Eve, then he could assume that Mar's intent to inform him that she had a sore throat on that date provides conclusive evidence that she spoke the truth. In these ordinary conditions, Mary's intention to inform Peter of her past sore throat would be fulfilled by making Peter recognize her intention. This is not an exceptional way of fulfilling an intention to inform an audience. We can, most generally, describe the above situation as follows. Mary intends (a) her utterance "I had a sore throat on Christmas Eve" to produce in Peter the belief that she had a sore throat the previous Christmas Eve; (b) Peter to recognize her intention (a); and (c) Peter's recognition of her intention (a) to function as at least part of his reason for his belief.

MUTUAL BELIEF AND RECOGNIZING INTENTIONS

Understanding the role that people's communicative intentions play in interpersonal communication requires study of the recognition–implies–fulfillment condition. Successful communication, however, demands that speakers do more than simply make their utterances and hope that listeners, or readers, somehow draw the right inferences about what they intend to convey. Speakers and listeners must coordinate their mutual knowledge, beliefs, and attitudes (i.e., their common ground to increase the probability that what is intended will be recognized and thus understood (Clark & Carlson, 1981). In this view, communicative intentions are *not* merely private mental acts but social products that are jointly constructed by all participants. Consider some interpersonal situations where the joint construction of communicative intentions results in both successful and unsuccessful exchanges. Each of these examples illustrates the role of mutual beliefs in distinguishing *authorized* from *unauthorized* inferences (Clark, 1978; Gibbs & Mueller, 1987).

The first example seems simple but involves some complexity: Rick is sitting in the living room reading a book when Sally walks in, leaving the door open. Rick says to Sally, "It's cold in here." He means for Sally to understand this sentence as a polite request to close the door, and she understands him to mean just that. Sally has therefore drawn an authorized inference, one that she believes Rick meant for her to infer. Sally derives this correct inference because she assumes that both she and Rick know that leaving a door open will cause a draft making the room feel cold. Sally uses this piece of shared knowledge in conjunction with the cooperativeprinciple (Grice, 1975) to infer exactly what communicative intention Rick wishes for her to recover.

The second example is even more complex: Helen and Karen are talking on the telephone about their upcoming final examinations. Karen asks Helen "How's the studying going?" and Helen replies, "I've been smoking a lot of cigarettes." Although Helen's answer is not a direct response to the questionshe intends Karen to understand it to mean "I'm studying quite hard," because Helen always smokes cigarettes when she studies. Karen knows this information, which is shared between Helen and Karen, and Karen correctly infers that Helen intends her to use this shared knowledge in understanding the response to her original question. The inference that Karen draws then is authorized. Note that if Karen incorrectly believes that Helen isn't studying very hard because she's spending all her time smoking cigarettes due to anxiety, then she would probably draw the unauthorized inference that Helen meant "I'm not studying very hard." Once again, a listener's understanding of a recognition–implies–fulfillment intention is based on his or her joint appraisal with a speaker of information in their common ground.

People on occasion draw unauthorized inferences about speakers' intentions, particularly in communicative situations in which they are trying to get their own way (e.g., when making requests, excuses, explanations of behavior). For example, one couple recalled a typical argument in which both maintained that they had not gone to a party because the other had not wanted to go (Tannen, 1982, p. 220). Each partner denied having expressed any disinclination to go. In this case, the mixup was traced to the following reconstructed conversation:

Wife:	John's having a party. Wanna go?
Husband:	OK.
(Later)	
Wife:	Are you sure you want to go to the party?
Husband:	OK, let's not go. I'm tired anyway.

When the couple later discussed the misunderstanding, the wife reported that she had merely been asking what her husband wanted to do without considering her own preference. She claimed that she was about to go to the party for her husband's sake and tried to make sure of his preference by asking him a second time. The wife felt she was being solicitous and considerate. The husband said that by bringing up the question of the party, his wife was letting him know that she wanted to go, so he agreed. But when she brought it up again, he thought that she was letting him know that she had changed her mind and now did not want to go. So he found a reason not to go, to make her feel all right about getting her way. Thus, the husband was also being solicitous and considerate. This brief conversational exchange shows how people can misunderstand the communicative intentions of others even when both conversants were being attentive, polite, and trying quite to assess what might be in their common ground.

The social coordination needed to infer speakers' communicative intentions suggests, once again, that it is best to conceive of intentions as the joint product of an interaction between a speaker/listener, writer/reader, or artist/observer rather than as purely, individual, private mental acts (Searle, 1990). Discourse is collective behavior; that is, it is a joint accomplishment of two or more people. Examples of collective action are ubiquitous in everyday life—jointly pushing a car, checking out in a supermarket, orchestral performances, dancing with others, executing a hit–and–run play in baseball, and engaging in conversation are all common examples. Collective behavior is not just helpful behavior. Engaging in a prizefight is an example of collective behavior in which the pugilists have agreed to cooperate, even if the two contestants are competing against one another.

Searle (1990) argues that individual intentionality is not by itself sufficient to account for collective action and hence discourse. He maintains that what is needed is a characterization of *collective intentions*. Collective behavior is not the same as a summation of individual actions: the difference between the two resides in the intentions of the actors. When engaged in collective activity, people are guided by collective intentions, sometimes termed *we-intentions*. On the other hand, even when engaged in collective activity, only individuals act, and these acts are caused by collective intentions. But how do collective intentions relate to the individual intentions that cause the individual actions constitutive of the collective behavior? Searle argues that collective actions are primitive and cannot be reduced to individual intentions supplemented with mutual beliefs. Instead, each agent *we-intends* to achieve the collective goal by means of having an individual intention to do his or her part. Collective intentionality presupposes that each person assumes the existence of a sense of other agents as candidates for collaboration.

Under this view, communicative intentions are social products created through the interaction of mutual beliefs between relational participants. The ongoing context of interaction is not reducible to either the intentions or actions of individuals. When issues of intent arise, participants negotiate and construct a mutually shared social reality with individual and relational implications. Much of the current work on collaboration in interpersonal communication may be profitably understood in terms of how people we-intend rather than merely in terms of how each individual expresses his or her own private intentions and how one person privately infers the communicative intentions of others. Exactly how we-intentions are established is an important topic for future research.

COORDINATION OF INTENTIONS IN NONVERBAL COMMUNICATION

An important part of the intentions that people convey to others is found in nonverbal behavior. One popular belief is that people's body "language" can communicate different messages from what people say (e.g., my body says "yes," while my words state "no"; Fast, 1970). Psychological and anthropological studies have explored aspects of how people communicate what they truly believe or intend by their body postures, facial expressions, gestures, and so on, in contrast to what their words often express. Many scholars presume that nonverbal behaviors are natural (i.e., signs) and, therefore, not specifically performed with the intention to be recognized as conveying communicative meanings (Kendon, 1981). But detailed studies of gesture and speech suggest that the two are highly coordinated and arise from the same computational source (McNeill, 1992). These studies show, at the very least, that gestures accompanying spoken language often facilitate listeners' understandings of speakers' messages (cf. Krauss, Morrel-Samuels, & Colasante, 1991). This conclusion may be extended to suggest that most body gestures, facial expressions, and so on are specifically produced to be understood as part of a person's overall communicative intentions and must be recognized as such for successful interpersonal interactions to occur.

My hypothesis is that listeners and observers interpret nonverbal behaviors to distinguish between natural and communicative behaviors. For instance, I may be seated across from another person at a boring lecture. Suppose that at one point I yawn. Now in some circumstances, such as when I catch the other person's eye before yawning, he or she might understand this gesture/facial expression as intended to communicate that I believe the lecture to be boring, whereas in other circumstances the person will simply understand my gesture as being a natural act without any specific communicative purpose. People generally observe others' nonverbal behaviors for clues to their possible communicative intentions. Despite the large body of research on nonverbal communication, there is surprisingly little work on the extent to which people ordinarily distinguish between behaviors that reflect communicative intentions, and thus are recognition–implies–fulfillment intentions, and behaviors that are natural and not communicative.

Another aspect of nonverbal communication that requires an examination of individual and collective intentions is people's understanding and appreciation of artworks. To conceive of something as an artwork, it is necessary to conceive of or experience that object or event as an artifact and not a natural object or event. For example, a photograph of a crack in the sidewalk has a different status as an artifact than does the sidewalk crack itself (Dipert, 1993). In conceiving of an artifact like a photograph, people necessarily conceive of an agent who has a communicative (or an expressive) intention, although the identity of the agent (e.g., the photographer) and of the intention itself need not be contemplated in any detail. People may conceive of the agent as having means–ends beliefs, and may link these intentions to a supposed plan (although again they may only assume that an agent has some such means–ends beliefs). Many artworks are not conceived to have finite, specific communicative meanings. But most are conceived to be recognized as artworks and part of people's understanding of them as such is possible through this recognition.

A wonderful example of how artists' intentions play a direct role in nonverbal interpersonal communication appears in a series of nonrepresentational paintings by two artists, Marilyn Hammond and Thelka Levin. Concerned that the visual impact of art was getting lost in excessive verbiage, the two painters decided to undertake a project titled "Epistolary Paint: A Visual Correspondence." The artists agreed on some ground rules for the size of the paintings and restricted their colors to the simple palette of red, green, white, and gold. They agreed to talk by telephone about the logistics of the project, but never about the actual art. Ten times from October 1992 to July 1995, Hammond shipped a finished piece from her Berkeley, California studio to Levin in Brookline, Massachusetts. In turn, Levin interpreted each of Hammond's 10 paintings and responded with a painting of her own for Hammond to interpret. Back and forth the correspondence went, with each painting raising the stakes for their project. The exhibition of the correspondence in pictures at the Richmond Art Center in Richmond, California, in fall 1995 provides a vivid testimony to Levin's and Hammond's intellectual and artistic sparrings. The paintings were hung in sequence starting with Levin's opening piece and ending with Hammond's final response. Walking through the exhibit, viewers could immediately see a contrast in styles despite the general similarities in the two artists' work as abstract painters. Levin painted with bold edges and simple patterns. On the other hand, Hammond, as she later admitted, added complexity to each painting, by applying layers of color to make things ambiguous and, as she put it, "ask a lot of questions."

Levin and Hammond not only created their respective paintings but also kept separate journals of their thoughts and musings as they painted and reacted to each other's visual "letters." The two artists' journals offer a fascinating glimpse into the role of communicative intentions in the creation and interpretation of artworks. Visitors at the Richmond Art Center exhibition spent considerable time reading through these journals; in fact, they spent as much if not more time reading the journals than they did looking at the painting dialogue. To take just one instance, Levin wrote upon receiving number 10 (the artists agreed not to give titles to their pieces):

> Despair—a profound despair and hopelessness overwhelms me. This painting makes manifest the leitmotif that has haunted me throughout our project—or maybe throughout my life—the suspicion that communication between people isn't just difficult, it is most probably impossible . . . I suggest multiplicity, you simplify, I suggest ambiguity, you reduce, object, you insist on non-representational shapes . . . I feel that I have been discounted. Denied. Ignored. Refuted. Abandoned. Reduced. Closed out. Maybe we are communicating!

These observations about their visual correspondence dramatically illustrate how important it was for Hammond and Levin to have their communicative intentions understood. Of course, the very nature of their collaboration forced both painters, and also the observers, to wonder about the interplay of intentions in the creation of artworks. Yet taken as a whole, as Hammond noted at the end of the project, the epistolary paint exhibition "shows that the paintings could carry all of that conversation, all of that emotion, all of these ideas, and when we started we weren't sure of that." This project provides wonderful testimony to the importance of intentions in interpersonal communication that is nonverbal and jointly produced by individuals not in close physical proximity.

SKEPTICISM ABOUT INTENTIONS IN COMMUNICATION

The examples above illustrate the importance of communicative intentions in the interpretation of meaning in different interpersonal situations. For most cognitive scientists, it is hard to imagine how people can ever communicate successfully without some understanding of what speakers intend to mean by what they say. One edited volume on intentions in communication, which included contributions by many cognitive scientists, did not even consider the idea that communicative intentions might be an ephemeral byproduct of linguistic understanding instead of a critical part of how utterances are understood (Cohen, Morgan, & Pollack, 1990).

Nevertheless, scholars in various disciplines in the humanities and the social sciences have often expressed skepticism about the role of intentions in interpreting meaning (cf. Iseminger, 1992). Many theorists, for instance, argue that understanding written language differs from comprehending verbal speech because written language tends to be more "decontextualized," with fewer cues about an author's possible communicative intentions (Olson, 1977). Finding the meaning in a text cannot depend on recovering anything about an author's intentions because there is no common ground between author and reader. Other scholars argue that intentions are often inscrutable because whatever a speaker may intend, there are always other meanings at other levels that are conveyed simultaneously (Lyas, 1992). For example, a person might say one thing but communicate other meanings via body gestures or other means. Which meanings an actor specifically intends can never be known for certain. Moreover, an individual's communicative intention can be especially problematic when he or she assumes various, perhaps competing, personae. A speaker, author, or artist might assume a literal posture at one time and an ironic posture at another. In many cases, intentions may be ambiguous or indeterminate, reflecting the mixed intentions of a particular individual at a particular time.

These problems with defining an individual's putative communicative intentions have led many philosophers, literary theorists, and legal scholars to proclaim that authorial intentions do not constrain the interpretation of literary, philosophical, or legal texts (Barthes, 1977; Berger, 1977; Derrida, 1973, 1976, 1978; Dworkin, 1985; Foucault, 1979; Lyon, 1990). These scholars argue that although authors may think they know what they intend, their thought and language are at the mercy of socioeconomic, psychological, and historical forces that cause them to mean something other than what they *think* they intend. This blindness makes what authors intend far less interesting than the operation of these external forces as revealed in their work (De Man, 1983). Anti-intentionalist theorists and critics contend that textual meaning can be determined by conducting close analyses of the "meanings in the text" (Wimsatt & Beardsley, 1954) or deconstructed by recognizing a text's infinite number of possible meanings in the "endless web of texts past and present" (Derrida, 1973). Once again, what an author might have intended to communicate in writing has little or no value in determining how a text should be construed. Similar claims have been advanced for how critics should interpret artworks: What an artist might have intended to convey should pose no limits on observers' interpretations of this art (Beardsley, 1958).

Although most critics of intentions focus on their role in the interpretation of written texts, which are a significant part of interpersonal communication, some anthropologists argue that the assessment and recovery of speakers' intentions are not primary in the ways that many cultures interpret speech in ordinary social contexts (Duranti, 1988; Ochs, 1982; Rosaldo, 1982). For instance, Duranti (1988), reporting on the interpretive strategies of the Samoans, noted the absence of means for distinguishing an utterance from its underlying intention. What an utterance means depends on what others take it to mean. Consequently a Samoan speaker will not "reclaim the meaning of his words by saying *I didn't mean it*" (p. 49).

Samoans often ignore a speaker's alleged intentions and concentrate on the consequences of someone's words. Rather than going back to speculate on what someone intended to say (a phrase that cannot be translated into Samoan), participants in a speech event rely on the dynamics between the speaker's words and the surrounding circumstances, which include the audience's responses, to assign interpretations (Duranti, 1988). In some cases, the audience may be asked to say more about an utterance's meaning than the person who originally uttered it. Samoans practice interpretation as a way of publicly controlling social relationships rather than as a way of figuring out what a given person intended to communicate (Duranti, 1988).

Western and Samoan ideologies of meaning are further contrasted in the character of their caregiver–child interactions (Ochs, 1982). When a young child has said something unintelligible, American white middle-class caregivers express a guess at what meaning the child *intended*, whereas Samoan caregivers normally do not. American caregivers' linguistic interactions conform to a cultural theory of communication in which speakers' personal intentions are critical to the interpretation of an utterance or action. But this theory is limited to certain cultural practices and does not accurately reflect the linguistic practices of many non-Western societies.

RESPONDING TO THE SKEPTICISM

This discussion of literary interpretation and Samoan discourse practices suggests that the interpretation of meaning in interpersonal communication may not limited, or constrained in any way, by the recognition of speakers' or authors' intentions. Yet, at the same time, the arguments of literary theorists and the Samoan data do not directly imply that listeners *never* seek out speakers' complex intentions as part of their immediate, mostly unconscious, processing of linguistic meaning. After all, in Samoan discourse, the analysis of what people say or do in response to what other speakers say focuses on the *products* of understanding, not on the mental *processes* by which people come to their interpretations of linguistic meaning (Gibbs, 1993). Listeners might immediately and unconsciously seek to recover speakers' intentions but then go beyond these intentions when they publicly respond to what has been said. In other words, it is quite possible to derive meanings from utterances that vary from what speakers intend when making these utterances.

Similarly, the attempts by philosophers, legal theorists, and literary critics to deconstruct the meanings of texts focus on the numerous possible interpretations texts might offer. However, these possible meanings are conscious *products* of these critics' interpretative practices and do not necessarily reflect anything about the automatic, unconscious mental *processes* that operate when a critic reads and elaborates on textual meaning. Literary critics and theorists might, just like ordinary speakers and listeners studied by cognitive scientists, immediately and unreflectively attempt to infer something about an author's communicative intentions before they consciously and reflectively analyze or deconstruct what a text could otherwise mean.

Determining what role communicative intentions have in the interpretation of language depends partly on which aspect of the temporal experience of understanding scholars most closely study. Philosophers, linguists, anthropologists, and literary theorists focus their attention on the later products of conscious interpretation and have not generally concern themselves with very fast, unconscious comprehension processes. Cognitive scientists, especially cognitive psychologists and psycholinguists, generally focus on the fast, on-line mental processes that occur during the first several seconds of linguistic processing. The issue here is whether it is appropriate to infer something about early, unconscious mental processes from an analysis of later, reflective products, and vice versa. Is it appropriate to infer something about the role of speakers' or authors' intentions in early on-line processing from an analysis of whether speakers' or authors' intentions constrain textual meaning?

My claim is that such reasoning is faulty and leads to the very different conclusions of cognitive scientists and humanities scholars in the controversy over intentions in interpretation. Many theorists mistakenly assume that a theory constructed to explain one temporal moment of linguistic understanding can be easily generalized to account for *all* aspects of understanding. It is incorrect to conclude that speakers' or authors' communicative intentions are irrelevant to the early processes of language comprehension simply because people can, at times, consciously interpret an utterance without direct appeal to what they think a speaker really intended. To say that people do not seek communicative intentions because they interpret an utterance in a way that apparently deviates from a speaker's or author's intention makes an unwarranted inference about an early process of understanding from an examination of a later product of understanding. Philosophers and literary critics are simply wrong when they proclaim that the "death of the author" eliminates *any* consideration of how authorial intentions constrain people's reading of texts.

In fact, there is experimental evidence demonstrating that people find it easier to understand writtenlanguage if it is assumed to have been composed by intentional agents (i.e., people) rather than by computer programs without intentional agency (Gibbs, Kushner, & Mills, 1991). Participants were presented with comparison statements and were told that these were either written by famous 20th-century poets or were randomly constructed by a computer program. The participants' task in one study was to rate the "meaningfulness" of the comparisons; in another study they read and pushed a button when they had comprehended the statements. Readers found metaphorical expressions, such as "Cigarettes are time bombs," more meaningful when such statements were supposedly written by famous 20th-century poets (intentional agents) than when these same metaphors were seen as random constructions of a computer program. People also took much less time to comprehend the comparisons when they were told that the statements were written by the poets than by the computer program. Moreover, readers took longer to reject as "meaningless" anomalous utterances when these were supposedly written by poets. Readers presume that poets have specific communicative intentions in designing their utterances, an assumption that does not hold for computer programs. Consequently, people spend much more effort trying to understand anomalous phrases, such as "A scalpel is like a horseshoe," when they are supposedly written by poets. But people more immediately rejected as "meaningless" these same anomalous expressions when told that they were written by a computer program because computers are assumed to lack communicative intentions.

These data testify to the powerful role of authorial intentions in people's understanding of writtenexpressions (also see Boswell, 1986). Other studies demonstrate that readers who actively infer something about an author's communicative intentions perform significantly better on various tests of comprehension and recall for expository material than do students who employ less sophisticated reading strategies (Shanahan, 1992; Tierney, LaZansky, Raphael, & Cohen, 1987). Thus, much evidences supports the idea that reading texts also involves significant consideration of people's communicative intentions. Some scholars now view reading as a conversation with an author (Nystrand, 1986; Shanahan, 1992).

GOING BEYOND INTENTIONS IN INTERPERSONAL COMMUNICATION

In Western discourse there are numerous instances of listeners deriving meanings that go beyond what speakers specifically intend to communicate. In these situations, listeners do not misunderstand what a speaker intends, but instead understand what a speaker says along with something more that might be appropriate to the context. In the following example, a speaker's utterance can be understood ironically even if the speaker had no ironic intention (Gibbs, 1994: 388). This scene, from the 1971 television documentary series *An American Family,* occurs fairly late in the series after the husband and wife, Bill and Pat, have separated because of, among many reasons, Bill's infidelity. In this scene, Bill's teenage daughter, Delilah, visits him and he begins the conversation by asking her about one of her brothers, Kevin:

(1) *Bill*:	What's Kevin doing?
(2) *Delilah*:	He studies a lot.
(3) *Bill*:	Is he . . .
(4) *Delilah*:	Yeah
(5) *Bill*:	working pretty hard? . . . Got any girl friend? . . .
(6) *Delilah*:	A lot of girls like him though
(7) *Bill*:	Yeah, Kevin's got that irresistible charm. He wants to get back to Hong Kong
(8) *Delilah*:	Takes after Dad
(9) *Bill*:	Yeah, isn't that the truth

Delilah's comment in (8) that Kevin takes after his father in having irresistible charm is clearly a jocular remark; more ironically, in a previous episode Bill's wife accused him of having irresistible charm that led to his numerous affairs. Delilah seems unaware of this and does not recognize the true irony of her remark in (8). But Bill recognizes the ironic truthfulness in what Delilah says and becomes noticeably embarrassed, and mumbles with intended irony "Yeah, isn't that the truth."

One set of experimental studies investigated readers' processing of intended and unintended verbal irony (Gibbs, O'Brien, & Doolittle, 1995). Consider the following two situations:

John and Bill were taking a statistics class together. Before the final exam, they decided to cooperate during the test. So they worked out a system so they could secretly share answers. After the exam John and Bill were really pleased with themselves. They thought they were pretty clever for beating the system. Later that night, a friend happened to ask them if they ever tried to cheat. John and Bill looked at each other and laughed, then John said, "I would never be involved in any cheating."

John and Bill were taking a statistics class together. They studied hard together, but John was clearly better prepared than Bill. During the exam, Bill panicked and started to copy answers from John. John didn't see Bill do this and so didn't know he was actually helping Bill. John took the school's honor code very seriously. Later than night, a friend happened to ask them if they ever tried to cheat. John and Bill looked at each other, then John said, "I would never be involved in any cheating."

These situations both end with the same statement which is understood as verbal irony. The speaker in the first story specifically intends for his audience to understand what is said as ironic, but the speaker in the second situation does *not* intend his utterance to be understood ironically. In the second story, only the addressees and overhearers see the irony in what the speaker said. People can understand a speaker's utterance as irony even when the speaker did not intend the utterance to be thus understood. Several experimental studies showed that people understand utterances in stories like the second one above as ironic even if the speaker did not intend for the utterance to be understood in this way (Gibbs et al., 1995). In fact, readers rate unintentionally ironic final statements as being more ironic than intentionally ironic statements. Thus, although irony often reflects speakers' communicative goals to identify aspects of ironic situations, speakers may unintentionally create irony by what they say.

CONCLUSION

Cognitive and social psychologists have learned a great deal about how speakers and listeners, and to a lesser extent writers and readers, collaborate in the production and interpretation of language in interpersonal communication. But the varieties of intentions that speakers, writers, and artists communicate suggests that relatively simple task-oriented experiments, such as the referential communication games studied by experimental psychologists, do not capture the complexity of interpersonal communication. As was shown earlier in the doctor–patient dialogue, speakers often convey multiple intentions. Even a single conversational utterance may convey multiple communicative intentions. Consider the following dialogue between a husband and wife (Robertson, Black, & Johnson, 1981, p. 316):

Wife: Why were you out so late last night?
Husband: I went out bowling with the boys.
Wife: I thought you hated bowling.

Each utterance can be jointly understood by wife and husband as reflecting a complex set of intentions. The wife's first utterance, for instance, reflects four interacting goals—to seek information about her husband's whereabouts the previous night, to seek information about his motivation for staying out late, to express anger over his absence, and to regain equilibrium in the relationship. Each intention fits together to produce the wife's initial utterance; the husband's answer partly attempts to respond to some of these intentions. When he responds, he satisfies his wife's goal of seeking information about his location last night, but the goal of seeking information about the husband's motivation for doing so remains active. This goal results in the wife's second statement. Conversational utterances are often made to satisfy multiple goals, which reflect the complexity of people's intentions in speaking with one another. A challenge for psychological accounts of interpersonal communication is to explain how multiple intentions are expressed and understood by conversational participants. A key part of this challenge is accounting for how participants create joint intentions, or we-intentions.

The meanings people infer from linguistic and nonlinguistic situations are not restricted to what speakers, authors, or artists specifically intend. Another challenge for psychological theories of interpersonal communication is to explain how and when addressees go beyond communicative intentions to create meaningful interpretations. It is important to note, again, that these "beyond intentions interpretations" are not mistakes in the sense of an addressee's failing to comprehend what a speaker or author intends to convey. Rather, people often draw inferences that they accurately recognize are not intended but that still appear relevant, either contextually, because of the situation, or personally, for the addressee.

Finally, whether intentions contain interpersonal communication depends on what aspect of communication is being considered. People may automatically and very quickly recover something about what speakers or writers intend to communicate in all situations but then optionally draw additional inferences that vary from communicative intentions at later, usually more conscious, moments of processing. The ultimate determination of how people jointly construct communicative intentions, and when they do and do not do so, requires different methodologies for analyzing the variety of moments at which the apprehension of meaning in interpersonal situations occurs. Whatever the final answers to questions about the roles of intentions in interpersonal communication, scholars must acknowledge the diversity of ways that intentions are communicated and the research of individuals in many academic disciplines that focus on the different ways meaning can be expressed and understood.

REFERENCES

Anscombe, G. (1963). *Intention*. Ithaca, NY: Cornell University Press.

Barthes, R. (1977). *Image, music, text*. New York: Hill & Wang.

Beardsley, M. (1958). *Aesthetics*. New York: Harcourt, Brace, & World.

Berger, R. (1977). *Government by judiciary*. Cambridge, MA: Harvard University Press.

Boswell, D. (1986). Speaker's intentions: Constraints on metaphor comprehension. *Metaphor and Symbolic Activity, 1*, 153–170.

Bratman, M. (1987). *Intention, plans, and practical reason*. Cambridge, MA: Harvard University Press.

Cassell, E. (1985). *Talking with patients: Volume 2, Clinical technique*. Cambridge, MA: MIT Press.

Clark, H. (1978). Inferring what is meant. In W. Levelt & G. Flores d'Arcais (Eds.), *Studies in the perception of language* (pp. 45–71). London: Wiley.

Clark, H., & Carlson, T. (1981). Context for comprehension. In J. Long & A. Baddeley (eds.), *Attention and performance XI* (pp. 313–330). Hillsdale, NJ: Lawrence Erlbaum Associates.

Cohen, P., Morgan, J., & Pollack, M. (Eds.) (1990). *Intentions in communication*. Cambridge, MA: MIT Press.

De Man, P. (1983). *Blindness and insight: Essays in the rhetoric of contemporary criticism*. Minneapolis, MN: University of Minnesota Press.

Derrida, J. (1973). *Speech and phenomena*. Evanston: Northwestern University.

Derrida, J. (1976). *Of grammatology*. Baltimore: Johns Hopkins Press.

Derrida, J. (1978). *Writing and difference*. Chicago: University of Chicago Press.

Dipert, R. (1993). *Artifacts, art works, and agency*. Philadelphia: Temple University Press.

Duranti, A. (1988). Intention, language, and the social action in a Samoan context. *Journal of Pragmatics, 12*, 13–34.

Dworkin, R. (1985). *A matter of principle*. Cambridge, MA: Harvard University Press.

Fast, J. (1970). *Body language*. New York: Lippincott.

Foucault, M. (1979). What is an author? In J. Harari (Ed.) *Textual strategies: Perspectives in post-structuralist criticism* (pp. 35–51). Ithaca, NY: Cornell University Press.

Gibbs, R. (1993). The intentionalist controversy and cognitive science. *Philosophical Psychology, 6*, 175–199.

Gibbs, R. (1994). *The poetics of mind: Figurative thought, language, and understanding*. New York: Cambridge University Press.

Gibbs, R., Kushner, J., & Mills, R. (1991). Authorial intentions in metaphor comprehension. *Journal of Psycholinguistic Research, 20*, 11–30.

Gibbs, R., & Mueller, R. (1987). Conversational meaning as coordinated, cooperative interaction. In S. Robertson, W. Zachery, & J. Black (Eds.), *Cognition, computing and interaction* (pp. 95–114). Norwood, NJ: Ablex.

Gibbs, R., O'Brien, J. E., & Doolittle, S. (1995). Inferring meanings that are not intended: Speakers' intentions and irony comprehension. *Discourse Processes, 20,* 187–203.

Grice, H. P. (1957). Meaning. *Philosophical Review, 64,* 377–388.

Grice, H. P. (1969). Utterer's meaning and intention. *Philosophical Review, 78,* 147–177.

Grice, H. P. (1975). Logic and conversation. In P. Cole & J. Morgan (Eds.), *Syntax and semantics: 3, Speech acts* (pp. 41–58). New York: Academic Press.

Iseminger, G. (Ed.). (1992). *Intention and interpretation.* Philadelphia: Temple University Press.

Kendon, A. (Ed.). (1981). *Nonverbal communication, interaction, and gesture.* New York: Mouton.

Krauss, R. M., Morrel-Samuels, P., & Colasante, C. (1991). Do conversational hand gestures communicate? *Journal of Personality and Social Psychology, 61,* 743–754.

Levinson, S. (1983). *Pragmatics.* Cambridge: Cambridge University Press.

Lyas, C. (1992). Wittgensteinian intentions. In G. Iseminger (Ed.), *Intention and interpretation* (pp. 132–151). Philadelphia: Temple University Press.

Lyon, D. (1990). Basic rights and constitutional interpretation. *Social Theory and Practice, 16,* 337–357.

McNeill, D. (1992). *Hand in mind.* Chicago: University of Chicago Press.

Nystrand, M. (1986). *The structure of written communication: Studies in reciprocity between writers and readers.* Orlando, FL: Academic Press.

Ochs, E. (1982). Talking to children in Western Samoan. *Language in Society, 11,* 72–104.

Olson, D. (1977). From utterance to text: The bias of language in speech and writing. *Harvard Educational Review, 47,* 257–281.

Robertson, S., Black, J., & Johnson, P. (1981). Intention and topic in conversation. *Cognition and Brain Theory, 4,* 303–326.

Rosaldo, S. (1982). The things we do with words: Ilongot speech acts and speech act theory in philosophy. *Language in Society, 11,* 203–237.

Searle, J. (1990). Collective intentions and actions. In P. Cohen, J. Morgan, & M. Pollack (Eds.), *Intentions in communication* (pp. 401–416). Cambridge, MA: MIT .

Shanahan, T. (1992). Reading comprehension as a conversation with an author. In M. Pressley, K. Harris, & J. Guthrie (Eds.), *Promoting academic competence and literacy in schools* (pp. 129–148). San Diego: Academic Press.

Sperber, D., & Wilson, D. (1986). *Relevance: Communication and cognition.* Cambridge, MA: Harvard University Press.

Tierney, R., LaZansky, J., Raphael, T., & Cohen, P. (1987). Author's intentions and reader's interpretations. In R. Tierney, P. Andes, & J. Mitchell (Eds.), *Understanding readers' understanding* (pp. 205–226). Hillsdale, NJ: Lawrence Erlbaum Associates.

Tannen, D. (1982). Ethnic style in male–female conversation. In J. Gumperz (Ed.), *Language and social identity* (pp. 217–231). Cambridge: Cambridge Univ. Press.

Wimsatt, W., & Beardsley, M. (1954). The intentional fallacy. In W. Wimsatt & M. Beardsley (Eds.), *The verbal icon: Studies in the meaning of poetry* (pp. 4–5). Lexington: University of Kentucky Press.

— 3 —

Communication in Standardized Research Situations: A Gricean Perspective

Norbert Schwarz

University of Michigan

Much knowledge of human behavior is based on the reports that research participants provide in response to a researcher's questions. From testing social science theories to determining the nation's unemployment rate, and from assessing public opinion to predicting future health care needs, researchers rely on the verbal reports that respondents provide in surveys. To gain an understanding of human cognition and judgment, we expose participants in psychological experiments to carefully constructed reasoning tasks. To reduce unwanted variation and to render research participants' answers comparable, the communication in these settings is highly standardized. Interviewers are trained to read the questions verbatim and to provide standardized explanations, if any, should a respondent ask for clarification. Similarly, experimenters are trained to follow a tightly designed script, even under conditions where their utterances are to appear as spontaneous. Moreover, research participants are expected to provide their answers in a predefined format, by checking a number on a rating scale or by endorsing one of several response alternatives presented to them.

As many researchers have noted (e.g., Bless, Strack, & Schwarz, 1993; Clark & Schober, 1992; Hilton, 1995; Strack, 1994a, b; Strack & Schwarz, 1992), standardizing communication in research settings precludes the mutual negotiation of meaning that characterizes communication in everyday life. Nevertheless, research participants are likely to bring to the research situation the tacit assumptions that govern the conduct of conversation in daily life. These tacit assumptions, described in Grice's (1975, 1978) logic of conversation, hold that conversations follow a cooperative principle that enjoins speakers to make their contributions informative, relevant, truthful, and clear.

In this chapter, I review research suggesting that the application of these tacit assumptions to research situations contributes to a wide range of phenomena that are typically assumed to reflect artifacts in survey measurement or inherent shortcomings and biases in human judgment. In survey interviews, for example, some 30% of respondents in any representative sample are likely to report an opinion on an issue that they can not know anything about because it was invented by the researcher (e.g., Schuman & Presser, 1981). Moreover,

39

respondents are likely to report that they watch more television (Schwarz, Hippler, Deutsch, & Strack, 1985), or have more frequent medical complaints (Schwarz & Scheuring, 1992), when the response scale on which they report their answers offers high- rather than low-frequency response alternatives. In experimental research, participants are likely to draw on useless information provided to them by experimenters; they rely, for example, on personality information of dubious diagnosticity at the expense of more diagnostic base-rate information (e.g., Kahneman & Tversky, 1973). When we consider findings of this type in light of the assumptions that govern the conduct of conversation outside research settings, they seem less surprising than their treatment in the psychological literature would suggest. Having no reason to assume that a researcher would ask a question about a nonexistent issue, would present a scale that is haphazardly designed, or would provide useless information, research participants are likely to search for meaning in a researcher's contributions. Little do they know that researchers violate every norm of conversational conduct that they would be likely to observe outside the research setting by providing information that is not relevant, informative, truthful, or clear. Researchers, however, are likely to evaluate research participants' responses relative to normative models that draw only on the semantic meaning of the information provided and ignore its pragmatic implications. As a result, many apparent artifacts and biases may, in part, reflect violations of conversational norms in research settings, rather than inherent shortcomings of human judgment.

Below, I first introduce the key assumptions of the Gricean logic of conversation. Subsequently, I illustrate their operation in research situations, focusing on survey interviews and psychological experiments.

THE LOGIC OF CONVERSATION

To understand the meaning of an utterance, a listener must go beyond the semantic meaning of the words to infer what the speaker intended to convey. As Clark and Schober (1992, p. 15) put it, it is a "common misperception that language use has primarily to do with words and what they mean. It doesn't. It has primarily to do with people and what *they* mean. It is essentially about *speakers' intentions*." To determine the meaning intended by a speaker and to design their reply, a listener relies on a set of tacit assumptions that have been described by Grice (1975, 1978), a philosopher of language. These assumptions can be expressed in the form of four deceptively simple maxims, which jointly make up a cooperative principle of conversation. Table 3.1, adapted from Levinson's (1983, pp. 101–102) discussion, summarizes these maxims.

TABLE 3.1

The Logic of Conversation

The Cooperative Principle

Make your contribution such as is required, at the stage at which it occurs, by the accepted purpose or direction of the talk exchange in which you are engaged.

Maxim of Manner

Be perspicuous, and specifically:
  1. Avoid obscurity.
  2. Avoid ambiguity.
  3. Be brief.
  4. Be orderly.

Maxim of Relation

Make your contributions relevant to the ongoing exchange.

Maxim of Quantity

  1. Make your contribution as informative as is required for the current purposes of the exchange.
  2. Do not make your contribution more informative than is required.

Maxim of Quality

Try to make your contribution one that is true, specifically:
  1. Do not say what you believe to be false.
  2. Do not say anything for which you lack adequate evidence.

Note: Adapted *Pragmatics* (pp. 101–102), by S. C. Levinson, 1983,Cambridge, England: Cambridge University Press. Copyright 1983 by Cambridge University Press. Adapted with permission.

A *maxim of manner* asks speakers to make their contribution such that it can be understood by their audience. To do so, speakers must avoid ambiguity and wordiness. Moreover, they must consider the characteristics of their audience and design their utterances in a way that the audience can figure out what they mean—and speakers are reasonably good at doing so (Krauss & Fussell, 1991). At the heart of this process are speakers' assumptions about the information that they share with recipients, that is, the common ground (Schiffer, 1972; Stalnaker, 1978). Listeners, in turn, assume that speakers observe this maxim and interpret speakers' utterances against what they assume to constitute the common ground (e. g., Clark, Schreuder, & Buttrick, 1983; Fussell & Krauss, 1989a, 1989b). Each successful contribution to the conversation extends the participants' common ground, reflecting that "in orderly discourse, common ground is cumulative" (Clark & Schober, 1992, p. 19).

This cumulative nature of the common ground reflects, in part, the operation of a *maxim of relation* that enjoins speakers to make all contributions relevant to the aims of the ongoing conversation. This maxim entitles listeners to use the context of an utterance to disambiguate its meaning by making bridging inferences (Clark, 1977). Moreover, this maxim implies that speakers are unlikely to assume that a contribution to a conversation is irrelevant to its goal, unless it is marked as such. As an example, suppose *A* asks, "Where is Bill?" and *B* responds, "There's a yellow Volkswagen (VW) outside Sue's home" (Levinson, 1983, p. 102). If taken literally, *B's* contribution fails to answer *A's* question and thus violates (at least) the maxim of relation and the maxim of quantity (to be addressed below). When people read this exchange, however, they are unlikely to consider *B's* contribution an inappropriate change of topic. Rather, they infer that Bill probably has a yellow VW and that the location of the yellow VW suggests that Bill is at Sue's home. These inferences, and the ease with which readers draw them, reflect the implicit assumption that *B* is a cooperative communicator whose contribution is relevant to *A's* question. As Sperber and Wilson (1986, p. vi) put it, "Communicated information comes with a guarantee of relevance" and if in doubt, it is the listener's task to determine the intended meaning of the utterance by referring to the common ground or by asking for clarification.

In addition, a *maxim of quantity* requires speakers to make their contributions as informative as is required, but not more informative than is required. That is, speakers should respect the established, or assumed, common ground by providing the information that a recipient needs, without reiterating information that the recipient already has or may take for granted (Clark & Haviland, 1977; Haviland & Clark, 1974). Finally, a *maxim of quality* enjoins speakers not to say anything that they believe to be false or lack adequate evidence for.

As Grice (1975) noted, these maxims apply most directly to situations in which participants attempt to exchange information to get things done. Conversations that are characterized by other goals, such as entertaining one another, are less likely to follow these rules (see Higgins, 1981; Higgins, Fondacaro, & McCann, 1982). Because this chapter is concerned with conversational processes in research settings, however, the adjustments required by different conversational goals do not need further elaboration. In general, research participants are likely to perceive the research situation as a task-oriented setting in which participants attempt to exchange information as accurately as possible; thus, the assumptions underlying task-oriented conversations are highly relevant.

In summary, on the basis of the tacit assumptions that govern the conduct of conversation in daily life, "Communicated information comes with a guarantee of relevance" (Sperber & Wilson, 1986, p. vi), and listeners are entitled to assume that speakers try to be informative, truthful, relevant, and clear. Moreover, listeners interpret speakers' utterances "on the assumption that they are trying to live up to these ideals" (Clark & Clark , 1977, p. 122).

Implications for Research Settings

Grice's (1975) maxims have important implications for research settings. As noted earlier (see also Bless et al., 1993; Clark & Schober, 1992; Strack, 1994a, b; Strack & Schwarz, 1992), "conversations" in research settings differ from natural conversations by being highly constrained. Whereas speakers and addressees collaborate in unconstrained natural conversations to establish the intended meaning of an utterance, their opportunity to do so is severely limited in research settings, because of the researcher's attempt to standardize the interaction. Typically, the standardization of instructions, or of the questions asked, prevents the utterances from being tailored to meet different common grounds. Moreover, when research participants ask for clarification, they often may not receive additional information. Rather, the previously given instructions may be repeated or a well-trained survey interviewer may respond, "Whatever it means to you," when asked to clarify a question's meaning. In some cases, as when a respondent is asked to complete a self-administered questionnaire, nobody may be available to ask for clarification. As a result, a mutual negotiation of intended meaning is largely precluded in many research situations.

Nevertheless, research participants attempt to cooperate by determining the intended meaning of a researcher's contributions to the constrained conversation. To do so, they need to rely even more on the tacit assumptions that govern the conduct of conversation in daily life than they would under less constrained conditions. Unfortunately, however, they are bound to miss one crucial point: Whereas the researcher is likely to comply with conversational maxims in almost any conversation he or she conducts outside a research setting, the researcher is much less likely to do so in the research setting itself. In fact, a researcher may violate every maxim of conversation by providing information that is neither relevant, truthful, informative nor clear—and may have explicitly designed the situation to suggest otherwise. A considerable body of research suggests that this misunderstanding about the cooperative nature of the research conversation is at the heart of many apparent biases, shortcomings, and artifacts that have been observed in psychological experiments and survey measurements (for reviews see Bless et al., 1993; Clark & Schober, 1992; Hilton, 1995; Schwarz, 1994, 1996; Strack, 1994a, b; Strack & Schwarz, 1992).

I next address two implications in more detail. The first implication pertains to Grice's maxim of relation and holds that research participants consider every contribution of researchers relevant and draw on it in determining the nature of their task and in arriving at an appropriate answer. In a research situation, the researcher's contributions include previously asked questions as well as apparently formal features of questionnaire design, such as the response scales provided to respondents, in addition to explicit instructions and other information. Hence, I first review what respondents infer from contextual information provided in a questionnaire and subsequently turn to the conversational relevance of information provided in psychological experiments. The second implication pertains to Grice's maxim of quantity, which enjoins speakers to provide information that recipients need rather than to reiterate information that the recipient already has. Respondents' attempts to obey this maxim in designing their answers contribute to a diverse set of apparent judgmental biases, including the emergence of assimilation and contrast effects.

THE RELEVANCE OF THE RESEARCHER'S CONTRIBUTIONS: CONTEXTUAL INFORMATION PROVIDED IN QUESTIONNAIRES

Survey researchers have long been aware that minor variations in the wording of a question or the design of a questionnaire may strongly affect the obtained responses (see Payne, 1951; Schuman & Presser, 1981; Sudman & Bradburn, 1974), and researchers have wondered how meaningful the obtained answers are. Although the observed findings have often been considered artifacts of survey measurement, recent research suggests that they reflect participants' application of conversational norms to the survey interview (e.g., Schwarz, 1995; Schwarz & Hippler, 1991; Strack, 1994a, b). Facing an ambiguous question or an otherwise difficult task, respondents draw on contextual information presented in a questionnaire to arrive at a meaningful interpretation. In doing so, they assume that the contributions of the researcher are relevant to the task at hand, as the examples in this section illustrate.

Making Sense of Ambiguous Questions

As an extreme example, consider questions about highly obscure or even completely fictitious issues, such as the "Agricultural Trade Act of 1978" (e.g., Bishop, Oldendick, & Tuchfarber, 1986; Schuman & Presser, 1981). In a typical study, some 30% of the respondents of a representative sample are likely to report an opinion on these issues, despite the fact that they cannot know anything about it. Why researchers ask such a question in the first place? The rationale for these studies is survey researchers' concern that the "fear of appearing uninformed" may induce "many respondents to conjure up opinions even when they had not given the particular issue any thought prior to the interview" (Erikson, Luttberg, & Tedin, 1988, p. 44). At first glance, asking questions about a fictitious issue provides a direct way to address this concern. From this perspective, the observation that many respondents are willing to report an opinion on a fictitious issue casts doubt on the reports provided in survey interviews in general and suggests that many responses are based on a "mental flip of coin" (Converse, 1964, 1970).

A conversational perspective suggests, however, that these responses may be more meaningful than has typically been assumed in public opinion research. The sheer fact that a question about an issue is asked presupposes that the issue exists—otherwise, asking a question about it would violate the norms of cooperative conduct. Respondents, however, have no reason to assume that researchers would ask meaningless questions and hence they try to make sense of the questions (see Sudman, Bradburn, & Schwarz, 1996, chap. 3, for general discussions of respondents' tasks in a survey interview). If a question is highly ambiguous and an interviewer does not provide additional clarification, respondents are likely to turn to the context of the ambiguous question to determine its meaning, much as they would be expected to do in any other conversation. Once respondents have assigned a particular meaning to an issue and have thus transformed the fictitious issue into a better defined issue that makes sense in the context of the interview, they may have no difficulty in reporting a subjectively meaningful opinion. Even if they have not given the particular issue much thought, they may easily identify the broader set of issues to which this particular one apparently belongs. If so, they can use their general attitude toward the broader set of issues to determine their attitude toward this particular one.

A study by Strack, Schwarz, and Wänke (1991, Experiment 1) illustrates this point. In this study, German college students were asked to report their attitude toward the introduction of an "educational contribution" allegedly discussed in a state parliament. For some participants, this target question was preceded by a question that asked them to estimate the average tuition fees that students pay at U.S. universities (in contrast to Germany, where university education is free). Others had to estimate the amount of money that the Swedish government pays every student as financial support. After having reported their own opinion on the introduction of an "educational contribution," respondents were asked what the "educational contribution" implied. Content analyses of their definitions of the fictitious issue indicated that they used the context of the question to determine its meaning. Hence, they inferred that "educational contributions" implied that students receive money when preceded by Swedish support question, but that students have to pay money when preceded by the American tuition question. Not surprisingly, their opinions reflected these interpretation and they favored the introduction of an "educational contribution" in the former case, but opposed it in the latter.

In summary, respondents turned to the contents of related questions to determine the meaning of an ambiguous question. In doing so, they interpreted the ambiguous question in a way that made sense of it and subsequently provided a subjectively meaningful response to *their* definition of the question. Accordingly, it is no surprise that responses to fictitious issues do *not* conform to a model of mental coin flipping as Converse (1964) and other early researchers hypothesized. Rather, they show a meaningful pattern that is systematically related to respondents' attitudes in substantively related domains (e.g., Schwarz, Strack, Hippler, & Bishop, 1991; see also Schuman & Kalton, 1985). What is at the heart of reported opinions about fictitious issues is not that respondents are willing to give subjectively meaningless answers, but that researchers violate conversational rules by asking meaningless questions in a context that suggests otherwise.

Open- Versus Closed-Question Formats

Although most researchers would agree that a question about a fictitious issue presents a formidable interpretation task, they have often overlooked the extent to which much simpler questions require elaborate inferences to determine their meaning. As Grice (1975) emphasized, answering any question requires more than an understanding of the semantic meaning of the words—it requires a pragmatic understanding of a speaker's intended meaning: What is it that the questioner wants to know? Suppose, for example, that you are asked to report what you have done today. Most likely, you would not include in your report that you took a shower, that you dressed, and so on. If these activities were included in a list of response alternatives, however, you would probably endorse them. This thought experiment reflects a set of standard findings from the survey methodology literature (for a review, see Schwarz & Hippler, 1991). Experimental studies on the impact of open- and closed-response formats have consistently demonstrated that these response formats yield considerable differences in the marginal distribution as well as in the ranking of items (e.g., Bishop, Hippler, Schwarz, & Strack, 1988; Schuman & Presser, 1977). On one hand, any opinion is less likely to be volunteered in an open-response format than to be endorsed in a closed-response format, if presented. On the other hand, opinions that are omitted from the set of response alternatives in a closed format are unlikely to be reported at all, even when an "other" category, which respondents in general rarely use, is explicitly offered, (Bradburn, 1983; Molenaar, 1982).

Several processes are likely to contribute to these findings. Most importantly, respondents are unlikely to spontaneously report, in an open-answer format, information that seems self-evident or irrelevant. In refraining from these responses, they follow the conversational maxim that an utterance should be informative and should provide the information that the recipient is interested in. This practice results in an under-reporting of presumably self-evident information that is eliminated by closed-response formats, where the explicit presentation of the proper response alternative indicates the investigator's interest in this information. Moreover, respondents may frequently be uncertain if information that comes to mind does or does not belong to the domain of information the investigator is interested in. Again, closed-response formats may reduce this uncertainly, resulting in higher responses. Finally, a generic "other" response provides little information and would be considered inadequate as an answer in most conversations. Hence, it is rarely checked.

The response alternatives may also remind respondents of options that they may otherwise not have considered. The literature in survey methodology has typically focused on this possibility, which implies that closed-response formats may suggest answers that respondents would never think of themselves. This assumption is to some degree supported by the observation that less well-educated respondents are more likely to refuse to answer in an open-response format, but are more likely to provide an answer in a closed-response format, than are well-educated respondents (Schuman & Presser, 1981). However, a conversational analysis suggests that the bulk of the obtained differences is more plausibly traced to the clarification of the questioner's interest that is provided by a closed-response format. Most important, the assumption that respondents may lack the information required for an answer, and hence pick one from the response alternatives, may hold to some degree for complex knowledge questions but does not hold for questions about daily activities such as, "What have you done today?" Nevertheless, the same differences are obtained for questions of this type, and they are most pronounced for activities that a questioner may take for granted, such as taking a shower or getting dressed (see Schwarz & Hippler, 1991, for an extended discussion).

Numeric Values of Rating Scales

Although it may not seem surprising that respondents draw on the content of substantive response alternatives to determine a question's intended meaning, similar processes have been observed for highly formal response alternatives, such as the numeric values presented as part of a rating scale. In constructing a rating scale, researchers typically pay attention to the verbal end anchors used and to the number of scale points presented (for a review see Dawes & Smith,

1985). Having settled for a 7-point rating scale, for example, they are less likely to worry whether those 7 points should be represented by unnumbered boxes, by numbers ranging from 1 to 7, or by numbers ranging from - 3 to + 3.

Empirically, however, the specific numerical values used may strongly affect the obtained responses. For example, Schwarz, Knäuper, Hippler, Noelle-Neumann, and Clark (1991, Experiment 1) asked a representative sample of German adults, "How successful would you say you have been in life?" This question was accompanied by an 11-point rating scale, with the endpoints labeled "not at all successful" and "extremely successful." In one condition, the numeric values of the rating scale ranged from 0 ("not at all successful") to 10 ("extremely successful"), whereas in the other condition they ranged from - 5 ("not at all successful") to + 5 ("extremely successful"). The results showed a pronounced effect from the numeric values used. Whereas 34% of the respondents endorsed a value between 0 and 5 on the 0 to 10 scale, only 13% endorsed one of the formally equivalent values between - 5 and 0 on the - 5 to + 5 scale. After both scales were coded from 0 to 10, this pattern resulted in mean ratings of $M = 6.4$ on the 0 to 10, but $M = 7.3$ on the - 5 to + 5 version of the scale.

Subsequent experiments (Schwarz, Knäuper, et al., 1991) indicated that the impact of numeric values reflects differential interpretations of the ambiguous endpoint label "not at all successful." When this label was combined with the numeric value 0, respondents interpreted it to refer to the absence of noteworthy success. When the same label was combined with the numeric value - 5, they interpreted it to refer to the presence of explicit failure. This differential interpretation reflects that a minus-to-plus format emphasizes the bipolar nature of the dimension that the researcher has in mind, implying that one endpoint label refers to the opposite of the other. Hence, "not at all successful" is interpreted as reflecting the opposite of success, that is, failure. In contrast, a rating scale format that presents only positive values suggests that the researcher has a unipolar dimension in mind. In this case, the scale values reflect different degrees of the presence of the crucial feature. Hence, "not at all successful" is now interpreted as reflecting the mere absence of noteworthy success, rather than the presence of failure. This differential interpretation of the same term as a function of its accompanying numeric value also affects the inferences that judges draw on the basis of a report given along a rating scale. For example, in a follow-up experiment (Schwarz, Knäuper, et al., 1991, Experiment 3), a fictitious student reported his academic success along one of the described scales and checked either a - 4 or a formally equivalent 2. As expected, when judges were asked to estimate how often this student had failed an exam, they assumed that the student failed twice as often when he checked a - 4 than when he checked a 2, although both values are formally equivalent along the rating scales used.

Moreover, respondents' use of numeric values in making sense of verbal labels is not restricted to variations that include or omit negative numbers. For example, Grayson and Schwarz (1995) asked undergraduates how often they engaged in a variety of low frequency activities. In all conditions, the 11-point rating scale ranged from "rarely" to "often." "Rarely," however, was combined with the numeric value 0 in one condition and the numeric value 1 in the other. As expected, respondents interpreted "rarely" to mean "never" when combined with 0, but to mean "low frequency" when combined with 1. As a result, they provided higher mean frequency ratings along the 0 to 10 ($M = 2.8$) than along the 1 to 11 scale ($M = 1.9$; scale recoded to 0 to 10).

In combination, these findings illustrate that "even the most unambiguous words show a range of meaning, or a degree of semantic flexibility that is constrained by the particular context in which these words occur" (Woll, Weeks, Fraps, Pendergrass, & Vanderplas, 1980, p. 60). Assuming that all contributions to an ongoing conversation are relevant, respondents turn to the context of a word to disambiguate its meaning, much as they would be expected to do in daily life. In a research situation, however, the contributions of the researcher include apparently formal features of questionnaire design, and render these features an important source of information, which respondents use. Far from demonstrating superficial and meaningless responding, findings of this type indicate that respondents systematically exploit the information available to them in an attempt to understand their task and to provide meaningful answers.

At the same time, these findings emphasize that researchers must be sensitive to the informational implications of their research instruments to use them to advantage. For instance, the previous findings suggest that rating scales with a continuum from negative to positive values may indicate that a researcher has a bipolar conceptualization of the respective dimension in mind, whereas scales with only positive values may indicate a unipolar conceptualization. If so, the choice of numeric values may either facilitate or dilute the polarity implications of the endpoint labels provided to respondents. Accordingly, researchers should ensure that the numeric values provided to respondents match the intended conceptualization of the underlying dimension as uni- or bipolar.

Frequency Scales

The same theme is reiterated in a related line of research, bearing on the impact of response alternatives on behavioral frequency reports (for a review, see Schwarz, 1990). Survey respondents are often asked to report the frequency with which they engage in a behavior by checking the appropriate value from a set of frequency response alternatives. Again, the range of response alternatives can serve as a source of information for respondents. In general, respondents assume that researchers construct a meaningful scale that reflects appropriate knowledge about the distribution of the behavior. Accordingly, values in the middle range of the scale are assumed to reflect "average" or "typical" behavior, whereas the extremes of the scale are assumed to correspond to the extremes of the distribution. These assumptions influence respondents' interpretations of the question, their behavioral reports, and related judgments.

Question Interpretation. Suppose, for example, that respondents are asked to indicate how frequently they were "really irritated" recently. Before respondents can answer, they must decide what the researcher means by "really irritated." Does the phrase refer to major irritations such as fights with a spouse, or does it refer to minor irritations such as having to wait for service in a restaurant? To determine the intended meaning, respondents may turn to the information provided by the frequency range of the response scale. High-frequency response alternatives presumably indicate that the researcher is interested in relatively frequent events, whereas low-frequency response alternatives indicate an interest in rare events. Because major irritations are less frequent than minor irritations, this presumption bears on the kinds of irritations the researcher may be interested in. Consistent with this assumption, Schwarz, Strack, Müller, and Chassein (1988) observed that respondents reported minor irritations when the response scale ranged from "several times daily" to "less than once a week," but reported major irritations when the scale ranged from "several times a year" to "less than once every three months." Thus, respondents drew on the information provided by the response scale and on their knowledge of the differential frequency of major and minor annoyances to determine the intended meaning of the question. Accordingly, identical question stems in combination with different frequency scales result in different interpretations, and hence assess different experiences.

Frequency Estimates. Even if the behavior under investigation is reasonably well defined, however, the range of response alternatives may strongly affect respondents' frequency estimates. This observation reflects the fact that mundane behaviors of a high frequency, such as watching television, are not represented in memory as distinct episodes (for reviews, see Bradburn, Rips, & Shevell, 1987; Schwarz, 1990). Rather, the various episodes blend together in a generic representation of the behavior that lacks temporal markers. Accordingly, respondents cannot recall the episodes to determine the frequency of the behavior but can only rely on an estimation strategy (see Menon, 1994, for a more detailed discussion). In doing so, they may use the range of the scale presented to them as a frame of reference. This results in higher frequency estimates along scales that present high- rather than low-frequency response alternatives.

The results of a study on television consumption, shown in Table 3.2, illustrate this effect (Schwarz, Hippler, Deutsch, & Strack, 1985, Experiment 1). In this study, 37.5% of a quota sample of German adults reported watching TV for 2.5 hours or more a day when they were presented with the high frequency response alternatives shown in Table 3.2, whereas only 16.2% reported doing so when presented with the low frequency response alternatives.

TABLE 3.2

Reported Daily TV Consumption as a Function of Response Alternatives

Low-Frequency Alternatives	Percentage	High-Frequency Alternatives	Percentage
Up to $\frac{1}{2}$ h	7.4%	Up to $2\frac{1}{2}$ h	62.5%
$\frac{1}{2}$ h to 1 h	17.7%	$2\frac{1}{2}$ h to 3 h	23.4%
1h to $1\frac{1}{2}$ h	26.5%	3h to $3\frac{1}{2}$ h	7.8%
$1\frac{1}{2}$ h to 2 h	14.7%	$3\frac{1}{2}$ h to 4 h	4.7%
2h to $2\frac{1}{2}$ h	17.7%	4h to $4\frac{1}{2}$ h	1.6%
More than $2\frac{1}{2}$ h	16.2%	More than $4\frac{1}{2}$ h	0.0%

Note. $N = 132$.

Adapted from "Response scales: Effects of category range on reported behavior and comparative judgments," by N. Schwarz, H. J. Hippler, B. Deutsch, & F. Strack, F., 1985, *Public Opinion Quarterly, 49*, 388–395. Copyright 1985 by University of Chicago Press. Adapted with permission.

Not surprisingly, respondents' reliance on the frame of reference suggested by response alternatives increases as their knowledge about relevant episodes decreases (Menon, Raghubir, & Schwarz, 1995; Schwarz & Bienias, 1990) or the complexity of the judgmental task increases (Bless, Bohner, Hild, & Schwarz, 1992). More important, however, the impact of response alternatives is eliminated when the informational value of the response alternatives is called into question. For example, telling respondents that they were participating in a pretest designed to explore the adequacy of the response alternatives wiped out the otherwise obtained scale effect (see Schwarz & Hippler, 1991, reported in Schwarz, 1996). Again, these findings illustrate that respondents assume researchers to be a cooperative communicators, whose contributions are relevant to the ongoing conversation, unless the implicit guarantee of relevance is called into question.

Comparative Judgments. In addition, the frequency range of the response alternatives has been found to affect subsequent comparative judgments. On the basis of the assumption that the scale reflects the distribution of behavior, checking a response alternative is the same as locating one's own position in the distribution. Accordingly, respondents extract comparison information from their own locations on the response scale and use this information in making subsequent comparative judgments.

For example, checking "2 h" on the low-frequency scale shown in Table 3.2 implies that a respondent's television consumption is above average, whereas checking the same value on the high-frequency scale implies that his or her television consumption is below average. As a result, respondents in the Schwarz et al. (1985) studies reported that television plays a more important role in their leisure time (Experiment 1) and described themselves as less satisfied with the variety of things they do in their leisure time (Experiment 2), when they had to report their television consumption on the low- rather than the high-frequency scale. Moreover, these frame of reference effects are not limited to respondents themselves, but influence the users of their reports as well. For example, in a study by Schwarz, Bless, Bohner, Harlacher, and Kellenbenz (1991, Experiment 2), experienced medical doctors considered that a patient's having the same physical symptom twice a week reflected a more severe medical condition when "twice a week" was a high-rather than a low-response alternative on the symptoms checklist presented to them.

Conclusions

Findings of the type reviewed in this section have usually been considered measurement artifacts. From a conversational viewpoint , however, they simply reflect that respondents bring the assumptions that govern the conduct of conversations in daily life to the research situation. Hence, they assume that every contribution is relevant to the goal of the ongoing conversation—and in a research situation, these contributions include preceding questions as well as apparently formal features of the questionnaire, such as the numeric values presented as part of a rating scale or the response alternatives presented as part of a frequency question. As a result, the scales used are far from neutral measurement devices. Rather, they constitute a source of information that respondents actively use in determining their tasks and in constructing reasonable answers. Whereas researchers have traditionally focused on the information that is provided by the wording of the question stem, they need to pay equal attention to the information conveyed by apparently formal features of the questionnaire.

THE RELEVANCE OF THE RESEARCHER'S CONTRIBUTIONS: PRESENTING "IRRELEVANT" INFORMATION IN EXPERIMENTS

Given that survey respondents draw on apparently formal features of questionnaire design to determine the intended meaning of questions presented by researchers, it is no surprise that participants in psychological experiments are equally likely to consider all contributions of experimenters as relevant to their task (for a review, see Bless et al., 1993). This observation is particularly problematic in studies in which an experimenter deliberately presents information that is irrelevant from the perspective of normative models of judgment. Having no reason to assume that an experimenter may violate all norms of conversational conduct by presenting information that is not relevant, truthful, or clear, participants are likely to do their best to find relevance in the information provided to them—or else, why would the experimenter have presented it in the first place?

Recent research has demonstrated that this basic misunderstanding about the cooperative nature of researchers' conversational conduct has systematically contributed to some of the more dramatic demonstrations of judgmental shortcomings. Relevant examples include the fundamental attribution error (e.g., Wright & Wells, 1988), over reliance on nondiagnostic individuating information at the expense of more diagnostic base-rate information (e.g., Schwarz, Strack, Hilton, & Naderer, 1991), and the emergence of leading-question effects in eyewitness testimony (e.g., Dodd & Bradshaw, 1980). Like most robust phenomena, these biases are undoubtedly overdetermined, and it would be misleading to trace their operation solely to violations of conversational norms. Nevertheless, we are unlikely to understand their operation in natural contexts when our experimental procedures give rise to them for reasons that are unlikely to hold outside of the psychological laboratory. Below, I illustrate this point with one example, namely a classic study on base-rate neglect reported by Kahneman and Tversky (1973; for extensive reviews, see Hilton, 1995; Schwarz, 1994, 1996).

Conversational Relevance of "Irrelevant" Information

Numerous studies have demonstrated a pronounced bias to rely on individuating information of little diagnostic value at the expense of more diagnostic base-rate information (for a review, see Nisbett & Ross, 1980). Although the initial conclusion that individuating information typically overwhelms the impact of base-rate information has been qualified by subsequent research (for a review, see Ginossar & Trope, 1987), the specific conditions under which people will or will not use base-rate information are still poorly understood. Unfortunately, the research paradigm most frequently used in this domain may have contributed to this state of affairs.

In what is probably the best-known demonstration of base-rate neglect, Kahneman and Tversky (1973) told their participants that a target person described to them "shows no interest in political and social issues and spends most of his free time on his many hobbies which include home carpentry, sailing, and mathematical puzzles" (p. 241). These participants predicted that the target person was most likely an engineer, independently of whether the base-rate probability for any target's being an engineer was .30 or .70. An analysis of the instructions used in this study proves informative. Specifically, the instructions read (emphases added):

> A panel of *psychologists* have *interviewed* and administered *personality tests* to 30 (resp. 70) engineers and 70 (resp. 30) lawyers, all successful in their respective fields. On the basis of *this* information, thumbnail descriptions of the 30 engineers and 70 lawyers have been written. You will find on your forms five descriptions, chosen at random from the 100 available descriptions. For each description, please indicate your probability that the person described is an engineer, on a scale from 0 to 100.

> The same task has been performed by a panel of *experts* who were *highly accurate* in assigning probabilities to the various descriptions. You will be paid a bonus to the extent that your estimates come close to those of the expert panel" (Kahneman & Tversky, 1973, p. 241).

The first part of the instructions informs participants that the individuating information was compiled by psychologists on the basis of respected procedures in their profession, namely interviews and tests. Given that laypeople generally assume psychologists to be experts on issues of personality (rather than on baserates), this introduction emphasizes the relevance of the individuating information. Moreover, other experts—most likely psychologists as well, to judge by the present context—are said to be highly accurate in making these judgments, a statement that further increases the relevance of the individuating information. The participants' task is then defined as determining a probability that matches the judgments of the experts. If these experts are assumed to be psychologists, participants can infer that the experimenter wants them to use the same information that these experts used—most likely the personality information compiled by their colleagues.

Finally, as the experiment proceeds, participants are asked to judge several target persons for whom different individuating information is presented. The base-rate information about the sample from which the targets are drawn, on the other hand, is held constant. This practice further suggests that the individuating information is of crucial importance: The information provides different clues for each judgment, and in the absence of this information all tasks would have the same solution. Thus, the instructions and procedures of Kahneman and Tversky's classic study allowed participants to infer (however incorrectly) the experimenter's intention that they should base their judgment on the individuating information. It therefore comes as little surprise that participants relied on it when making their judgments.

To test this conversational analysis of the base-rate fallacy, Schwarz, Strack, Hilton, et al. (1991, Experiment 1) tried to undermine the guarantee of relevance that characterizes human communication in a modified partial replication of Kahneman and Tversky's study. Some participants were told that the person description was written by a psychologist, replicating the instructions used by Kahneman and Tversky. This wording entitles recipients to assume that the presented information obeys the tacit rules of conversational conduct and reflects a particular communicative intention on the part of the experimenter. Other participants were told that the (identical) description was compiled by a computer drawing a random sample of descriptive sentences bearing on the target person. Obviously, the cooperative principle does not directly apply to the resulting communication, and the communicative intention cannot be unambiguously inferred. Although the database from which the computer drew the sentences was said to have been compiled by psychologists, the collection drawn by the computer is of dubious relevance.

As expected, undermining the implicit guarantee of relevance greatly attenuated participants' reliance on the individuating information. Specifically, participants in the replication condition estimated the likelihood of the target being an engineer as .76, despite a low base-rate of .30. But, when the same information was allegedly selected by a computer, respondents' likelihood estimates dropped to .40. This finding indicates that participants' reliance on individuating information at the expense of base-rate information reflects, in part, their assumption that the experimenter is a cooperative communicator who does not present irrelevant information. Once this assumption is called into question, participants are free to disregard the individuating information, and the otherwise obtained base-rate neglect is largely attenuated. In a similar vein, Krosnick, Li, and Lehman (1990) observed that the utilization of base-rate information varied as a function of the relative importance of the base-rate and the individuating information, which was conveyed by the order in which the information was presented.

Conclusions

As these findings illustrate, participants are likely to assume that the information provided to them is relevant to their task, unless the implicit guarantee of relevance characterizing human communication in most settings is called into question. Similar conversational analyses have been offered for other judgmental biases that reflect reliance on normatively irrelevant information, including the fundamental attribution error (e.g., Wright & Wells, 1988) and misleading question effects in eyewitness testimony (e.g., Dodd & Bradshaw, 1980). In fact, when explicitly asked, participants often seem aware that the normatively irrelevant information is of little informational value (e.g., Miller, Schmidt, Meyer, & Colella, 1984). Nevertheless, they typically proceed to use it to make a judgment. A conversational analysis suggests that this observation reflects participants' (erroneous) assumption that the experimenter is a cooperative communicator whose contributions can be assumed to be informative, relevant, and clear. Once this assumption is undermined, participants are less inclined to see relevance in the information provided to them and the impact of normatively irrelevant information is attenuated.

This analysis suggests that the typical procedures used in psychological research are likely to result in an overestimation of the size and pervasiveness of judgmental biases. I reiterate, however, that a conversational analysis does not imply that violations of conversational norms are the sole source of judgmental biases. Like most robust phenomena, judgmental biases are likely to have many determinants. To understand their operation in natural contexts, however, we must ensure that the emergence of biases in laboratory experiments does not reflect the operation of determinants that are unlikely to hold in other settings.

MAKING ONE'S ANSWER INFORMATIVE: QUESTION REPETITION AND MEANING CHANGE

The preceding examples illustrated how research participants draw on conversational maxims to interpret researchers' contributions. Not surprisingly, research participants also heed the maxims underlying their conduct of conversation in daily life when they design their answers to researchers' questions. Adhering to the maxim of quantity, they observe the common ground and try to provide information that is new to the researcher, rather than information they have previously given. Unfortunately, researchers may not always appreciate participants' attempts to avoid redundancy, as the following example from the domain of survey measurement illustrates (see Schwarz, 1994, for applications to other research domains).

Partially Redundant Questions: Context Effects in Attitude Measurement

Schwarz, Strack, and Mai (1991; see also Strack, Martin, & Schwarz, 1988) asked survey respondents to report their marital satisfaction as well as their general life satisfaction and varied the order in which they presented the two questions. The first column of Table 3.3 shows the resulting correlations between marital and life satisfaction. When the life satisfaction question preceded the marital satisfaction question, both measures were moderately correlated, $r = .32$. Reversing the question order, however, increased the correlation to $r = .67$.

This finding reflects the possibility that answering the marital satisfaction question increased the accessibility of marriage-related information in memory. The quality of a person's marriage clearly bears on the overall quality of his or her life, and respondents included this information when they evaluated their lives as a whole. This interpretation is supported by a highly similar correlation of $r = .61$ when a reworded version of the general question explicitly asked respondents to take their marriages into account. Moreover, these differences in correlations were also reflected in respondents' mean reports of general life satisfaction. As expected, happily married respondents reported higher, and unhappily married respondents lower, general life satisfaction when the preceding question brought their marriages to mind than they did when the general question was asked first.

In a third condition, however, Schwarz and Mai (1991) deliberately evoked the conversational norm of nonredundancy. To do so, they introduced both questions with a joint lead-in that read, "We now have two questions about your life. The first pertains to your marital satisfaction and the second to your general life-satisfaction." Under this condition, the same question order that resulted in $r = .67$ without a joint lead-in now produced a low and nonsignificant correlation of $r = .18$. This finding suggests that respondents

TABLE 3.3

Correlation of Relationship Satisfaction and Life-Satisfaction as a Function of Question Order and Conversational Context

Condition	*Number of Specific Questions*	
	One	*Three*
General–specific	.32*	.32*
Specific–general	.67*	.46*
Specific–general, with joint lead-in	.18	.48*
Specific–general, explicit inclusion	.61*	.53*
Specific–general, explicit exclusion	.20	.11

*Correlations marked by an asterisk differ from chance, $p < .05$.

Note. $N = 50$ per cell, except $N = 56$ for "Specific–general, with joint lead-in." Adapted from "Assimilation and Contrast Effects In Part-Whole Question Sequences: A Conversational Logic Analysis," by N. Schwarz, F. Strack, & H. P. Mai, 1991, *Public Opinion Quarterly, 55,* 3–23. Copyright 1991 by University of Chicago Press. Adapted with permission.

deliberately ignored information that they had already provided in response to a specific question when making a subsequent general judgment. Apparently, they interpreted the general question as if it were worded, "Aside from your marriage, which you already told us about, how satisfied are you with other aspects of your life?" Consistent with this interpretation, a nearly identical correlation of $r = .20$ was obtained when the general question was reworded in this way.

Again, these differences in correlations were also reflected in respondents' mean reports of general life satisfaction. When respondents were induced to disregard previously considered information about their marriage, unhappily married respondents reported higher general life satisfaction, and happily married respondents reported lower life satisfaction, than when the conversational norm of nonredundancy was not evoked. Thus, contrast effects were obtained when a joint lead-in elicited the exclusion of previously provided information, whereas assimilation effects were obtained without a joint lead-in (see Schwarz & Bless's, 1992, inclusion–exclusion model of assimilation and contrast effects for a detailed discussion of the underlying cognitive processes).

Note, however, that the applicability of the norm of nonredundancy may vary as a function of the number of specific questions that precede the general one. If only one specific question precedes the general one, the repeated use of the information on which the answer to the specific question was based renders the response to the general question redundant. Suppose, however, that several specific questions precede the general one. For example, respondents may be asked to report on their job satisfaction, their leisure time satisfaction, and their marital satisfaction before a general life satisfaction question is presented. In this case, they may interpret the general question in two different ways: as a request to consider still other aspects of their life, (much as if the question were worded, "Aside of what you already told us, . . .") or as a request to integrate the previously reported aspects into an overall judgment, (much as if it were worded, "Taking these aspects together, . . .") This interpretational ambiguity does not arise if only one specific question is asked. In this case, an interpretation of the general question in the sense of "taking all aspects together" would make little sense because only one aspect was addressed, thus rendering this interpretation of the general question completely redundant with the specific one. If several specific questions are asked, however, both interpretations are viable. In this case, an integrative judgment is informative because it does provide "new" information about the relative importance of the respective domains. Moreover, summing up at the end of a series of related thoughts is acceptable conversational practice whereas if only one thought is offered there is little to sum up.

To explore these possibilities, other respondents of the Schwarz, Strack, and Mai (1991) study were asked three specific questions, pertaining to their leisure time satisfaction, their job satisfaction, and their marital satisfaction. As shown in the second column of Table 3.3, the correlation between marital satisfaction and life satisfaction increased from $r = .32$ to $r = .46$ when answering the specific questions first brought information about marriage to mind. This increase was less pronounced than when the marital satisfaction question was the only specific question that preceded the general one ($r = .67$), a finding reflecting that the three specific questions brought a more varied set of information to mind. More importantly, introducing the three specific and the general question by a joint lead-in did *not* reduce the emerging correlation, $r = .48$. This finding indicates that respondents adopted a "taking-all-aspects-together" interpretation of the general question when it was preceded by three, rather than one, specific questions. This interpretation is further supported by a highly similar correlation of $r = .53$ when the general question was reworded to request an integrative judgment and a highly dissimilar correlation of $r = .11$ when the reworded question required the consideration of other aspects of life.

In combination, these findings further illustrate that the interpretation of an identically worded question may change as a function of conversational variables and may result in markedly different responses. Moreover, the emerging differences are not restricted to the means or margins of the response distribution, as social scientists have frequently assumed. Rather, context variables may result in different correlational patterns. This finding violates the assumption that context effects are restricted to differences in the means, whereas the relationship between variables is "form resistant" (Schuman & Duncan, 1974; Stouffer & DeVinney, 1949). Obviously, we would draw very different substantive conclusions about the contribution of marital satisfaction to overall life satisfaction, depending on the order in which these questions are presented and the perceived conversational context evoked by their introduction (see Sudman, Bradburn, & Schwarz, 1996, for a general discussion of context effects in survey measurement).

Conclusions

This example illustrates that research participants observe the maxim of quantity, which enjoins them to provide new information rather than to reiterate information the recipient already has. As a result, they reinterpret otherwise redundant questions in a way that turns them into a request for information that has not yet been provided. In the case of context effects in survey measurement, observation of the maxim of quantity underlies a set of otherwise puzzling findings illustrating that asking a specific question before a general one may elicit assimilation as well as contrast effects (see Turner & Martin, 1984, pp. 5–7). As the previous analysis indicates, the effect obtained depends on the number of specific questions asked and their perceived conversational relatedness—variables that determine the degree to which drawing on the same information twice would result in redundancy. Obviously, respondents' attempts to avoid redundancy deserve as much attention as the information that is inadvertently conveyed by researchers (discussed in the preceding sections).

CONCLUSIONS

The research reviewed in this chapter indicates that research participants bring to the research situation the tacit assumptions that govern the conduct of conversation in daily life. The default assumption is that researchers are cooperative communicators, whose contributions are informative, relevant, and clear—and when researchers do not live up to these ideals, participants draw on the context to determine the meanings of the researchers' utterances. They have little other choice: The standardized nature of research interactions does not allow for a mutual negotiation of meaning (see Strack & Schwarz, 1992). Moreover, the most directly apparent meanings are presumably those that researchers intended to convey, or else researchers would have taken proper precautions, as Clark and Schober (1992) noted. This perspective has important implications for the analysis of "artifacts" in social and psychological research as well as for the analysis of judgmental biases and shortcomings. I address both aspects in turn.

Artifacts and Demand Characteristics

Psychological researchers have long been concerned with the social psychology of psychology experiments (for an overview, see Kruglanski, 1975). Following Orne's (1962, 1969) seminal discussion of demand characteristics, this work has been guided by the assumption that participants are motivated to look for cues in experimental situations that provide them with the experimenter's hypothesis. Depending on their motivation to play the role of a "good subject," they may then react in line with the suspected hypothesis. Accordingly, most research in this tradition has focused on participants' motivation to detect and to act according to experimenters' hypotheses, rather than on the process by which participants extract information from the research procedures used.

In contrast, a conversational analysis suggests that special assumptions about motivations germane to participating in an experiment are unnecessary. Rather, this analysis indicates that participants' behavior in an experiment or research interview is guided by the *same* assumptions and motivations that govern the conduct of conversation in any other setting (see Bless et al., 1993, for a detailed comparison of Orne's analysis and a conversational perspective and Kihlstrom, 1995, for a related discussion). From a conversational viewpoint, the key difference between experiments and conversations in natural settings is only that experimenters are less likely to comply to conversational rules in conducting an experiment than in conducting any other conversation, although participants have no reason to suspect that experimenters are not cooperative communicators. As a result, participants apply to research settings the tacit assumptions usually governing the conduct of conversation and go beyond the literal information provided to them by drawing inferences on the basis of the conversational context. Hence, many emerging artifacts reflect normal social behavior rather than unique features of experimental research. The problem is not that participants behave in unusual ways once they enact the role of research participant. Rather, the problem is that we are likely to behave in unusual ways once we enact the role of researcher, while our participants have no reason to suspect us doing so.

Biases and Shortcomings

What are the implications of this perspective for the emergence of biases and shortcomings in social judgment? Many studies have documented pronounced biases in human judgment, but a conversational analysis of the procedures used suggests that some of the more dramatic illustrations may have painted an overly negative picture of human rationality (for extensive reviews, see Hilton, 1995; Schwarz, 1994, 1996). In many cases, people do not seem to lack the ability to make adequate judgments; they lack the insight that we as researchers do not live up to the standards we would typically observe in any other conversation . Research participants simply give us more credit than we deserve by assuming that the information we provide is relevant to the task at hand, truthful, informative, and clear. Unless we learn to observe these standards in our conduct of research and in our interpretation of results, we may run the risk of severely overestimating the size and pervasiveness of judgmental biases and shortcomings. Once again, however, I emphasize that violations of conversational norms are *not* the only source of judgmental biases. Like most robust phenomena, judgmental biases are likely to be overdetermined and some of them have been documented under conditions that do not involve the violation of conversational norms (for a review, see Nisbett & Ross, 1980). To fully understand the operation of biases in natural contexts, however, we must ensure that their operation in our laboratories does not reflect determinants that are unlikely to be similarly powerful outside of our labs.

To use a distinction introduced by Funder (1987), the errors that research participants commit in our studies by relying on conversational maxims are less likely to result in mistakes in everyday contexts, where communicators try to conform to conversational norms, provide information that is relevant to the judgment at hand, and make the task clear rather than ambiguous—and where recipients are indeed expected to use contextual cues to disambiguate the communication, should the communicator not live up to the ideal. Thus, behavior that leads to errors in experimental contexts may be adaptive in everyday settings. As Funder (1987, p. 82) noted in a related context, "It seems ironic that going beyond the information given in this way is so often interpreted by social psychologists as symptomatic of flawed judgment. Current thinking in the field of artificial intelligence is that this propensity is exactly what makes people smarter than computers."

REFERENCES

Bishop, G. F., Hippler, H. J., Schwarz, N., & Strack, F. (1988). A comparison of response effects in self-administered and telephone surveys. In R. M. Groves, P. Biemer, L. Lyberg, J. T. Massey, W. L. Nicholls, & J. Waksberg (Eds.), *Telephone survey methodology* (pp. 321–340). New York: Wiley.

Bishop, G. F., Oldendick, R. W., & Tuchfarber, R. J. (1986). Opinions on fictitious issues: the pressure to answer survey questions. *Public Opinion Quarterly, 50,* 240–250.

Bless, H., Bohner, G., Hild, T., & Schwarz, N. (1992). Asking difficult question: Task complexity increases the impact of response alternatives. *European Journal of Social Psychology, 22,* 309–312.

Bless, H., Strack, F., & Schwarz, N. (1993). The informative functions of research procedures: Bias and the logic of conversation. *European Journal of Social Psychology, 23,* 149–165.

Bradburn, N.M. (1983). Response effects. In P.H. Rossi, & J.D. Wright (Eds.), *The handbook of survey research* (pp. 289–328). New York: Academic Press.

Bradburn, N. M., Rips, L. J., & Shevell, S. K. (1987). Answering autobiographical questions: The impact of memory and inference on survey. *Science, 236,* 157–161.

Clark, H. H. (1977). Inferences in comprehensio. In D. La Berge, & S. Samuels, (Eds.), *Basic processes in reading: Perception and comprehension* (pp. 243–263). Hillsdale, NJ: Lawrence Erlbaum Associates.

Clark, H. H., & Clark, E. V. (1977). *Psychology and language.* New York: Harcourt, Brace, Jovanovich.

Clark, H. H., & Haviland, S. E. (1977). Comprehension and the given–new contract. In R. O. Freedle (Ed.), *Discourse production and comprehension* (pp. 1–40). Hillsdale, NJ: Lawrence Erlbaum Associates

Clark, H. H., & Schober, M. F. (1992). Asking questions and influencing answers. In J. M. Tanur (Ed.), *Questions about questions* (pp. 15–48). New York: Russell Sage.

Clark, H. H., Schreuder, R., & Buttrick, S. (1983). Common ground and the understanding of demonstrative reference. *Journal of Verbal Learning and Verbal Behavior, 22,* 245–258.

Converse, P. E. (1964). The nature of belief systems in mass politics. In D. Apter (Ed.), *Ideology and discontent* (pp. 238–245). New York: Free Press of Glencoe.

Converse, P. E. (1970). Attitudes and non-attitudes: Continuation of a dialogue. In E. R. Tufte (Ed.), *The quantitative analysis of social problems* (pp. 188–189). Reading, MA: Addison-Wesley.

Dawes, R. M., & Smith, T. (1985). Attitude and opinion measurement. In G. Lindzey & E. Aronson (Eds.), *Handbook of social psychology* (Vol. 2, pp. 509–566). New York: Random House.

Dodd, D. H. & Bradshaw, J. M. (1980). Leading questions and memory: Pragmatic constraints. *Journal of Verbal Learning and Verbal Behavior, 19,* 695–704.

Erikson, R. S., Luttberg, N. R., & Tedin, K.T. (1988). *American public opinion* (3rd ed.). New York: Macmillan.

Funder, D. C. (1987). Errors and mistakes: Evaluating the accuracy of social judgment. *Psychological Bulletin, 101,* 75–90.

Fussell, S. R., & Krauss, R. M. (1989a). The effects of intended audience on message production and comprehension: Reference in a common ground framework. *Journal of Experimental Social Psychology, 25,* 203–219.

Fussell, S. R., & Krauss, R. M. (1989b). Understanding friends and strangers: The effects of audience design on message comprehension. *European Journal of Social Psychology, 19,* 509–525.

Ginossar, Z., & Trope, Y. (1987). Problem solving and judgment under uncertainty. *Journal of Personality and Social Psychology, 52,* 464–474.

Grayson, C. E., & Schwarz, N. (1995). *When "rarely" is "never": The numeric value of rating scales and the interpretation of scale labels.* Manuscript: University of Michigan.

Grice, H. P. (1975). Logic and conversation. In P. Cole, & J. L. Morgan (Eds.), *Syntax and semantics: 3 Speech acts* (pp. 41–58). New York: Academic Press.

Grice, H. P. (1978). Further notes on logic and conversation. In P. Cole, (Ed.), *Syntax and semantics: 9 Pragmatics* (pp. 113–128). New York: Academic Press.

Haviland, S., & Clark, H. H. (1974). What's new? Acquiring new information as a process in comprehension. *Journal of Verbal Learning and Verbal Behavior, 13,* 512–521.

Higgins, E. T. (1981). The "communication game": Implications for social cognition and communication. In E. T. Higgins, M. P. Zanna, & C. P. Herman (Eds.), *Social cognition: The Ontario Symposium* (Vol. 1, pp. 343–392). Hillsdale, NJ: Lawrence Erlbaum Associates.

Higgins, E. T., Fondacaro, R. A., & McCann, C. D. (1982). Rules and roles: The "communication game" and speaker–listener processes. In W. P. Dickson (Ed.), *Children's oral communication skills* (pp. 289–312). New York: Academic Press.

Hilton, D. J. (1995). The social context of reasoning: Conversational inference and rational judgment. *Psychological Bulletin, 118,* 248–271.

Kahneman, D., & Tversky, A. (1973). On the psychology of prediction. *Psychological Review, 80,* 237–251.

Kihlstrom, J. F. (1995, June). *From the subject's point of view: The experiment as conversation and collaboration between investigator and subject.* Invited address presented at American Psychological Society, New York.

Krauss, R. M., & Fussell, S. R. (1991). Perspective-taking in communication: Representations of others' knowledge in reference. *Social Cognition, 9,* 2–24.

Krosnick, J. A., Li, F., & Lehman, D. R. (1990). Conversational conventions, order of information acquisition, and the effect of base rates and individuating information on social judgment. *Journal of Personality and Social Psychology, 59,* 1140–1152.

Kruglanski, A. W. (1975). The human subject in the psychology experiment: Fact and artifact. In L. Berkowitz (Ed.), *Advances in experimental social psychology* (Vol. 8, pp. 101–147). New York: Academic Press.

Levinson, S. C. (1983). *Pragmatics.* Cambridge, England: Cambridge University Press.

Menon, G. (1994). Judgments of behavioral frequencies: Memory search and retrieval strategies. In N. Schwarz & S. Sudman (Eds.), *Autobiographical memory and the validity of retrospective reports* (pp. 161–172). New York: Springer Verlag.

Menon, G., Raghubir, P., & Schwarz, N. (1995). Behavioral frequency judgments: An accessibility–diagnosticity framework. *Journal of Consumer Research, 22,* 212–228.

Miller, A. G., Schmidt, D., Meyer, C., & Colella, A. (1984). The perceived value of constrained behavior: Pressures toward biased inferenc in the attitude attribution paradigm. *Social Psychology Quarterly, 47,* 160–171.

Molenaar, N. J. (1982). Response effects of formal characteristics of questions. In W. Dijkstra & J. van der Zouwen (Eds.), *Response behavior in the survey intervie* (pp. 49–90). New York: Academic Press.

Nisbett, R. E., & Ross, L. (1980). *Human inference: Strategies and shortcomings of social judgment.* New York: Prentice Hall.

Orne, M. T. (1962). On the social psychology of the psychological experiment: With particular reference to demand characteristics and their implications. *American Psychologist, 17,* 776–783.

Orne, M. T. (1969). Demand characteristics and the concept of quasi-controls. In R. Rosenthal & R. L. Rosnow (Eds.), *Artifact in behavioral research* (pp. 143–179). New York: Academic Press.

Payne, S. L. (1951). *The art of asking questions.* Princeton: Princeton University Press.

Schiffer, S. (1972). *Meaning.* Oxford, England: Clarendon Press.

Schuman, H., & Duncan, O. D. (1974). Questions about attitude survey questions. In H. L. Costner (Ed.), *Sociological methodology.* San Francisco: Jossey-Bass.

Schuman, H., & Kalton, G. (1985). Survey methods. In G. Lindzey, & E. Aronson (Eds.), *Handbook of social psychology* (Vol. 1, pp. 635–698). New York: Random House.

Schuman, H., & Presser, S. (1977). Question wording as an independent variable in survey analysis. *Sociological Methods and Research, 6,* 151–176.

Schuman, H., & Presser, S. (1981). *Questions and answers in attitude surveys.* New York: Academic Press.

Schwarz, N. (1990). Assessing frequency reports of mundane behaviors: Contributions of cognitive psychology to questionnaire construction. In C. Hendrick & M. S. Clark (Eds.), *Research methods in personality and social psychology* (Review of Personality and Social Psychology, Vol. 11, pp. 98–119). Beverly Hills, CA: Sage.

Schwarz, N. (1994). Judgment in a social context: Biases, shortcomings, and the logic of conversation. In M. Zanna (Ed.), *Advances in experimental social psychology* (Vol. 26, pp. 123–162). San Diego, CA: Academic Press.

Schwarz, N. (1995). What respondents learn from questionnaires: The survey interview and the logic of conversation. *International Statistical Review, 63,* 153–177.

Schwarz, N. (1996). *Cognition and communication: Judgmental biases, research methods and the logic of conversation.* Hillsdale, NJ: Lawrence Erlbaum Associates.

Schwarz, N., & Bienias, J. (1990). What mediates the impact of response alternatives on frequency reports of mundane behaviors? *Applied Cognitive Psychology, 4,* 61–72.

Schwarz, N., & Bless, H. (1992). Constructing reality and its alternatives: An inclusion/exclusion model of assimilation and contrast effects in social judgment. In L. Martin & A. Tesser (Eds.), *The construction of social judgment* (pp. 217–245). Hillsdale, NJ: Lawrence Erlbaum Associates.

Schwarz, N., Bless, H., Bohner, G., Harlacher, U., & Kellenbenz, M. (1991). Response scales as frames of reference: The impact of frequency range on diagnostic judgment. *Applied Cognitive Psychology, 5,* 37–50.

Schwarz, N., & Hippler, H.J. (1991). Response alternatives: The impact of their choice and ordering. In P. Biemer, R. Groves, N. Mathiowetz, & S. Sudman (Eds.), *Measurement error in surveys* (pp. 41–56). Chichester, England: Wiley.

Schwarz, N., Hippler, H. J., Deutsch, B., & Strack, F. (1985). Response scales: Effects of category range on reported behavior and subsequent judgments. *Public Opinion Quarterly, 49,* 388–395.

Schwarz, N., Knäuper, B., Hippler, H. J., Noelle-Neumann, E., & Clark, F. (1991). Rating scales: Numeric values may change the meaning of scale labels. *Public Opinion Quarterly, 55,* 570–582.

Schwarz, N., & Scheuring, B. (1992). Selbstberichtete Verhaltens- und Symptomhäufigkeiten: Was Befragte aus Anwortvorgaben des Fragebogens lernen. (Frequency-reports of psychosomatic symptoms: What respondents learn from response alternatives of questionnaires.) *Zeitschrift für Klinische Psychologie, 22,* 197–208.

Schwarz, N., Strack, F., Hilton, D. J., & Naderer, G. (1991). Judgmental biases and the logic of conversation: The contextual relevance of irrelevant information. *Social Cognition, 9,* 67–84.

Schwarz, N., Strack, F., Hippler, H. J., & Bishop, G. (1991). The impact of administration mode on response effects in survey measurement. *Applied Cognitive Psychology, 5,* 193–212.

Schwarz, N., Strack, F., & Mai, H. P. (1991). Assimilation and contrast effects in part–whole question sequences: A conversational logic analysis. *Public Opinion Quarterly, 55,* 3–23.

Schwarz, N., Strack, F., Müller, G., & Chassein, B. (1988). The range of response alternatives may determine the meaning of the question: Further evidence on informative functions of response alternatives. *Social Cognition, 6,* 107–117.

Sperber, D., & Wilson, D. (1986). *Relevance: Communication and cognition.* Cambridge, MA: Harvard University Press.

Stalnaker, R. C. (1978). Assertion. In P. Cole, (Ed.), *Syntax and semantics: Vol. 9, Pragmatics* (pp. 315–332). New York: Academic Press.

Stouffer, S. A., & DeVinney, L. C. (1949). How personal adjustment varied in the army—By background characteristics of the soldiers. In S. A. Stouffer, E. A. Suchman, L. C. DeVinney, S. A. Star, & R. M. Williams (Eds.), *The American soldier: Adjustment during army life.* Princeton, NJ: Princeton University Press.

Strack, F. (1994a). Response processes in social judgment. In R. S. Wyer & T. K. Srull (Eds.), *Handbook of social cognition* (2nd ed., Vol. 1, pp. 287–322). Hillsdale, NJ: Lawrence Erlbaum Associates.

Strack, F. (1994b). *Zur Psychologie der standardisierten Befragung: Kognitive und kommunikative Prozesse* (On the psychology of standardized interviews: Cognitive and communicative processes.) Heidelberg, Germany: Springer Verlag.

Strack, F., Martin, L. L., & Schwarz, N. (1988). Priming and communication: The social determinants of information use in judgments of life-satisfaction. *European Journal of Social Psychology, 18,* 429–442.

Strack, F., & Schwarz, N. (1992). Communicative influences in standardized question situations: The case of implicit collaboration. In K. Fiedler & G. Semin (Eds.), *Language, interaction and social cognition* (pp. 173–193). Beverly Hills, CA: Sage.

Strack, F., Schwarz, N., & Wänke, M. (1991). Semantic and pragmatic aspects of context effects in social and psychological research. *Social Cognition, 9,* 111–125.

Sudman, S., & Bradburn, N.M. (1974). *Response effects in surveys: A review and synthesis.* Chicago: Aldine.

Sudman, S., Bradburn, N., & Schwarz, N. (1996). *Thinking about answers: The application of cognitive processes to survey methodology.* San Francisco, CA: Jossey-Bass.

Turner, C. F., & Martin, E. (Eds.) (1984). *Surveying subjective phenomena* (Vol. 1). New York: Russell Sage.

Woll, S. B., Weeks, D. G., Fraps, C. L., Pendergrass, J., & Vanderplas, M. A. (1980). Role of sentence context in the encoding of trait descriptors. *Journal of Personality and Social Psychology, 39,* 59–68.

Wright, E. F., & Wells, G. L. (1988). Is the attitude-attribution paradigm suitable for investigating the dispositional bias? *Personalit and Social Psychology Bulletin, 14,* 183–190.

PART II

Indirect Speech and Figurative Language

— 4 —

Interpersonal Foundations of Conversational Indirectness

Thomas Holtgraves

Ball State University

People frequently speak indirectly. They hint, insinuate, give backhanded compliments, make polite requests and so on; in all instances they mean something more than the words literally impart. Indirectness presents a challenge for theories of language use and for theories of social interaction; the former must explain how such remarks are produced and understood, and the latter must explain why these remarks occur and what roles they play in social interaction. These two issues are related, and in this chapter I argue that an understanding of the production and comprehension of indirectness (the *how* of indirectness) involves a consideration of the interpersonal underpinnings of indirectness (the *why* of indirectness).

To do this, I first focus on speakers and describe briefly one of the major conceptual frameworks (Grice, 1975) for understanding how people speak indirectly. I then discuss research generated by politeness theory (P. Brown & Levinson, 1987), one of the major theoretical approaches that explains why a speaker might produce indirect remarks. After switching to the hearer's side, I discuss how both intended and unintended indirect meanings are recognized, with particular emphasis on the role played by interpersonal variables in this process. Finally, I briefly review research examining cultural and individual variability in both the production and the comprehension of indirectness.

INDIRECTNESS AS CONVERSATIONAL IMPLICATURE

One of the most popular approaches for understanding indirectness is Grice's (1975) model of conversational implicature. According to Grice, communication is possible because interactants mutually abide by a cooperative principle (CP). The CP consists of the four general maxims of relevance (make your contribution relevant to the exchange), quantity (be as informative as required), quality (say what is true), and manner (be clear). A speaker who conforms to these maxims produces remarks that are crisp, clear, and maximally efficient. But speakers can, and frequently do, deviate from these maxims and in so doing convey a nonliteral meaning. Specifically, if a hearer can assume that a speaker is being cooperative, then violations of the CP should cause the hearer to realize that the speaker means something other than what was literally conveyed. As a result, the hearer should then generate a conversational implicature (i.e., a nonliteral reading of what the speaker means).

In one sense, this interpretation is an exquisitely socio-psychological model of communication because of the reliance on interactants' coordination to successfully communicate. That is, conversational implicatures are possible only to the extent that interlocutors mutually assume adherence to the CP. If a hearer erroneously assumes cooperativeness on the part of a speaker, then the meaning of the speaker's remarks may be misinterpreted (e.g., see Schwarz, 1994; this volume). In another sense, however, this model is decidedly weak as a socio-psychological account of communication: There is no consideration of why people convey indirect meanings in the first place.

There are probably a variety of motives for violating conversation maxims and conveying indirect meanings.[1] Sometimes the violations are unintentional, a result of failing to understand the prior remark. But many times they are intentional. Why go through the trouble of violating a maxim to convey meaning indirectly, when it would be so much easier and efficient to convey meaning directly? Sometimes such violations are a means of expressing sarcasm (Slugoski & Turnbull, 1988) or humor and wit (Roberts & Kreuz, 1994; Kreuz, Kassler, & Coppenrath this volume). In face-to-face interaction, however, indirectness appears to be motivated, in large part, by interpersonal considerations, by interactants' mutual sensitivity to the thoughts and feelings of one another. People seem to use indirect meanings to say (or perhaps more accurately, to suggest) things to others in ways that attend to their own interpersonal needs. The interpersonal underpinnings of indirectness can be made clearer by contrasting human–human communication with human–computer communication. Communicating with a computer is always direct, efficient, and in compliance with the Gricean maxims. People do not suggest to their computers that they perform some task—they command them to do so. Because computers have no feelings or pride or sensitivity, they take no offense if ordered to do something. Humans, in contrast, do have sensitivities and might indeed be offended if commanded to do something. People use indirectness to perform many interpersonally sensitive actions in a nonthreatening manner.

---

[1] Although the notion of literal meaning is somewhat controversial (e.g., see Dascal, 1987; Gibbs, 1984), I take it here to refer to the sense and reference of an utterance derived from the words and rules of syntax alone, without any reference to the context in which the utterance occurs. Any other communicative meanings derived from the utterance are considered here to be indirect or nonliteral meanings.

FACE AND FACE–WORK

A useful and popular approach for conceptualizing how interpersonal needs are linguistically realized is P. Brown and Levinson's (1987) theory of politeness, a theory based on Goffman's (1967) seminal writings on face and face-work. Face, according to Goffman, is the public display of self, and face-work refers to communications designed to create, support, or challenge face. Face-work takes place in virtually all interactions and encompasses rituals whereby people indicate respect for one another (e.g., by not calling attention to another's faults) and reaffirm relationships (e.g., via compliments, greetings). Face-work (and hence face) is a collaborative venture. Face can be given only by others, and therefore it is in everyone's best interest to cooperate so as to maintain each other's face. A person's threats to another's face become threats to his or her own face; although insults, challenges, and so on occur, people are generally motivated to maintain each other's face.

P. Brown and Levinson (1987) adopted and subdivided the concept of face into two universal desires or wants: a desire for autonomy or freedom from imposition (*negative face*), and a desire for connectedness or solidarity with others (*positive face*). Although some researchers (Lim & Bowers, 1991; Tracy, 1990) have argued that face should be subdivided even further, attempts to delineate subtypes of face seem misguided. Rather, face is a basic concept involved in the presentation of any and all identities, and it loses its explanatory power if subdivided further.

Face is assumed to be fragile and subject to continued threat during social interaction. In the P. Brown and Levinson (1987) model, verbal acts can threaten the positive and/or negative face of the speaker and/or hearer. Requests, for example, threaten a hearer's negative face (i.e., they impose upon a hearer); disagreements threaten a hearer's positive face. A speaker's face may also be threatened. For example, promises threaten a speaker's negative face (by restricting his or her subsequent freedom), and apologies threaten a speaker's positive face (via an admission of wrongdoing).

Social interaction thus presents a dilemma for interactants. On the one hand, people are motivated to maintain each other's positive and negative face. On the other hand, they often need to perform acts that threaten these motivations. This dilemma is solved by engaging in face-work (Goffman, 1967), or more specifically by being polite (P. Brown & Levinson, 1987). In fact, face-work or politeness can be regarded as a prerequisite for orderly social interaction to emerge from the chaos of self-serving individuals. As R. Brown (1990) has noted, politeness extends far beyond the world of Emily Post.

The essence of politeness–face-work is the performance of a face-threatening act and the simultaneous attention to the face wants of the interactants. The manner in which this aim is accomplished can be seen most clearly with requests, the speech act most frequently studied in this regard.

INDIRECT REQUESTS

To make a request of another is to impose on the person and hence threaten his or her negative face. Requests that comply with the Gricean maxims would be performed with the imperative (e.g., "Close the door."). Although this form is clear and unambiguous, it also clearly threatens a hearer's negative face. Consequently, the imperative is rarely used, and requests are often performed indirectly (Ervin-Tripp, 1976). This observation has been recognized by many researchers, and several schemes have been proposed for categorizing these forms (e.g., see Blum-Kulka, Danet, & Gherson, 1985; Ervin-Tripp, 1976; Gibbs, 1986; Herrmann, 1983). I focus here on P. Brown and Levinson's (1987) scheme because of the clear articulation of the face-work underlying the forms.

Probably the most common way to perform a request is on-record with negative face redress (*negative politeness*). Negative politeness addresses recipients' negative face, or desire to not be imposed on. Any form that decreases the imposition on the hearer (primarily imposed by giving the hearer options) functions as a negatively polite strategy. A common way to do this is to question or assert any preconditions underlying the performance of a request (Gordon & Lakoff, 1975; Searle, 1975). For example, to comply with a request, a recipient must have the ability and willingness to do so. Thus, a speaker can perform a negatively polite request by questioning a hearer's ability or willingness to comply with the requested act (e.g., "Can you shut the door?" and "Would you shut the door?" respectively).

A second broad strategy is to perform the act on-record with positive face redress (Goffman's presentation rituals). Positive face-work is achieved through the use of mechanisms that implicate solidarity with the hearer. For example, the use of ingroup identity markers (e.g., slang, familiar address forms), jokes and presumptuous optimism (e.g., "You'll lend me your notes, won't you?"), all implicate a speaker's view that although a hearer is being imposed on, the relationship is relatively close (or else the speaker would not be imposing in this way).

The third strategy in the P. Brown and Levinson (1987) model is to perform the request off-record. Off-record strategies (similar to Goffman's protective measures) are clear instances of indirectness. They are inherently ambiguous and have the feature of deniability; the speaker can deny any one interpretation in favor of another. There are an infinite number of off-record forms, and there has been little systematic research on the specific mechanisms that might be used to perform them.

One possible mechanism has been termed a negative state remark (Holtgraves, 1994). This form involves the following principle: A speaker can perform a request by asserting (or questioning) the existence of a negative state (or state that a hearer can infer is negative) if there is some action that the hearer can perform to remedy the negative state. For example, in the appropriate context, "It's noisy in here" or "Isn't it noisy in here?" can be used as a request to shut a door or window, an action that remedies the negative state. Note that if the interactants are roughly equal in status, a recipient has the option of either complying with the indirect request or replying to the literal meaning of the remark (e.g., "Yes, it sure is noisy in here").

Performing requests with any of these three politeness strategies involves violations of the Gricean maxims. This fact is clear for off-record forms, and to a lesser extent, for negatively polite forms. But it is also the case for positively polite strategies. Many times these forms include the imperative (and hence are direct), but the imperative is embedded in verbal markers of closeness, an embedding that is unnecessary and hence violates the quantity maxim (do not say more than is necessary). In addition, positively polite strategies can sometimes involve more indirect meanings, as is the case with irony (P. Brown, 1995).

Performing a request indirectly rather than directly implicates politeness on the part of the speaker. But how much politeness? P. Brown and Levinson (1987) proposed that the politeness of these strategies can be ordered (from least to most polite) as follows: Bald (no face-work), positive politeness, negative politeness, off-record. This order is based, in large part, on the degree of imposition, or cost, for a hearer. Off-record forms (e.g., "It seems cold in here.") impose very little on a hearer; he or she can simply respond to the literal meaning ("Yes, it is cold in here."). Negative politeness forms are less polite than off-record forms because the request intent is clearer (it is on-record), and hence these forms are more restrictive of a hearer's autonomy. The request intent with positively polite forms is very clear; hence they are less polite than are negatively polite forms. Still, the attention paid to a recipient's positive face makes these forms more polite than a bald strategy.

This ordering has some empirical support. For example, Holtgraves and Yang (1990) found the perceived politeness of these strategies, with one exception, was as predicted by the theory, for both Americans and South Koreans. The one exception was that the ratings of the negatively polite and off-record forms were reversed (in both cultures). There are several possible reasons for this reversal. Although off-record forms do not impose on hearers in terms of restricting their autonomy, they do impose on hearers in so far as they must make an effort to understand a speaker's intended meaning. Moreover, a speaker may appear manipulative if an off-record form is used (see Lakoff, 1977; Leech, 1983) and this may detract from the face-work that is accomplished.

Within-strategy variations in politeness are also possible. The number of negative politeness requests is very large, and these requests vary in the extent to which a hearer's negative face is threatened (Clark & Schunk, 1980). For example, "May I ask you where Jordan Hall is?" is less imposing (the speaker is asking permission to ask a question), and hence more polite than, "Would you tell me where Jordon Hall is?" Research has demonstrated that the perceived politeness of negatively polite requests varies with the implied cost for a hearer (Clark & Schunk, 1980, 1981; but see Kemper & Thissen, 1981); this finding has occurred for Americans and South Koreans (Holtgraves & Yang, 1990).

Requests illustrate how politeness can be conveyed by violating the Gricean maxims and performing a request indirectly. But face can be managed without indirectness. For example, a speaker can use a prerequest (e.g., "Are you busy?") and in this way orient to hearers' potential inability to perform the request (Levinson, 1983). If a recipient affirms a lack of ability, the first speaker can manage the face of both by avoiding making a request with which the other would not comply. In addition, the manner in which face-work can be performed nonverbally (e.g., via smiles, distance, etc.) is now beginning to be explored (Ambady, Koo, Lee, & Rosenthal, 1996). In short, indirectness is a very important mechanism for managing face, but it is not the only mechanism.

INTERPERSONAL VARIABLES

One of the major attractions of P. Brown and Levinson's (1987) model is that it links face-threat, and hence politeness, with the fundamental interpersonal dimensions of power and distance. Greater face-threat, and hence greater politeness, is assumed to result from greater addressee power, psychological distance, and act imposition. Accordingly, people should tend to be more polite to those higher in power, with whom they are less familiar, and for acts that are more imposing. In terms of the politeness of requests, there has been relatively strong support for the power variable. It appears that people are more polite (or at least report being more polite) to people higher in power (e.g., Blum-Kulka, Danet, & Gherson, 1985; R. Brown & Gilman, 1989; Holtgraves & Yang, 1990; 1992; Leichty & Applegate, 1991), and it is possible that this relation is invariant over cultures (e.g., Holtgraves & Yang, 1992). In addition, there is moderate support for the imposition variable: Speakers are generally more polite the more imposing the request (R. Brown & Gilman, 1989; Holtgraves & Yang, 1992; Leichty & Applegate, 1991; but see Baxter, 1984).

Research on the relationship variable has been much more mixed. Some researchers have reported increasing politeness associated with increasing distance (as predicted by the theory; Holtgraves & Yang, 1992); others have reported the reverse (Baxter, 1984). The underlying logic for this variable is that in unfamiliar relationships the potential for aggression is unknown and so politeness is used to signal the lack of an aggressive intent. Such a concern is assumed to be less important between familiars. A potential problem with the distance variable is the confounding of psychological distance (i.e., familiarity) with relationship affect or liking. There appears to be a positive relationship between politeness and liking, but a negative relationship between familiarity and politeness (R. Brown & Gilman, 1989; Slugoski & Turnbull, 1988).

The degree and nature of politeness implies a person's view of the interpersonal setting. That is, by speaking indirectly (or not), a person communicates not only varying degrees of concern for others' face, but also indirectly conveys his or her sense of an interpersonal situation. The logic here is straightforward. If higher status speakers use less polite forms than lower status speakers for performing the same act, then the use of less polite forms should result in perceptions of higher status on the part of a speaker, other things being equal. There is some support for this idea. In a cross-cultural study using participants from the United States and South Korea, Holtgraves and Yang (1990, Experiment 3) found that less polite forms were associated with perceptions of greater power on the part of a speaker. This effect was similar for South Koreans and Americans and occurred for relatively minor wording changes. For example, "Would you get the mail?" resulted in perceptions of greater speaker power than "Could you get the mail?" In a similar way, powerful language (in general, more direct speech) also conveys speaker power (Erickson, Lind, Johnson, & O'Barr, 1978). In short, violating the maxims as a means of performing a request indirectly conveys not only concern for the face of a hearer, but the degree of expressed concern implicates varying degrees of status on a speaker's part.

Speech Acts Other Than Requests: Disagreements

There has been much less research on speech acts other than requests, and hence whether the findings for requests generalize to other speech acts is not clear. What is clear, however, is that many speech acts other than requests do raise interpersonal concerns, and these concerns should motivate the manner in which these acts are performed. In this section, I briefly sketch how the face management implications of disagreements may motivate their indirect performance.

To disagree with another person represents a clear threat to the person's positive face (rather than negative face, as is the case with requests). Simple reflection suggests that people only occasionally perform these acts with maxim efficiency (i.e., in accord with the Gricean maxims) and instead attempt to mitigate the implied face-threat of this act. To investigate this issue, I asked unacquainted college students to discuss a controversial topic (e.g., abortion) on which they disagreed (Holtgraves, 1997a). Interactants in these discussions displayed many of the positively polite strategies described by P. Brown and Levinson (1987, pp. 112–117). For example, participants often sought out and discussed "safe" topics; in one abortion discussion there was a lenthy discussion of the current status of abortion laws, a topic that could be pursued painlessly by people with differing opinions on abortion. In addition, participants frequently provided token agreement (e.g., "Yes, but . . . ") with the other's position. Overall, the most frequent strategy was to hedge opinions (e.g., "I kinda think x," etc.).

Some conversation-analytic research also nicely illustrates this phenomenon. A fundamental insight of conversation analysis is that verbal interactions reveal a preference organization (Atkinson & Drew, 1979; Levinson, 1983; Pomerantz, 1984; Sacks, 1987; Schegloff, 1968). That is, conversations (particularly adjacency pairs such as questions and answers) have a "preferred" structure: Not all next actions are equivalent. For example, preferred responses to assessments and offers are agreements and acceptances, and nonpreferred responses are disagreements and refusals, respectively (Atkinson & Drew, 1979; Drew, 1984; Heritage, 1984; Levinson, 1983; Pomerantz, 1984).

In general, nonpreferred responses are marked in some way (Pomerantz, 1984). They frequently are delayed within a turn or over a series of turns and are syntactically complex and often implicit (see also Drew, 1984). In addition, they are often prefaced in some way, such as with hesitating prefaces ("Well . . . "), requests for clarification of the preceding turn, or inclusion of weak agreement with the preceding turn. In other words, nonpreferred replies are face-threatening acts; a fact manifested in the performance of these acts in a less than optimally efficient manner.

Disagreements appear to be performed primarily with positive rather than with negative politeness. In fact, it is difficult to imagine negative politeness strategies for performing these acts. Moreover, positively polite strategies are perceived as more polite than negatively polite strategies for these acts (Lim & Bowers, 1991). This finding suggests that P. Brown and Levinson's (1987) invariant ordering of negative politeness as more polite than are positive politeness may be incorrect (see also Tracy, 1990). Rather, more politeness may be conveyed by orienting to the specific type of face threatened by the act (i.e., negatively polite strategies for threats to negative face such as requests, and positively polite strategies for threats to positive face such as disagreements).

Performing a disagreement with positive politeness implicates concern for another's face, although a speaker's intended meaning is often relatively clear. Are there more indirect strategies for performing these acts? The answer seems to be "yes." Because disagreements (and many other speech acts such as criticisms, accounts, and self-disclosures) are often replies to a preceding turn (e.g., a question or assessment), a person can perform these acts indirectly (when they occur as replies) by violating the relevance maxim (cf. Sperber & Wilson,

1986). This act is accomplished by responding to a remark with an utterance whose surface meaning is not directly relevant to the intended meaning of the prior remark. For example, the reply "That's really a hard course" in response to the question "How are you doing in chemistry?" represents a violation of the relevance maxim. In most instances such a reply would be interpreted indirectly as indicating that a speaker is doing poorly in the class.

Relevance violations can convey indirect meanings because remarks must be interpreted in the context of the remark that precedes them (Heritage, 1984; Schegloff, 1968). Thus, even though the literal meaning of a reply might be completely irrelevant to the preceding remark, the reply will be interpreted as (indirectly) addressing the prior remark (Labov & Fanshel, 1977; see also Levinson, 1995).

Although there has been theoretical attention paid to the relevance maxim (e.g., Levinson, 1995; Sperber & Wilson, 1986), empirical research has been lacking. This area is important for investigation because relevance violations are common. Except for the initial remark in an exchange, every remark is a reply to a preceding turn, and hence could be performed indirectly in this way. Moreover, Sperber and Wilson (1986) have argued that the four Gricean maxims are reducible to the overarching maxim of relevance. Relevance violations also reveal in important ways a fundamental tension between abiding by the Gricean maxims and attending to the face wants of self and others. People tend to produce relevant remarks when face concerns are absent, but prefer to violate the relevance maxim when such concerns are activated (Bavelas, Black, Chovil, & Mullett, 1990; Holtgraves, 1986).

COMPREHENSION

Recognition of Speaker Meaning

Indirect communication, by virtue of a hearer's recognizing its occurrence, conveys varying degrees of politeness and hence the speaker's view of the interpersonal situation. Successful communication, of course, requires that a hearer not only recognize the conveyed politeness, but also the act that is being indirectly performed (i.e., speaker meaning). How does this recognition happen? The standard Gricean (1975) model (see also Searle, 1975) presumes an initial activation of the literal meaning of a remark, a recognition that this meaning violates the CP and thus that a speaker must mean something else, and finally a determination by a hearer of what the speaker's intended meaning might be.

Is this statement an accurate characterization of how indirect meanings are comprehended? Early research by Clark and Lucy (1975) indicated that it is. They found that participants took much longer to verify the truth of sentences such as "I'll be very happy/sad unless you color the circle blue" than of sentences such as "I'll by very happy/sad if you color the circle blue," even though the sentences had the same conveyed meaning (i.e., a request to either color the circle blue or refrain from coloring the circle blue). This finding suggests that participants were recognizing the literal meaning of these sentences before their recognition of the indirect meaning (see also Carrell, 1981).

Results consistent with this model are provided by many studies (e.g., Clark & Schunk, 1980; Holtgraves & Yang, 1990) demonstrating that the perceived politeness of a request varies with the literal meaning of the request; this result would not occur if the literal meaning was not recognized.[2] Finally, it appears that people spontaneously remember, at better than chance levels, the politeness wording used to perform requests (Holtgraves,1997b), and this finding too indicates some activation of the literal meaning.

More recent studies, however, have demonstrated that the literal meaning of indirect remarks is not always activated (see Gibbs, 1984, 1994). Many studies of figurative language have demonstrated that the comprehension of idioms (Glucksberg, Gildea, & Bookin, 1982; Titone & Connine, 1994), and metaphors (Blasko & Connine, 1993) does not involve an initial activation and subsequent rejection of the literal meaning. Similar results have been found for certain types of indirect requests (Gibbs, 1983). Although the specifics of these studies vary, there does seem to be an emerging consensus that the literal reading of potentially indirect remarks need not be activated to comprehend a speaker's intended meaning.

Are all indirect remarks comprehended without a Gricean inference process? Probably not, and it becomes important to determine when an inference process is required. For requests, one important factor is the conventionality of the form. Although there is some disagreement about this issue, conventional indirect requests are instances of negative politeness that have the following features: (a) They can be performed by asserting or questioning the preparatory conditions underlying the requested act (e.g., "Could you shut the door?" questions the ability precondition); (b) the imperative is part of the utterance; and (c) the word *please* can be inserted in the utterance. Nonconventional indirect requests are off-record forms that do not meet these three criteria. There are probably infinite nonconventional forms (including nonverbal actions), but one principled and relatively common form is a negative state remark (i.e., questioning or asserting the existence of a negative state: "It's warm in here" as a request for a hearer to open a window).

The results of several experiments designed to investigate the comprehension of conventional and nonconventional indirect requests suggest that a Gricean

---

[2]It is possible, however, that indirect forms have conventional politeness values that are recognized independent of the remark's literal meaning.

inference process is not required for the comprehension of the former, but sometimes is necessary for the comprehension of the latter (Holtgraves, 1994). For example, the results of a priming study (Experiment 3) indicated that the literal meaning of conventional indirect requests was not activated (consistent with Gibbs, 1983), but that the literal meaning of the nonconventional forms (when a speaker was relatively low in status) was activated. The latter is consistent with the operation of a Gricean inference process.

More important, conventional and nonconventional indirect requests differed in terms of whether they were affected by a speaker's ostensible status. Consistent with the idea that conventional indirect forms are comprehended without an inference process, a speaker's status did not play a role in recognizing a speaker's intended meaning with conventional indirect requests. That is, whether a speaker was high or low status made no difference in the speed with which these forms were comprehended. In contrast, the comprehension of nonconventional forms was affected by a speaker's status. Participants were faster at comprehending these forms when a speaker was higher in status than when he was not, and the priming experiments (Experiments 2 and 3) indicated that both the literal and the indirect meanings were activated for these forms when a speaker was lower in status.[3] Thus, a Gricean inference process does appear to be necessary for comprehending nonconventional indirect requests performed by a lower status speaker.

The Role of the Interpersonal Context

The effect of speaker status on the comprehension of nonconventional indirect requests demonstrates the role played by the interpersonal context in comprehension. These results make sense because variables affecting the production of remarks (e.g., speaker status) should (via the necessity of speaker–hearer coordination, Clark, 1985) also play a role in remark comprehension.

But exactly how and why did speaker status play a role in the comprehension of these remarks? There are at least two possibilities. First, knowledge that a speaker is high status can facilitate an inference process (if one is required). That is, rejection of the literal reading is dependent on the possibility that alternative readings of a remark are available (Sperber & Wilson, 1986). Because high status people can and do direct the actions of others, directive interpretations for many of their remarks are possible. The existence of

---

[3]This finding might appear inconsistent with research demonstrating that lower status interactants are more likely than are high status interactants to speak indirectly (e.g., Holtgraves & Yang, 1992). Although indirect forms are more appropriate for lower status speakers (at least for requests), this does not facilitate comprehension of these forms because directives (regardless of how they are performed) are less appropriate for lower status interactants, as subsequently discussed.

these interpretations increases the likelihood that the literal meaning is rejected. Moreover, because the literal meaning of a remark is rejected, knowledge that the speaker is high status can increase the likelihood that a directive interpretation (rather than some other interpretation) is adopted (see also Holtgraves, Srull, & Socall, 1989).

A second possibility is that knowledge that a speaker is high status may totally circumvent the need for a Gricean inference process, so that the directive interpretation is recognized before any activation of a remark's literal meaning. That is, when a speaker is high status, a hearer may be inclined to interpret the speaker's remarks a priori as directives (cf. Ervin-Tripp, Strage, Lampert, & Bell, 1987). To examine this possibility, I conducted a priming experiment in which participants read descriptions of situations in which speaker status was varied and then made sentence verification judgments of targets that either were or were not possible directives in this situation (Holtgraves, 1994, Experiment 4). Unlike the other priming studies in this research, participants saw only a description of the context, not a remark. Speaker status alone (without a remark) was sufficient to prime directives. That is, when a speaker was high status, sentence verification speeds were significantly faster for directives than for related control targets (i.e., a priming effect), and this result did not occur when a speaker was low status.

Although empirical research is scarce, it is likely that interpersonal variables other than status play a role in remark comprehension. One important factor in this regard is face management, a primary reason for people's indirectness in the first place. Specifically, a hearer's recognition that face concerns are important in a setting should prompt the hearer to look for an ulterior meaning. For example, with replies to questions asking for personal information (e.g., "How are you doing in chemistry?"), a reply violating the relevance maxim (e.g., "I watched the Pacer's game last night") is likely to be interpreted as conveying negative information (i.e., I'm not doing very well in chemistry). A hearer is likely to believe that the information is negative via the recognition that a speaker is attempting to manage face. If the requested information was positive (i.e., he or she was doing well in chemistry), there would usually be no need to respond indirectly.[4] In this instance, the comprehension of a nonliteral meaning requires the recognition of a reason for a speaker to speak indirectly.

Recognition of a reason for the occurrence of indirectness is one mechanism that may guide a hearer in determining what is really meant with a remark. It is important to identify such mechanisms because a fundamental weakness of the Gricean model is the lack of clear guidelines about which specific conversational implicature (out of a virtually unlimited number of possible implicatures) a

---

[4]In certain situations people may be indirect even when the information is positive (e.g., as a means of being modest).

hearer will make. Grice (1975) argued that the implicature will be one that is relevant for the exchange, but this description is vague and more specific proposals have been articulated. For example, Sperber and Wilson (1986) have argued that the inference made is the most relevant one (i.e., has the greatest number of easily derived contextual implications) in context. Hobbs, Stickel, Appelt, and Martin (1993) have argued for interpretation as abduction, or inference to the best explanation for why a remark would be true. All these proposals, however, ignore the role of interpersonal variables (the very variables that may have given rise to the maxim violations in the first place) in guiding the inference process.

Unintended Inferences

The successful performance of an indirect speech act results in a hearer's recognizing a speaker's indirect meaning and, by virtue of that meaning's being conveyed indirectly rather than directly, a certain degree of politeness on a speaker's part. A speaker intends both the indirect meaning and the politeness to be recognized. But language use in context is a rich source of information about the motives, intentions, and personality of others, and sometimes interactants may make unintended inferences about a speaker. It seems likely that the Gricean maxims play a role in the formation of unintended as well as intended inferences.

On the basis of the CP, hearers who notice the violation of a Gricean maxim should first attempt to discern an intended ulterior meaning (Levinson, 1995). But sometimes it may be impossible to construct an intended meaning that makes sense of the violation. Still, recipients should usually attempt to derive an explanation for the violation (e.g., Hastie, 1984), even if it is only that a speaker was not paying attention. These explanations may then serve as the basis for inferences about a speaker and his or her motives.

I examined this possibility by manipulating the testimony of a defendant in a mock jury study (Holtgraves & Grayer, 1994). Participants read testimony in which the responses of a defendant (Experiment 1) or the questions of a prosecutor (Experiment 2) were varied; sometimes the responses violated the quantity maxim by being overinformative (i.e., the answer provided more information than was required by the question). For example, in Experiment 1, the prosecutor asked whether the defendant was insured as a driver. In some conditions the defendant replies "Yes, I've never lost my insurance because of speeding tickets." The defendant has provided more information (by mentioning speeding tickets) than is required by the Yes–No question, and thereby has violated the quantity maxim. It would be difficult for a hearer to determine what meaning a speaker might intend to convey with this violation, even though the quantity maxim can be intentionally violated to implicate, for example, the opposite of the remark's literal meaning (e.g., see Gruenfeld & Wyer, 1992). As a result, hearers should, and do, generate inferences about a speaker's motives (that he is or she trying to convey a favorable image), personality (that he or she is nervous and anxious), and guilt in an attempt to explain the violation.

Conceptually similar results have been reported for violations of the relevance maxim (Davis & Holtgraves, 1984). In this research, a politician who failed to provide relevant answers to debate questions was perceived more negatively on several dimensions than was a politician whose answers were relevant. Participants noticed these violations and explained them in terms of the speaker's motives (e.g., he was trying to avoid the issues) and personality (e.g., competence). It seems clear, then, that the Gricean maxims can provide a framework for the construction of unintended (as well as intended) inferences about a speaker.

INDIVIDUAL AND CULTURAL DIFFERENCES IN INDIRECTNESS

As my review suggests, whether people speak indirectly and look for indirect meanings in others' remarks is heavily influenced by the social context. But it is doubtful that the situation alone explains all of the variability in indirectness. Regardless of the situation, some people seem to speak more indirectly than others; similarly, some people seem to be more likely to look for indirect meanings in others' remarks.

The possibility of both individual and cultural differences in indirectness has been noted by many writers. Tannen (1981), for example, has argued that indirectness is an important component of conversational style and a source of misunderstanding between people who fail to appreciate one another's style. Also, the behavioral manifestations of individualism and collectivism may include variability in indirectness (Triandis, 1994). People with a collectivist orientation (and an interdependent self) are described as being more attuned to the face wants of each other than are people with an individualistic orientation (and an independent self; Ting-Toomey, 1988). As a result, the former should be more likely to speak indirectly and to look for possible indirect meanings in the remarks of others.

Despite the relatively widespread acknowledgment of the existence and importance of individual variability in indirectness, there has been surprisingly little empirical research on this issue. Recently, however, I have developed a conversational indirectness scale (CIS) as an initial step in exploring these differences (Holtgraves, 1997c). The CIS is a 19-item self-report measure of a person's tendency to look for indirect meanings in others' remarks (an interpretation dimension) and to speak indirectly (a production dimension). Preliminary results indicate that this measure of indirectness is valid and reliable, with both micro- and macrolevel implications. For example, consistent with current theorizing about individualism–collectivism (Triandis, 1994), South Korean college students scored far higher on both the production and interpretation dimensions than did college students from the United States.[5] At the microlevel, the interpretation dimension is associated with differences in the comprehension of indirect remarks. Specifically, people scoring high on this dimension are more likely to comprehend certain indirect meanings, and to be significantly faster at doing so, than are those scoring low on this dimension.

It is possible that some individual and cultural variability in conversational indirectness is a result of differing perceptions of an interpersonal situation. For example, people who speak more indirectly may, relative to their more direct counterparts, tend to perceive themselves as relatively low in status and more distant from their partners. Thus, they may perceive any act as relatively more face threatening and hence think that greater indirectness is called for. Similarly, people in some cultures may tend to assume greater distance between unacquainted others than do those in other cultures, and these differences can then result in people in the former culture tending to be more indirect than those in the latter culture (Holtgraves & Yang, 1992; Scollon & Scollon, 1981).

CONCLUSIONS

People speak indirectly for a reason: as one way of being attentive to each other's face. To do so they must assess the interpersonal situation to determine the appropriate level of indirectness. Thus, a person's view of an interpersonal setting (including his or her self-view) is revealed in his or her talk. Hearers, of course, must be attentive to the same features of the interpersonal context and operate with the same conversational rules to recognize a speaker's intended meaning and politeness. In short, people must coordinate to communicate (cf. Clark, 1985), and this coordination extends to the interpersonal level. People perform not only speech acts when they use language; they simultaneously perform interpersonal acts. Although this fact has long been recognized (e.g., Watzlawick, Beavin, & Jackson, 1967), empirical research on the interpersonal underpinnings of language has been somewhat rare. An understanding of language use in general, and indirectness in particular, requires a consideration of the interpersonal foundations of language.

ACKNOWLEDGMENTS

Correspondence should be addressed to Thomas Holtgraves, Department of Psychological Science, Ball State University, Muncie, IN 47306. Email: 00T0HOLTGRAV@BSUVC.BSU.EDU.

---

[5]Reliable gender differences with this measure did not occur in either country.

REFERENCES

Ambady, N., Koo, J., Lee, F., & Rosenthal, R. (1996). More than words: Linguistics and nonlinguistic politeness in two cultures. *Journal of Personality and Social Psychology, 70,* 996–1011.

Atkinson, J. M., & Drew, P. (1979). *Order in the court.* London: Macmillan.

Bavelas, J. B., Black, A., Chovil, N., & Mullett, J. (1990). *Equivocal communication.* Newbury Park, CA: Sage.

Baxter, L. A. (1984). An investigation of compliance gaining as politeness. *Human Communication Research, 10,* 427–456.

Blasko, D. G., & Connine, C. M. (1993). Effects of metaphor aptness on metaphor processing. *Journal of Experimental Psychology: Learning, Memory, and Cognition, 19,* 295–308.

Blum-Kulka, S., Danet, B., & Gherson, R. (1985). The language of requesting in Israeli society. In J. Forgas (Ed.), *Language and social situations* (pp. 113–139). New York: Springer-Verlag.

Brown, P. (1995). Politeness strategies and the attribution of intentions: The case of Tzeltal irony. In E. Goody (Ed.), *Social intelligence and interaction* (pp. 153–174). Cambridge, England: Cambridge University Press.

Brown, P., & Levinson, S. (1987). *Politeness: Some universals in language usage.* Cambridge, England: Cambridge University Press.

Brown, R. (1990). Politeness theory: Exemplar and exemplary. In I. Rock (Ed.), *The legacy of Solomon Asch: Essays in cognition and social psychology* (pp. 23–38). Hillsdale, NJ: Lawrence Erlbaum Associates.

Brown, R., & Gilman, A. (1989). Politeness theory and Shakespeare's four major tragedies. *Language in Society, 18,* 159–212.

Carrell, P. L. (1981). Children's understanding of indirect requests: Comparing child and adult comprehension. *Journal of Child Language, 8,* 329–345.

Clark, H. H. (1985). Language use and language users. In G. Lindzey & E. Aronson, (Eds.), *Handbook of social psychology* (pp. 179–231). New York: Random House.

Clark, H. H., & Lucy, P. (1975). Understanding what is meant from what is said: A study in conversationally conveyed requests. *Journal of Verbal Learning and Verbal Behavior, 14,* 56–72.

Clark, H. H., & Schunk, D. (1980). Polite responses to polite requests. *Cognition, 8,* 111–143.

Clark, H. H., & Schunk, D. (1981). Politeness in requests: A rejoinder to Kemper and Thissen. *Cognition, 9,* 311–315.

Dascal, M. (1987). Defending literal meaning. *Cognitive Science, 11,* 259–281.

Davis, D., & Holtgraves, T. (1984). Perceptions of responsive others: Attributions, attraction, understandability, and memory for their utterances. *Journal of Experimental Social Psychology, 20,* 383–408.

Drew, P. (1984). Speakers' reportings in invitation sequences. In J. M. Atkinson & J. Heritage (Eds.), *Structures of social action* (pp. 129–151). Cambridge, England: Cambridge University Press.

Erickson, B. E., Lind, A., Johnson, B. C., & O'Barr, W. (1978). Speech style and impression formation in a court setting. *Journal of Experimental Social Psychology, 14,* 266–279.

Ervin-Tripp, S. (1976). Is Sybil there? The structure of some American English directives. *Language in Society, 5,* 25–66.

Ervin-Tripp, S., Strage, M., Lampert, M., & Bell, N. (1987). Understanding requests. *Linguistics, 25,* 107–143.

Gibbs, R. W., Jr. (1983). Do people always process the literal meanings of indirect requests? *Journal of Experimental Psychology: Learning, Memory, and Cognition, 9,* 524–533.

Gibbs, R. W., Jr. (1984). Literal meaning and psychological theory. *Cognitive Science, 8,* 275–304.

Gibbs, R. W., Jr. (1986). What makes some indirect speech acts conventional? *Journal of Memory and Language, 25,* 181–196.

Gibbs, R. W., Jr. (1994). *The poetics of mind.* Cambridge, England: Cambridge University Press.

Glucksberg, S., Gildea, P., & Bookin, H. (1982). On understanding nonliteral speech: Can people ignore metaphor? *Journal of Verbal Learning and Verbal Behavior, 21,* 85–98.

Goffman, E. (1967). *Interaction ritual: Essays on face to face behavior.* Garden City, NY: Anchor Books.

Gordon, D., & Lakoff, G. (1975). Conversational postulates. In P. Cole & J. Morgan (Eds.), *Syntax and semantics: Vol. 3, Speech acts,* (pp. 83–196). New York: Academic Press.

Grice, H. P. (1975). Logic and conversation. In P. Cole & J. Morgan (Eds.), *Syntax and semantics: Vol. 3, Speech acts,* (pp. 41–58). New York: Academic Press.

Gruenfeld, D. H., & Wyer, R. S., Jr. (1992). Semantics and pragmatics of social influence: How affirmations and denials affect beliefs in referent propositions. *Journal of Personality and Social Psychology, 62,* 38–49.

Hastie, R. (1984). Causes and effects of causal attribution. *Journal of Personality and Social Psychology, 46,* 44–56.

Heritage, J. (1984). *Garfinkel and ethnomethodology.* Cambridge, England: Polity.

Herrmann, T. (1983). *Speech and situation.* New York: Springer-Verlag.

Hobbs, J. R., Stickel, M. E., Appelt, D. E., & Martin, P. (1993). Interpretation as abduction. *Artificial Intelligence, 63,* 69–142.

Holtgraves, T. M. (1986). Language structure in social interaction: Perceptions of direct and indirect speech acts and interactants who use them, *Journal of Personality and Social Psychology, 51,* 305–314.

Holtgraves, T. M. (1994). Communication in context: Effects of speaker status on the comprehension of indirect requests. *Journal of Experimental Psychology: Learning, Memory and Cognition, 20,* 1205–1218.

Holtgraves, T. M. (1997a). Yes, but . . . : Positive politeness in conversation arguments. *Journal of Language and Social Psychology, 16,* 222–239.

Holtgraves, T. M. (1997b). Politeness and memory for the wording of remarks. *Memory & Cognition, 25,* 106–116.

Holtgraves, T. M. (1997c). Styles of language use: Individual and cultural variability in conversational indirectness. *Journal of Personality and Social Psychology, 73,* 624-637.

Holtgraves, T., & Grayer, A. (1994). I am not a crook: Effects of denials on perceptions of a defendant's personality, motives, and guilt. *Journal of Applied Social Psychology, 24,* 2132–2150.

Holtgraves, T., Srull, T., & Socall, D. (1989). Conversation memory: The effects of speaker status on memory for the wording of conversation remarks. *Journal of Personality and Social Psychology, 56,* 149–160.

Holtgraves, T., & Yang, J. N. (1990). Politeness as universal: Cross-cultural perceptions of request strategies and inferences based on their use. *Journal of Personality and Social Psychology, 59,* 719–729.

Holtgraves, T., & Yang, J. N. (1992). The interpersonal underpinnings of request strategies: General principles and differences due to culture and gender. *Journal of Personality and Social Psychology, 62,* 246–256.

Kemper, S. & Thissen, D. (1981). How polite? A reply to Clark and Schunk. *Cognition, 9,* 305–309.

Kreuz, R. J., Kassler, M. A., & Coppenrath, L. (1998). The use of exaggeration in discourse: Cognitive and social facets. In S. R. Fussell & R. J. Kreuz (Eds.), *Social and cognitive approaches to interpersonal communication.* Mahwah, NJ: Lawrence Erlbaum Associates.

Labov, W., & Fanshel, D. (1977). *Therapeutic discourse: Psychotherapy as conversation.* New York: Academic Press.

Lakoff, R. (1977). Women's language. *Language and Style, 10,* 222–248.

Leech, G. N. (1983). *Principles of pragmatics.* London: Longman.

Leichty, G., & Applegate, J. L. (1991). Social-cognitive and situational influences on the use of face-saving persuasive strategies. *Human Communication Research, 17,* 451–484.

Levinson, S. (1983). *Pragmatics.* Cambridge, England: Cambridge University Press.

Levinson, S. (1995). Interactional biases in human thinking. In E. Goody (Ed.) *Social intelligence and interaction* (pp. 221–260). Cambridge, England: Cambridge University Press.

Lim, T. S., & Bowers, J. W. (1991). Face-work, solidarity, approbation, and tact. *Human Communication Research, 17,* 415–450.

Pomerantz, A. (1984). Agreeing and disagreeing with assessments: Some features of preferred/dispreferred turn shapes. In J. M. Atkinson & J. Heritage (Eds.), *Structures of social action* (pp. 57–101). Cambridge, England: Cambridge University Press.

Roberts, R. M., & Kreuz, R. J. (1994). Why do people use figurative language? *Psychological Science, 5,* 159–163.

Sacks, H. (1987). On the preferences for agreement and contiguity in sequences in conversation. In G. Button & J. R. E. Lee (Eds.), *Talk and social organization* (pp. 54–69). Clevedon, England: Multilingual Matters.

Schegloff, E. (1968). Sequencing in conversational openings. *American Anthropologist, 70,* 1075–1095.

Schwarz, N. (1994). Judgment in a social context: Biases, shortcomings, and the logic of conversation. In M. Zanna (Ed.), *Advances in experimental social psychology* (Vol. 26, pp. 123–162). San Diego, CA: Academic Press.

Schwarz, N. (1998). Communication in standardized research situations: A Gricean perspective. In S. R. Fussell & R. J. Kreuz (Eds.), *Social and cognitive approaches to interpersonal communication.* Mahwah, NJ: Lawrence Erlbaum Associates.

Scollon, R., & Scollon, S. (1981). *Narrative, literacy, and face in interethnic communication.* Norwood, NJ: Ablex.

Searle, J. (1975). Indirect speech acts. In P. Cole & J. Morgan (Eds.), *Syntax and semantics: Vol. 3, Speech acts* (pp. 59–82). New York: Academic Press.

Slugoski, B. R., & Turnbull, W. (1988). Cruel to be kind and kind to be cruel: Sarcasm, banter, and social relations. *Journal of Language and Social Psychology, 7,* 101–121.

Sperber, D., & Wilson, D. (1986). *Relevance.* Cambridge, MA: Harvard University Press.

Tannen, D. (1981). Indirectness in discourse: Ethnicity as conversation style. *Discourse Processes, 4,* 221–238.

Ting-Toomey, S. (1988). Intercultural conflict styles: A face-negotiation theory. In Y. Kim & W. Gudykunst (Eds.), *Theories in intercultural communication* (pp. 213–235). Newbury Park, CA: Sage.

Titone, D. A., & Connine, C. M. (1994). Comprehension of idiomatic expressions: Effects of familiarity and literality. *Journal of Experimental Psychology: Learning, Memory, and Cognition, 20,* 1126–1138.

Tracy, K. (1990). The many faces of face-work. In H. Giles and W. P. Robinson (Eds.), *Handbook of language and social psychology* (pp. 209–226). London: Wiley.

Triandis, S. (1994). *Individualism and collectivism.* Boulder, Co: Westview Press.

Watzlawick, P., Beavin, J. H., & Jackson, D. D. (1967). *Pragmatics of human communication: A study of interactional patterns, pathologies, and paradoxes.* New York: Norton.

— 5 —

The Use of Exaggeration in Discourse: Cognitive and Social Facets

Roger J. Kreuz,* Max A. Kassler,** and Lori Coppenrath*

*The University of Memphis and **Bell Communications Research

When people speak with one another, they frequently do not literally mean what they say. For example, someone might refer to a curvy road as a snake, or suggest that a mutual friend has let the cat out of the bag. Even though a speaker is not literally referring to snakes, cats, or bags, few listeners would have difficulties in figuring out the intended meanings of such statements.

Speakers also frequently say the opposite of what they mean. For example, a speaker might refer to a torrential downpour as "lovely weather" or to a disappointing announcement as "wonderful news." Although such ironic or sarcastic statements can be misinterpreted (Kreuz, 1996), most listeners are able to determine their intended meanings.

Finally, consider a third possibility: A speaker might refer to an event, but some aspect of the situation is exaggerated. In many cases, this is done by specifying a physically impossible quantity. People commonly complain that they have been waiting in line forever or that they have millions of reasons for not doing something. Many colloquial terms, such as *gobs*, *oodles*, or *zillions*, are frequently used to refer to extreme amounts of indefinite magnitude.

Traditionally, such statements have been classified as nonliteral language, because by definition they are nonveridical. They have been the focus of literary scholars and students of rhetoric for centuries, but they have also begun to attract the attention of researchers in psycholinguistics. Although there is some disagreement about the exact number of these forms, a fairly representative listing, along with definitions and examples, appears in Table 5.1.

Nonliteral language is of interest to psycholinguists because its existence poses considerable difficulties for simple models of language comprehension (e.g., Grice, 1978). Although many theories of communication have been proposed to explain such language (e.g., Grice, 1975; Sperber & Wilson, 1986), none of these proposals have met with universal acceptance.

One purpose of this chapter is to review the psychological research on extreme statements variously referred to as hyperbole, exaggerations, or overstatements. The theoretical ideas proposed to explain hyperbole will be reviewed, and the issue of degree of exaggeration will be discussed. We propose some simple hypotheses about degree of exaggeration and describe a series of studies that test these hypotheses.

TABLE 5.1

Eight Forms of Nonliteral Language (Based on Kreuz & Roberts, 1993)

Type	Definition	Example
Hyperbole	Deliberate exaggeration	"The cafeteria line was a mile long."
Idiom	Conventionalized nonliteral expression	"He kicked the bucket."
Indirect request	Request for actions stated obliquely	"Can you pass the salt?"
Irony	Opposite meaning intended	"What gorgeous weather!" (if spoken during a thunderstorm)
Metaphor	Implicit comparison	"The road was a snake."
Rhetorical question	Assertion framed as question	"Who do you think you are?"
Simile	Explicit comparison	"My job is like a jail."
Understatement	Deliberate underemphasis	"Mozart wrote some decent music."

NOTE: Based on "The Empirical Study of Figurative Language in Literature," by R. J. Kreuz and R. M. Roberts, 1993, *Poetics, 22,* pp. 151–169. Copyright 1993 by Elsevier Science Publishers BV.

PREVIOUS RESEARCH ON HYPERBOLE

Very little empirical work has been conducted on the phenomenon of hyperbole. In fact, it remains one of the most understudied forms of figurative language (Gibbs, 1993; 1994). This fact is somewhat surprising, given how frequently exaggeration is employed in discourse. A study by Kreuz, Roberts, Johnson, and Bertus (1996) assessed the relative frequency of figurative language usage in a random sampling of American short stories. The researchers catalogued all instances of hyperbole, idioms, indirect requests, irony, metaphors, rhetorical questions, simile, and understatements that appeared in the stories. Not surprisingly, metaphor was the most common figurative form (accounting for 29% of the corpus), but hyperbole was second and accounted for 27%. Metaphor has been extensively studied by the psychological community (for reviews, see

Kreuz & Roberts, 1993; Ortony, 1993); but hyperbole, which is almost as common, has been relatively neglected.

Interestingly, the logical opposite of hyperbole was infrequently registered in the Kreuz et al. (1996) corpus. *Meiosis* (understatement) accounted for only 3% of the figurative occurrences in the stories. This disparity has been noted by others, and it seems that understatement is more typical of British English than of American English (e.g., Hübler, 1983).

In fact, studies of overstatement and understatement have tended to emphasize cultural differences in the use of these two figures. In a study that compared the reporting of embarrassing situations in five European cultures (Greece, Italy, Spain, the United Kingdom, and West Germany), the British were found to understate their embarrassment, while the Greeks tended to overstate embarrassment (Edelman et al., 1989). Cohen (1987) claims that difficulties in the diplomatic relations between Egypt and the United States are partly caused by the Egyptian propensity for exaggeration.

Another interesting aspect of hyperbole is that it tends to co-occur with other forms of figurative language. Consider, for example, this utterance:

(1) The mere thought of his calculus midterm caused Bob's heart to race like a jet engine.

In (1), the simile is exaggerated to an impossible degree to suggest Bob's feelings about his upcoming test. It is also quite common for metaphoric and ironic statements to be very extreme, and this co-occurrence was seen repeatedly in the Kreuz et al. (1996) corpus.

To examine this phenomenon more closely, Kreuz and Roberts (1995) looked at the importance of exaggeration in the comprehension of ironic statements. Participants read brief scenarios and rated how ironic the final statements seemed to be. For example, in one scenario, Jane is moving out of her apartment, and her friend Gary is helping her. He attempts to move her grandfather clock but only succeeds in tipping it over, and it crashes to the floor. In one version of the scenario, Jane says to Gary:

(2) Thanks for your help!

This statement is clearly ironic, and the participants rated it as such. In another version, however, Jane says:

(3) I'll never be able to repay you for your help!

The statement in (3) is also ironic, but it is more exaggerated than the statement in (2). The participants rated exaggerated ironic statements as being significantly more ironic than were nonexaggerated ironic statements. It seems likely, therefore, that the use of exaggeration is a reliable cue for determining ironic intent (see Kreuz, 1996).

Exaggeration, however, can be used in discourse for other reasons. In their influential analysis of linguistic politeness, Brown and Levinson (1987) have suggested that people use hyperbole as one way of going "off record" (i.e., accomplishing a face-threatening act by being indirect). For example, an utterance like (4):

(4) There must have been a million people at the grocery store!

could be used by someone as an excuse for their lateness.

The many different uses of such language led Roberts and Kreuz (1994) to examine the variety of *discourse goals* that are fulfilled when speakers choose to speak nonliterally. Previous research had suggested that ironic statements are used to fulfill multiple discourse goals (Kreuz, Long, & Church, 1991), but Roberts and Kreuz's study explored the discourse goals satisfied by the eight different forms of nonliteral language mentioned earlier: hyperbole, idiom, indirect requests, irony, metaphor, rhetorical questions, simile, and understatement.

In the study, college students were shown examples of these eight types of figurative language and were asked to generate new examples of particular nonliteral forms. Finally, each participant was asked to list the reasons that a person might choose to express himself or herself in this particular way. A discourse goal taxonomy, based on the participants' responses, was devised. For hyperbole, the participants provided discourse goals such as "to clarify," "to emphasize," and "to be humorous."

It may seem paradoxical to think of clarification as one of the discourse goals of hyperbole, since such statements do not provide veridical information. Hyperbole, however, can often provide insight into *why* a particular statement has been uttered. Consider, for example, the utterance in (5):

(5) I've just watched the Pittsburgh football team lose for the thousandth time!

This hyperbolic statement provides specific information (that the Steelers lost), but it also informs listeners of the speaker's attitude about this information (in this case, disgust or disillusionment). So hyperbole can be used by speakers to make clear their feelings or states of mind.

There also exists some research on children's understanding of hyperbole. In a study by Winner et al. (1987, Experiment 2), 6-, 8-, and 10-year-old children viewed videotapes in which different forms of figurative language were used. The children were less successful in correctly interpreting hyperbole and understatement than they were in interpreting other statements such as sarcastic remarks. Although older children's interpretations were more accurate than were younger children's, there was some evidence across all age groups that the children interpreted exaggerated statements as lies (see also Winner, 1988).

Although children's interpretations of figurative language are often problematic, there is no doubt that even very young children are frequently exposed to such talk. A study by Sell, Kreuz, and Coppenrath (1997) examined the use of nonliteral language by parents to their 48- to 70-month-old children in free-play contexts. An analysis of 17 videotaped sessions of 30 minutes each revealed hundreds of figurative utterances by parents, including dozens of hyperbolic statements. In fact, the use of hyperbole was slightly more common than was the use of metaphor, although neither was as common as rhetorical questions or idioms. The discourse goals of the parents, however, seemed to be different from those observed in the Roberts and Kreuz (1994) study. The parents typically used hyperbole to encourage their children in their play activities (e.g., "We can fix anything, can't we?").

THEORETICAL EXPLANATIONS OF HYPERBOLE

Traditional pragmatic theory has dealt with hyperbole by classifying it as a violation of Grice's (1975) Maxim of Quality (Say what you believe to be true, Gibbs, 1994, p. 392), or as a violation of the Maxim of Quantity (Do not say more than is necessary, Brown & Levinson, 1987, p. 219). (For a description of Grice's framework, see Holtgraves, 1998, and Schwarz, 1998.) As Gibbs (1994) has pointed out, however, these formulations are less than satisfactory. It makes more sense to suggest that an exaggerator's comment should *resemble* his or her beliefs than for the statement and the belief to be identical. For example, when a speaker utters:

(6) It's raining cats and dogs out there!

he or she does not intend to be untruthful but to supply useful information about the intensity of the rain by using a hyperbolic, idiomatic statement. Accordingly, Gibbs suggests that Grice's Maxim of Quality should be broadened so that literally false but figuratively true statements can be incorporated into Grice's framework (Gibbs, 1994, pp. 392–394).

Another factor also makes hyperbole different from other types of figurative language. When speakers choose to express themselves in an exaggerated way, they have a great deal of latitude in specifying the *form* of their statements.

Consider the following utterances:

(7)   To get the tickets, I had to wait in line for hours!
(8)   To get the tickets, I had to wait in line for days!
(9)   To get the tickets, I had to wait in line for weeks!
(10) To get the tickets, I had to wait in line for months!
(11) To get the tickets, I had to wait in line for years!
(12) To get the tickets, I had to wait in line for decades!
(13) To get the tickets, I had to wait in line for centuries!
(14) To get the tickets, I had to wait in line forever!

Utterance (7) would strike most people as quite possible, and it clearly could be a literal statement. Utterance (8) is extremely unlikely, but within the realm of physical possibility. Utterances (9) to (14) are clearly nonliteral; listeners can draw on world knowledge to realize that a ticket line could never reach such lengths. It would not be unusual, however, to hear (9) through (14) uttered by an unhappy would-be concertgoer.

These issues can be explored at a deeper level. What does it mean to "draw on world knowledge?" Speakers must rely on implicit knowledge embodied in scripts and schemata. This must be the case because what is hyperbolic in one situation may be nonhyperbolic in another, and listeners must be sensitive to these differences. Consider, for example, a statement like (15):

(15) It took me years to find the perfect woman!

Regardless of the woman's perfection, it could certainly take years to find a compatible person. Compare this with (16):

(16) It took the waiter years to bring me the bill!

Because of listeners' knowledge of the restaurant script, (16) would be recognized as a hyperbolic statement; a literal translation might be (17):

(17) It took the waiter much more time than is normal to bring
      me the bill.

Although knowledge of scripts and schemata clearly helps listeners make sense of literal statements, this information may play an even greater role in helping to identify nonveridical, nonliteral statements. Although this issue has been explored with regard to metaphor (e.g., Allbritton, 1995), it has received less attention with regard to other forms of nonliteral language. One clear implication is that world knowledge allows listeners to correctly *detect* statements that are meant figuratively and to have greater certainty about these interpretations. For example, knowledge about horse racing would allow the reader of a racing story to determine whether certain descriptions (e.g., the speeds of the horses) were meant literally or hyperbolically (see Kreuz et al., 1996, pp. 93–94).

DEGREE OF EXAGGERATION

Consider once again examples (9) through (14). On the basis of script knowledge, it can be inferred that all these statements exceed some threshold of *physical possibility*. Therefore, these statements are clearly nonliteral, and they all suggest the same literal "translation"—the wait for tickets was longer than expected. Should we conclude, however, that statements like (9) through (14) are equivalent in terms of their effects on listeners? Clearly, these statements differ greatly in terms of specified magnitude. Are there psychological consequences for specifying varying degrees of impossible quantities? Why might a speaker choose one level of exaggeration over another? How are such statements perceived by their hearers? A number of possibilities can be entertained.

It may be the case, for example, that exaggeration makes the intended meaning of nonliteral statements clearer and less ambiguous. In other words, as the degree of exaggeration increases, the perceived appropriateness or effectiveness of a statement may also increase. This hypothesis is supported by the research on irony and exaggeration cited earlier (Kreuz & Roberts, 1995):

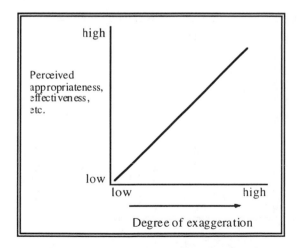

FIG. 5.1: Depiction of first hypothesis ("The More the Better" theory).

Participants were more likely to consider a nonliteral (and potentially ambiguous) remark as ironic when it was exaggerated than when it was not. This hypothesis can be diagrammed as shown in Figure 5.1, and can be expressed very simply: The more exaggeration, the better.

There are, however, other possibilities. Perhaps increasing the degree of exaggeration is effective only up to a certain point. After some optimal level of exaggeration is reached, any further exaggeration may be perceived as less appropriate or less effective. If a speaker exaggerates too little, for example, the nonliteral nature of a statement may be lost on the hearer. If a speaker exaggerates too much, the statement may seem absurd or bizarre. This hypothesis would predict an inverted-U relation between degree of exaggeration and perception, as shown in Figure 5.2. Just as in the story of the Three Bears, in which Goldilocks found different bowls of porridge to be too hot, too cold, or "just right," perhaps there is a preferred, or "just right" level of exaggeration for interpersonal communication.

A third possibility has been diagrammed in Figure 5.3. Perhaps a speaker must achieve some necessary threshold to clearly signal his or her nonliteral meaning. Going past this threshold, however, may not lead to any changes in how the utterance is perceived. In other words, once a "critical mass" has been reached, the exaggeration has its intended effect upon a hearer, and additional exaggeration is irrelevant. Although there are several additional possibilities, these three hypotheses illustrate some possible relationships between degrees of exaggeration and effects on listeners.

Consider once again the issue of physical possibility. If either the "just

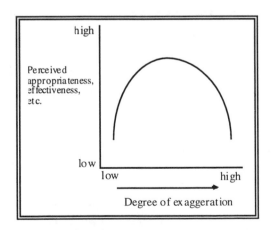

FIG. 5.2. Depiction of second hypothesis ("Just Right" theory).

right" or "critical mass" view of hyperbole is correct, at what points do participants' perceptions of exaggerated statements begin to change? It seems likely that the level of physical possibility is important, as statements that are physically impossible should be clearer with regard to their hyperbolic nature. The following experiments were conducted to quantify the relationship between exaggeration and listener judgments, and to determine the importance of physical possibility as a cue for nonliteral intent.

Experiment 1: Construction of Materials

We began the project by creating stimulus materials that could be used in a series of studies. We wrote 20 experimental scenarios, all with the same form: seven sentences that introduced two (or more) characters and a particular situation (e.g., moving a piano). The last sentence of each scenario contained a (potentially) hyperbolic remark uttered by one of the characters. That is, a character made reference to a quantifiable entity, such as weight, time, number, temperature, or speed. Two of these scenarios appear in the top portion of 5.2.

Once the scenarios had been constructed, they were given to undergraduate participants recruited from the psychology department participant pool. As shown in Table 5.2, the quantifiable entity in the scenarios was left blank. Participants were asked to read each scenario, and to provide six completions

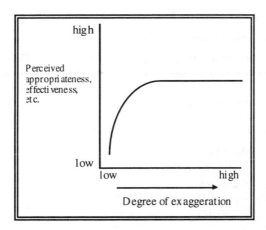

FIG. 5.3. Depiction of third hypothesis ("Critical Mass" theory).

TABLE 5.2

Examples of Scenarios Used in the Experiments

Example 1

Tim and Natalie were talking about their weekend plans.
Natalie asked, "Can we afford to see a movie and have dinner tonight?"
"Sure, I've got plenty of money for us to go out," Tim said.
"Where did you get the money from?" Natalie asked.
"There was a flyer in the psychology building about a professor looking for
help to move his furniture, so I called him, and helped him move this
afternoon," Tim replied.
"That's great!" Natalie said.
"Well, it was hard work—the guy had a grand piano that must have weighed
_____, but at least he paid pretty well," Tim added.

Average Values Provided by Participants in Experiment 1

Degree	Level of Exaggeration	Average Value
0	None (literal statement)	400 lbs.
1	Unlikely but possible	500 lbs.
2	Very unlikely but possible	700 lbs.
3	Physically impossible	A ton
4	Physically impossible and extreme	Five tons
5	Physically impossible and very extreme	A million lbs.

---

that would satisfy the six following criteria:

(1) Extremely likely
(2) Unlikely, but possible
(3) Very unlikely, but possible
(4) Physically impossible
(5) Physically impossible, and extreme
(6) Physically impossible, and very extreme

For each scenario, the mean, median, and mode of the participants' responses for
each of the six exaggeration levels were computed. For each exaggeration level

TABLE 5.2 (CONTINUED)

Examples Of Scenarios Used In The Experiments

Example 2

Mary and Ted were watching *Gone with the Wind* on television.
Mary had seen the movie many times, but Ted had never seen it before.
Unfortunately, Ted kept asking stupid questions, and Mary was rather
irritated with him.
"I don't get it," Ted was saying, "Why doesn't she just find somebody
else?"
"But Rhett is the love of her life!" Mary exclaimed, even more irritated by
Ted's questions.
Luckily for Mary, a commercial came on the TV, but now it was Ted's turn to
be annoyed.
"I hate this—just when the action gets going, they interrupt with _____
commercials!"

Average Values Provided by Participants in Experiment 1

Degree	Level of Exaggeration	Average Value
0	None (literal statement)	5
1	Unlikely but possible	10
2	Very unlikely but possible	12
3	Physically impossible	25
4	Physically impossible and extreme	1000
5	Physically impossible and very extreme	a million

we then attempted to select values that would be monotonic (i.e., greater than
the previous level[s]), and reflective of the central tendency of the participants'
responses.

In practice, this turned out to be somewhat difficult. Because most
exaggerated statements are general in nature (e.g., "I've been waiting here for a
thousand years!" as opposed to "I've been waiting here for 967.4 years!"), the
mean response was usually rejected as unsuitable. Instead, we examined the
median and mode for each level, and typically chose the rounder of these two
numbers (e.g., 40 was chosen over 43). If this choice resulted in an amount
equal to or lower than a previous level, we chose the value that would maintain

a monotonic ordering of values. Finally, in the case of bimodal distributions, we tended to select the median value. The selected values used in the two example scenarios appear in Table 5.2.

Experiment 2: Validation of Materials

In the next phase of the study, we made an attempt to validate the chosen values on a new group of participants. The participants were asked to read the 20 scenarios described in Experiment 1. These were presented on a computer screen, one sentence at a time. In the final sentence of each scenario, the participants were shown one of the six amounts selected in Experiment 1. Each participant saw only one version of each scenario (i.e., no one ever saw more than one exaggeration level for any scenario). After reading each scenario, the participants were asked "How exaggerated was the final statement?" They made their ratings on a 6-point scale, with endpoints labeled "not at all exaggerated" and "very exaggerated."

The results of this study confirmed that we had selected psychologically distinct values for the exaggeration levels. The data conformed to an extremely linear increasing function across the five levels of exaggeration ($R^2 = .99$). The mean values for each level appear in Table 5.3.

It should be noted, however, that the participants did not seem very sensitive to the threshold of physical possibility, as there was no sudden change in the ratings between the second (very unlikely, but possible) and the third (physically impossible) levels of exaggeration.

Experiment 3: Ratings of Sense

We designed the next study to assess the *semantic* aspects of hyperbole. After a new group of participants read the scenarios as they appeared on the computer

TABLE 5.3

Results From the Validation Study (Experiment 2)

Mean Ratings of Exaggeration by Degree of Exaggeration*					
0	*1*	*2*	*3*	*4*	*5*
2.45	3.09	3.77	4.35	4.85	5.21
(1.59)	(1.60)	(1.68)	(1.61)	(1.53)	(1.24)

*Standard deviations appear in parentheses.

TABLE 5.4

Results From the First Semantic Study (Experiment 3)

Mean Ratings of Sense by Degree of Exaggeration*					
0	1	2	3	4	5
4.49	3.92	3.78	3.28	3.04	2.69
(1.40)	(1.78)	(1.78)	(1.75)	· (1.69)	(1.80)

*Standard deviations appear in parentheses.

screens, they were asked to indicate how much *sense* the final comment in each story made. Once again, participants made their ratings on a 6-point scale, with endpoints labeled "no sense" and "a lot of sense."

The data from this study appear in Table 5.4. Interestingly, we found that the high levels of exaggeration (Levels 3, 4, and 5), were rated as making less sense than the level with no hyperbole or the first level with slight hyperbole. The data can be best described as an almost linear decreasing function ($R^2 = .99$), with no abrupt changes as the level of physical possibility is exceeded.

Because these results did not support any of the hypotheses mentioned earlier, they were surprising. It seemed as if the participants were equating the sense question with the degree of exaggeration, instead of considering the nonliteral aspects of the statement. This finding perhaps occurred because most of the statements evaluated by the participants were exaggerated. By definition, half the statements rated by participants were beyond the point of physical possibility (i.e., Levels 3, 4, and 5). Therefore, it is possible that the participants quickly became aware of the manipulation, and their awareness could have affected the results. This potential problem was addressed in a new experiment.

Experiment 4: Ratings of Sense with Filler Scenarios

Experiment 4 was a replication of Experiment 3, except that the presentation of the experimental scenarios was interspersed with 10 filler texts. The filler scenarios had the same form as the experimental scenarios, but they ended with veridical, nonexaggerated statements. In Experiment 4, participants provided sense ratings for the final statement in all 30 scenarios. In addition, the participants were asked if they were able to guess the purpose of this experiment. Before the debriefing at the conclusion of the study, the participants were asked,

"Now that you've finished the experiment, we'd like to know what you think this study is about. Use the index card next to the computer to record your response. If you have no idea what the experiment was about, write "I don't know" on the card. However, please try to make a guess about the purpose of the study." In all other respects the study was identical to Experiment 3.

As Table 5.5 shows, the results of this study were similar to those of Experiment 3. Although the results were somewhat attenuated and did not show the same monotonic function as in the previous study ($R^2 = .92$), statements with high levels of exaggeration were rated as making less sense than did statements with little or no hyperbole. Twenty-seven percent of participants reported at least partial awareness of the use of exaggeration in the scenarios, so the majority of the participants were not cognizant of the hyperbole manipulation.

TABLE 5.5

Results From the Second Semantic Study (Experiment 4)

*Mean Ratings of Sense by Degree of Exaggeration**					
0	*1*	*2*	*3*	*4*	*5*
4.33	4.38	3.98	3.60	3.59	3.32
(1.55)	(1.47)	(1.54)	(1.64)	(1.80)	(1.78)

*Standard deviations appear in parentheses.

Experiment 5: Ratings of Appropriateness

The next studies were designed to focus on the *pragmatic* aspects of hyperbole. Although the participants showed no sensitivity to the degree of physical possibility in the semantic studies (Experiments 3 and 4), it seemed reasonable to predict some sensitivity to this dimension when we asked about the communicative function of these statements.

Experiment 5 was similar in design to Experiment 3; participants were presented with the 20 experimental scenarios and were asked to make ratings on a 6-point scale. These participants, however, were asked how *appropriate* the final comment was. The scale used by the participants had endpoints labeled "not at all appropriate" and "very appropriate." As in Experiment 4, they were also asked to guess at the purpose of the study before the debriefing. As shown in Table 5.6, participants rated the most exaggerated statements (Level 5) as

TABLE 5.6

Results From the First Pragmatic Study (Experiment 5)

*Mean Ratings of Appropriateness by Degree of Exaggeration**					
0	*1*	*2*	*3*	*4*	*5*
3.89	3.90	3.66	3.71	3.54	3.07
(1.69)	(1.73)	(1.83)	(1.73)	(1.83)	(1.45)

*Standard deviations appear in parentheses.

being less appropriate than were the modal or slightly exaggerated statements. As in Experiment 4, 27% of participants reported awareness of the presence of exaggeration in the scenarios.

Experiment 6: Ratings of Likelihood of Use

Experiment 6 was designed to explore the pragmatic aspects of hyperbole from a different perspective. The participants in this study read the scenarios, and rated how *likely* it was that the character would have uttered the final comment. A 6-point rating scale was used, with endpoints labeled "not at all likely" and "very likely." The data from this study appear in Table 5.7. According to a multiple comparison test, the highly exaggerated statements (Levels 4 and 5) were less likely to be used than were statements with less or no exaggeration (Levels 1 to 3). Twenty percent of the participants reported some awareness of the exaggeration manipulation.

TABLE 5.7

Results From the Second Pragmatic Study (Experiment 6)

*Mean Ratings of Likelihood by Degree of Exaggeration**					
0	*1*	*2*	*3*	*4*	*5*
4.02	4.26	4.11	3.77	3.21	3.12
(1.82)	(1.61)	(1.65)	(1.81)	(2.00)	(2.03)

*Standard deviations appear in parentheses.

These data provide some support for the "just right" hypothesis described earlier; the participants seemed to think that moderate exaggeration was more likely than either no exaggeration or high exaggeration. The no exaggeration level, however, did not differ significantly from the low exaggeration levels (Levels 1 and 2). A more likely, and problematic, interpretation of the data is that participants were simply rating the literal *plausibility* of the statement in its context. This potential interpretation considerably clouds the results from Experiment 6 and possibly some of the other studies.

Experiment 7: Interpretations of the Hyperbolic Statements

A different approach was undertaken in Experiment 7. In this study, participants were asked to *interpret* the exaggerated sentences. After reading each story, participants were asked, "Why did the character say this?" As an example, we asked them to consider the case of John, who, after failing a test, said, "Now I'll never graduate!" We suggested that one interpretation of this statement was, "John was upset." The participants were specifically told to avoid restating or rewording the statement. Once again, we were interested in determining whether the degree of exaggeration would influence the interpretations. It seemed probable that participants would be more likely to mention emphasis or exaggeration when the statements were literally impossible (Levels 3, 4, and 5) than when they were not (Levels 1 and 2).

The interpretation data were coded by two of the experimenters. Among other dimensions, participants' responses were coded according to whether they mentioned exaggeration or emphasis. The codings of the judges were compared, and a Cronbach's alpha was computed to determine reliability. The alpha was .81, which was judged as acceptable.

The data from Experiment 7 appear in Table 5.8. Responses were coded as 1 if they mentioned exaggeration or emphasis and as 0 if they did not. Even in the case of the modal or literal condition, participants mentioned exaggeration or

TABLE 5.8

Results From the Interpretation Study (Experiment 7)

Mean Number of Mentions of Exaggeration or Emphasis by Degree of Exaggeration					
0	*1*	*2*	*3*	*4*	*5*
0.25	0.34	0.30	0.44	0.48	0.45

emphasis about a quarter of the time. In the case of the physically impossible exaggerations (Levels, 3, 4, and 5), however, participants mentioned exaggeration or emphasis nearly half the time.

After the participants in Experiment 7 provided their interpretations, they were asked to give confidence ratings for these interpretations. Once again, a 6-point scale was used; in this case, the endpoints were labeled "not very confident" and "very confident." The confidence ratings data appear in Table 5.9. There were no significant differences between the groups, a finding suggesting that interpretations of exaggerated statements are neither easier nor harder to make than those for nonexaggerated statements.

Experiment 8: A Recall Study

We undertook a final study to assess the mnemonic consequences of using hyperbole. Previous memory studies have shown that statements with high pragmatic involvement tend to be remembered better than are those that lack pragmatic involvement (Keenan, MacWhinney, & Mayhew, 1977; Kintsch & Bates, 1977). Statements with high pragmatic involvement (or interactional content, as Keenan et al. refer to it) contain information about speakers' intentions, beliefs, or attitudes toward a listener. It seems likely that nonliteral statements possess greater pragmatic involvement than do literal statements, as the goals of figurative language include many interpersonal factors (Roberts & Kreuz, 1994). In addition, previous research has suggested that there is some memory facilitation for ironic statements when compared to memory for literal equivalents (Kreuz, Long, & Church, 1991). Therefore, it seemed quite likely that a similar facilitation would be found with exaggerated statements.

Experiment 8 was disguised as an impression formation task. Participants read the scenarios and were asked to rate how much they liked one of the characters in each story. Their ratings were made on a 6-point scale, with

TABLE 5.9

Results From the Interpretation Study (Experiment 7)

Mean Confidence Ratings by Degree of Exaggeration*					
0	1	2	3	4	5
4.50	4.57	4.65	4.77	4.73	4.72
(1.20)	(1.28)	(1.17)	(1.13)	(1.24)	(1.29)

*Standard deviations appear in parentheses.

TABLE 5.10

Results From the Recall Study (Experiment 8)

Mean Recall Level by Degree of Exaggeration					
0	*1*	*2*	*3*	*4*	*5*
0.58	0.61	0.57	0.52	0.55	0.47

endpoints labeled "not at all" and "very much."

Ninety minutes after the putative conclusion of the study, the participants returned to the lab and received a surprise cued-recall task. For each scenario, the participants were provided with a complete transcript of the story, except for the amount or degree of the exaggerated term. They were instructed to provide the exact wording for the missing element, such as "a *million* miles" or "a *thousand* degrees below zero."

Responses were scored according to strict and more liberal criteria. The results are similar, so only the strict recall data are reported here. A response was scored as 0 if it did not match the original exactly and as 1 if it did. The data appear in Table 5.10, and according to a multiple comparison test, the only significant difference was that statements with slight exaggeration (Level 1) were remembered better than highly exaggerated statements (Level 5).

SUMMARY AND CONCLUSIONS

Taken as a whole, these experiments provide little or no support for the three hypotheses about degree of exaggeration proposed in this chapter. Hyperbolic statements were perceived as making less sense, as being less likely to be used, and as less appropriate than nonexaggerated statements. In addition, the hyperbolic nature of such statements does not seem to provide any mnemonic advantage. The interpretation data (Experiment 7), however, do provide some support for the idea that physical possibility is psychologically significant. These data thus seem to support a "literalist" hypothesis about nonliteral language use. The participants seem to have eschewed the extreme in favor of the literal, at least for the variables that we measured. These results, however, seem to be at odds with intuitive ideas about exaggeration. Because people use hyperbolic statements frequently, why would they do so if they did not confer particular advantages?

One possible problem with the studies reported here is that the materials might not have truly assessed the range of exaggerated statements. The participants in Experiment 1 provided relatively conservative quantities in the completion task, even when they were asked to be very extreme (as in Levels 4 and 5). For example, the most exaggerated value for the speed of an automobile was only 500 miles per hour, and the greatest length for a line of people waiting to use a photocopier was only 10 miles. This truncation perhaps provided values that were not truly reflective of how people use exaggeration in everyday discourse.

Another potential problem concerns the scenarios themselves. Although the scenarios were written to be relatively engaging, some communicative functions of hyperbole seem muted when they appear in short contexts about fictitious individuals. For example, although Roberts and Kreuz (1994) found that speakers intend hyperbole to be humorous, the amount of humor generated by these hyperbolic statements is rather low. The scenarios were written so that the characters shared common ground (Clark & Marshall, 1981), but the contexts were so short that not much involvement could be generated.

These studies also suggest that physical possibility does not play a major role in how hyperbolic statements are perceived. Once again, however, this interpretation is clouded by other possibilities. Although we attempted to choose topics that the participants were familiar with (e.g., winter temperatures, mosquito bites), perhaps physical possibility is less psychologically salient than it appears at first. Consider the first example scenario in Table 5.2. We assumed that undergraduates would have some familiarity with pianos, but it is doubtful that many of them had had experience in moving grand pianos. Although the quantities we chose did generate a linear function in Experiment 2 (see Table 5.3), the variance in these values may make any strict demarcation between "possible" and "impossible" values rather artificial. Unfortunately, the physical world provides few phenomena that can be unambiguously quantified, and variability in the participants' script knowledge adds another layer of uncertainty.

Further research on hyperbole is clearly needed, because of the ubiquity of this form of figurative language. Better ways of exploring this phenomenon need to be devised, and more sensitive measures may need to be employed. Perhaps most important, researchers must reassess current notions of pragmatics in order to bring hyperbole under a theoretical umbrella large enough to include all forms of nonliteral language.

ACKNOWLEDGMENTS

Portions of this chapter were presented in 1994 at the 35th annual meeting of the Psychonomic Society in St. Louis, Missouri. Susan Fussell and Tracie Stewart provided helpful feedback on earlier drafts of this chapter. Partial support for the preparation of this chapter was provided by a Center of Excellence grant from the state of Tennessee to the Department of Psychology at the University of Memphis.

REFERENCES

Allbritton, D. W. (1995). When metaphors function as schemas: Some cognitive effects of conceptual metaphors. *Metaphor and Symbolic Activity, 10,* 33–46.

Brown, P., & Levinson, S. C. (1987). *Politeness: Some universals of language usage.* Cambridge, England: Cambridge University Press.

Clark, H. H., & Marshall, C. R. (1981). Definite reference and mutual knowledge. In A. K. Joshi, B. Webber, & I. A. Sag (Eds.), *Elements of discourse understanding* (pp. 10–63). Cambridge, England: Cambridge University Press.

Cohen, R. (1987). Problems of intercultural communication in Egyptian-American diplomatic relations. *International Journal of Intercultural Relations, 11,* 29–47.

Edelman, R. J., Asendorpf, J., Contarello, A., Zammuner, V., Georgas, J., & Villanueva, C. (1989). Self-reported expression of embarrassment in five European cultures. *Journal of Cross-Cultural Psychology, 20,* 357–371.

Gibbs, R. W., Jr. (1993). Process and products in making sense of tropes. In A. Ortony (Ed.), *Metaphor and thought* (2nd ed., pp. 252–276). Cambridge, England: Cambridge University Press.

Gibbs, R. W., Jr. (1994). *The poetics of mind: Figurative thought, language, and understanding.* Cambridge, England: Cambridge University Press.

Grice, H. P. (1975). Logic and conversation. In P. Cole & J. Morgan (Eds.), *Syntax and semantics: Vol. 3, Speech acts* (pp. 41–58). New York: Academic Press.

Grice, H. P. (1978). Further notes on logic and conversation. In P. Cole (Ed.), *Syntax and semantics: Vol. 9, Pragmatics* (pp. 113–127). New York: Academic Press.

Holtgraves, T. (1998). Interpersonal foundations of conversational indirectness. In S. R. Fussell & R. J. Kreuz (Eds.), *Social and cognitive approaches to interpersonal communication.* Mahwah, NJ: Lawrence Erlbaum Associates.

Hübler, A. (1983). *Understatements and hedges in English.* Amsterdam: John Benjamins.

Keenan, J. M., MacWhinney, B., & Mayhew D. (1977). Pragmatics and memory: A study of natural conversation. *Journal of Verbal Learning and Verbal Behavior, 16,* 549–560.

Kintsch, W., & Bates, E. (1977). Recognition memory for statements from a classroom lecture. *Journal of Experimental Psychology: General, 118,* 374–386.

Kreuz, R. J. (1996). The use of verbal irony: Cues and constraints. In J. S. Mio & A. N. Katz (Eds.), *Metaphor: Implications and applications* (pp. 23–38). Hillsdale, NJ: Lawrence Erlbaum Associates.

Kreuz, R. J., Long., D. L., & Church, M. B. (1991). On being ironic: Pragmatic and mnemonic implications. *Metaphor and Symbolic Activity, 6,* 149–162.

Kreuz, R. J., & Roberts, R. M. (1993). The empirical study of figurative language in literature. *Poetics, 22,* 151–169.

Kreuz, R. J., & Roberts, R. M. (1995). Two cues for verbal irony: Hyperbole and the ironic tone of voice. *Metaphor and Symbolic Activity, 10,* 21–31.

Kreuz, R. J., Roberts, R. M., Johnson, B. K., & Bertus, E. L. (1996). Figurative language occurrence and co-occurrence in contemporary literature. In R. J. Kreuz & M. S. MacNealy (Eds.), *Empirical approaches to literature and aesthetics* (pp. 83–97). Norwood, NJ: Ablex.

Ortony, A. (Ed.). (1993). *Metaphor and thought* (2nd ed.). Cambridge, England: Cambridge University Press.

Roberts, R. M., & Kreuz, R. J. (1994). Why do people use figurative language? *Psychological Science, 5,* 159–163.

Schwarz, N. (1998). Communication in standardized research situations: A Gricean perspective. In S. R. Fussell & R. J. Kreuz (Eds.), *Social and cognitive approaches to interpersonal communication.* Mahwah, NJ: Lawrence Erlbaum Associates.

Sell, M. A., Kreuz, R. J., & Coppenrath, L. (1996). Parents' use of nonliteral language with preschool children. *Discourse Processes, 23,* 99–118.

Sperber, D., & Wilson, D. (1986). *Relevance: Communication and cognition.* Cambridge, MA: Harvard University Press.

Winner, E. G. (1988). *The point of words: Children's understanding of metaphor and irony.* Cambridge, MA: Harvard University Press.

Winner, E., Windmueller, G., Rosenblatt, E., Bosco, L., Best, E., & Gardner, H. (1987). Making sense of literal and nonliteral falsehood. *Metaphor and Symbolic Activity, 2,* 13–32.

— 6 —

Figurative Language in Emotional Communication

Susan R. Fussell* and Mallie M. Moss**

*Carnegie Mellon University and **University of Nebraska

Over the course of the past several decades, research on figurative language has been flourishing in psychology and related fields (for recent reviews, see Cacciari & Glucksberg, 1994; Gibbs, 1994a, 1994b; Kreuz & Roberts, 1993). One of the most noteworthy outcomes of this research is the recognition that figurative language is not deviant—not a form of communication that requires special or additional cognitive processes to understand and that occurs only in special circumstances. Rather, figurative language is ubiquitous in many forms of discourse (e.g., Mio & Katz, 1996), no more difficult to understand in context than literal language (e.g., Gibbs, 1983, 1986; Glucksberg, Gildea & Bookin, 1982), and, according to some theorists, fundamental to the way people conceptualize the world (Gibbs, 1979, 1994b; Kovecses, 1986; Lakoff, 1987; Lakoff & Johnson, 1980).

Despite the rapid growth of figurative language research, most studies have focused on its comprehension. Although there have been numerous single case or small sample studies of figurative speech in therapeutic contexts (e.g., Karp, 1996; McMullen & Conway, 1996; Pollio & Barlow, 1975) and in preplanned language in speeches and literary works (e.g., Kreuz, Roberts, Johnson, & Bertus, 1996; Williams-Whitney, Mio, & Whitney, 1992), there have been relatively few rigorous studies of figurative language in everyday conversation. Consequently, as Roberts and Kreuz (1994) observe, there is little understanding of when and why speakers use figures of speech such as idioms, metaphors, and irony in a particular context.

In this chapter we explore the production of figurative language as it occurs in the communication of emotional states. We chose the domain of affective communication because the subjective nature of emotional experiences appears to lend itself to figurative expression. As Asch (1958) observed quite some time ago,

> There is apparently no aspect of nature that does not serve to express psychological realities. . . . Conversely, there are, it seems, hardly any

psychological terms *sui generis,* denoting psychological operations exclusively." (Asch, 1958, p. 87)

A casual examination of everyday conversation suggests that English is rife with idioms (e.g., *hot under the collar, hit the roof*), similes (e.g., *mad as a wet hen*), metaphor (e.g., *down, blue*), and other figurative expressions for emotions. The prevalence of these expressions in the conventionalized affective lexicon has been documented by several investigators (e.g., Bush, 1973; Clore, Ortony, & Foss, 1987; Davitz, 1969; Johnson-Laird & Oatley, 1989; Ortony, Clore, & Collins, 1988; Ortony, Clore, & Foss, 1987; Roberts & Wedell, 1994). Studies of language use in psychotherapy likewise are replete with examples of figurative expressions, particularly metaphor (e.g., Davitz, 1969; Davitz & Mattis, 1964; Karp, 1996; McMullen & Conway, 1996; Pollio & Barlow, 1975; Siegelman, 1990).

In the remainder of this paper we first briefly reviewing prior research on speakers' and writers' use of figurative language in descriptions of autobiographical emotional experiences in laboratory studies and in therapeutic contexts. We then describe some limitations to our understanding of figurative language use, limitations that stem from using research paradigms in which each participant describes a different, personal, affective experience. Next, we describe a research methodology we have developed that uses objective stimuli—characters' experiences in brief film clips—as the emotional experiences to be expressed and review some of the issues we have been examining using this methodology. We conclude with some observations about areas for future investigation.

FIGURATIVE LANGUAGE IN DESCRIPTIONS OF AUTOBIOGRAPHICAL EMOTIONAL EXPERIENCES

Two basic research strategies have been used to examine figurative language in descriptions of emotional experiences. Both strategies focus on how people communicate their personal affective experiences: one in laboratory settings, in which people describe (in writing or verbally) emotions of a type specified by an investigator; the other in clinical settings, in which actual dialogues between patients and therapists are examined. In this section, we discuss each of these areas of research.

Laboratory Studies of Affective Communication

In his classic paper on the communicative functions of metaphor, Ortony (1975) argued that metaphors are used to fill gaps in the lexicon, to provide succinct ways of stating ideas that would be lengthy or awkward to formulate in literal terms, and to add vividness or intensity to a message. If Ortony's argument is correct, the domain of emotional communication should be ripe for the study of figurative language: Emotions are subjective experiences, and subjective experiences are often difficult to capture in literal terms. Emotions are also complex, made up not only of affective responses, but also of physiological reactions, cognitions, behavioral responses, and the like (e.g., Ekman & Davidson, 1994). Metaphor and other figurative expressions may serve to succinctly capture these diverse components of emotions. Emotional reactions also differ in their intensity, and metaphorical language may provide a way of communicating the level of intensity of an emotional experience.

Ortony's hypotheses were supported in a study by Fainsilber and Ortony (1987), who examined metaphor use in oral descriptions of autobiographical emotional experiences and in behaviors resulting from these experiences. In support of Ortony's view that metaphor is used for communicating ideas difficult or impossible to express in literal terms, Fainsilber and Ortony found that metaphor was used more often to describe subjective feeling states than to describe overt actions stemming from these states. They also found that figurative language was used more often to express intense emotional states than to express milder ones. On the whole, the metaphors used by Fainsilber and Ortony's participants were frozen rather than novel, an observation suggesting that people have a conventionalized figurative vocabulary for expressing emotions.

Williams-Whitney et al. (1992) expanded on Fainsilber and Ortony's results by examining metaphor use in written descriptions of intense experiences of pride and shame as a function of writing experience and context. They further manipulated the experiencer of the emotion (the participant him- or herself versus a person described in a vignette). Williams-Whitney et al. found that experienced writers used more metaphor than did inexperienced writers, and both groups used more metaphor for feelings than for actions. Although there was no difference between experienced and inexperienced writers in the amount of figurative language they used to describe their personal emotional states, experienced writers used more metaphor to describe others' feelings than did inexperienced writers, and more of their expressions were novel rather than frozen. On the whole, then, writing expertise appears to lead to more creative language use.[1]

---

[1]As Williams-Whitney et al., 1992, noted, even though judges may deem a metaphor novel, this does not ensure that a writer has not made it a frozen part of his orher verbal repertoire. Only an analysis of the same individual's writing over time would permit a separation of novel and frozen but idiosyncratic expressions with guaranteed accuracy.

As already noted, affective states are complex and consist of subjective feelings, physiological reactions, behavioral responses, and cognitive processes. As Fainsilber and Ortony's (1987) results suggest, however, these dimensions may differ in the extent to which they lend themselves to figurative description. To address this issue, one of us (Fussell, 1992) asked undergraduate students to write descriptions of specific instances in which they had experienced mild and intense feelings of anger, sadness, happiness, and pride. In contrast to Fainsilber and Ortony's study, there were no constraints on the content of participants' descriptions. Thus, it was possible to examine the frequency with which describers mentioned cognitive, affective, behavioral and bodily reaction components of affective experience as well as their use of figurative language in each of these domains.

Figure 6.1 shows metaphor use as a function of the nature and intensity of emotional state. Metaphor use varied substantially as a function of the type and intensity of the emotional state being expressed. As predicted, participants used significantly more figurative language when describing intense as opposed to mild emotional experiences. This effect was especially strong for sadness and happiness. These findings are consistent with Ortony's suggestion that one function of metaphor is to convey intensity.

Participants used figurative language when mentioning each component of an emotional experience. Examples of each type of figurative language are shown for ANGER in Table 6.1. For example, "I felt trapped by emotion," "my mind was

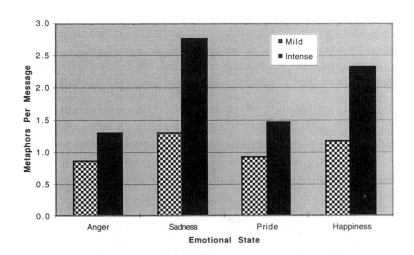

FIG. 6.1. Metaphors for feelings as a function of intensity of emotional state (Fussell, 1992).

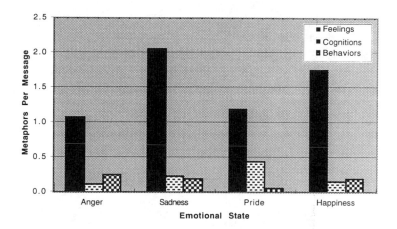

FIG. 6.2. Affective, cognitive, and bodily response metaphors as a function of emotional state (Fussell, 1992).

seething and boiling," and the other expressions in the top third of this figure express affective reactions, whereas "I'd like to dismember him and keep him in my drawers" appears to be a cognitive reaction. Finally, "My stomach was twisted in knots," and "my insides feel all hot," are descriptions of bodily responses that co-occur with the affective reactions. Although figures of speech were used for describing all these components of emotional experiences, however, they were most prevalent in descriptions of feelings. As shown in Figure 6.2, participants used one to two metaphors per message to describe their feelings, whereas they averaged much less than one per message when describing cognitive reactions or bodily responses.

Although most of the figurative expressions participants produced were conventional or frozen, it is apparent from the examples in Tables 6.1 and 6.2 that a substantial number of the expressions used were fairly novel. For example, "my mind was seething and boiling," and "my entire insides seemed ready to hurt," were used to express anger. At the same time, certain themes ran through a variety of figurative expressions, such as the feeling of something "missing" in oneself in descriptions of sadness, a feeling described, for example, as "hollowness," "emptiness," "having a piece missing," "a hole in the heart," (see Table 6.2). Similarly, a several participants mentioned that they felt "larger" or "bigger" when describing an instance of pride.

TABLE 6.1

Figurative expressions for affective, cognitive, and bodily responses
in descriptions of autobiographical experiences of *anger*

Affective Responses

I felt like a coiled spring.
Trapped by emotion.
Don't want to blow my top.
I felt "dark" and mean.
My temper burst.
I was RED HOT with anger.
My mind was seething and boiling.

Cognitive Reactions

I'd like to dismember him and keep him in my drawers.
I want to put somebody through the wall into the next planet.
[I had a] desire to crush the other.

Bodily Responses

My stomach was twisted in knots.
My entire insides seemed ready to hurt.
My insides feel all hot.
I feel like I'm going to burst.

NOTE: From *The Uses of Metaphor in Written Descriptions of Emotional States* by
S. R. Fussell, 1992. Unpublished manuscript, Carnegie Mellon University. Copyright
1992 by Susan R. Fussell. Published with permission.

The research we have reviewed thus far provides some insights into speakers' use of metaphor and idioms in emotional communication, but these examples are limited in that they focus primarily on metaphor in lieu of other figures of speech. In addition, all examples have dealt with single words or utterances extracted from conversational context; thus they are limited in what they reveal about the amount, type, and communicative functions of figurative language in dialogues. For example, the rate of figurative language use might be lower in conversational than in other settings because speakers feel pressured to prepare a message in a timely fashion; or, the rate might be higher because there is less risk of misunderstanding when feedback from the listener can be used to indicate that clarification is necessary (e.g., Clark & Wilkes-Gibbs, 1986; Kraut, Lewis, & Swezey, 1982). In addition, some theories about figurative language, such as the claim that metaphor use creates a sense of closeness between speaker and listener (Cohen, 1979; Gerrig & Gibbs, 1988), are difficult if not impossible to examine outside a meaningful social situation. In the next section we review work that has taken a broader, discourse-level approach to figurative language production.

Figurative Language in Conversations About Emotions

Most research on the role of figurative language in conversations about emotions has been done in the context of therapeutic discourse. Studies by clinicians have examined the frequency and type of figurative language in therapeutic contexts as well as the role of metaphor in creating positive treatment outcomes (e.g., Pollio & Barlow, 1975; Siegelman, 1990). In addition to these clinically oriented studies, there has been increasing attention to therapeutic discourse as a speech genre among sociologists, sociolinguistics, ethnomethodologists, and others (e.g., Capps & Ochs, 1995; Ferrara, 1994; Karp, 1996; Labov & Fanshel, 1977). These studies have found that figures of speech are rather common in clients' speech (Angus, 1996; Ferrara, 1994; McMullen, 1989; Pollio &

TABLE 6.2

Figurative expressions for autobiographical experiences of *sadness*

---

a sense of emptiness
feelings of hollowness
as if a small piece of a puzzle were missing and you can't find it anywhere
like I had lost a part of myself
I had a hole in my heart
like a part of me had been ripped away and I would never be whole again
a freezing fire
it just welled inside me slowly like a beach tide
I fall again into my frozen heart
like there's a black hole sucking in all my feelings and emotions
there was a darkness that hung over everything
I ached inside
as if I were silently sobbing
a deadness inside—a bottomless gloom.
everything was dark and destroyed
like I was drowning and there was nothing I could do about it
a sense of deflation, of being squeezed
as if I had a lead block in my chest

NOTE: From *The Uses of Metaphor in Written Descriptions of Emotional States* by S. R. Fussell, 1992. Unpublished manuscript, Carnegie Mellon University. Copyright 1992 by Susan R. Fussell. Published with permission.

Barlow, 1975) and also occur in therapists' messages to a lesser extent.

Several studies have found consistencies across clients in the metaphorical themes used to describe emotional states. For example, sociologist David Karp (1996) asked 50 former or current psychotherapy clients, all of whom had suffered from depression, to describe what the state was like. He found substantial uniformity in the figurative language used to describe experiences of depression. The most common expressions involved suffocating, falling down a pit, drowning, or being in a dark tunnel. As Karp points out, these expressions appear to be designed to capture the "downward spiral" of serious depression, in which people become increasingly absorbed by self-hatred, negative thoughts, and sadness. This interpretation is further supported by interviewees' statements that depressive states come to have "a life of their own." Unfortunately, Karp did not provide the exact percentages of people using each metaphor or the rate of metaphor use as a function of total words spoken.

Interpersonal consistency in metaphorical themes and expressions has also been demonstrated in a series of studies by McMullen and her colleagues (McMullen, 1985, 1989; McMullen & Conway, 1994, 1996). McMullen and Conway (1996), for example, analyzed 24 clients' discussions with their therapists across a number of sessions. They found that many clients described themselves in terms of fragmentation (e.g., "falling apart," "at loose ends"), and interestingly, the degree of fragmentation expressed appeared to be related to therapeutic outcome. McMullen and Conway also found repeated use of figurative expressions for anger and sadness that appear to fall neatly into conceptual schemas (e.g., ANGER AS HEAT, ANGER AS INSANITY, cf. Lakoff, 1987; Gibbs, 1994b).

Other insights into the communicative function of figurative language can be gleaned from studies of how speakers and listeners interactively construct metaphorical statements. In her excellent book on therapeutic discourse, Ferrara (1994) devoted an entire chapter to the collaborative creation of metaphor. She provided several examples of how the same metaphors, or variations on them, arise again and again during the course of a therapy session, not only repeated by the client but expanded upon in a variety of ways by the therapist. In the following example from Ferrara's transcripts (p. 140), the subsequent discussion developed and clarified the client's earlier statement that he was "floating down the river":[2,3]

---

[2]We have replaced people's names with labels reflecting their roles in the therapeutic process.

[3]Here and throughout the chapter we use bold text to indicate figurative language in quoted conversations.

Therapist: What's it like to be **floating down the river**?
                 Tell me more.
Client: It's comfortable. It's safe. Everything just **keeps on an
                 even keel**, you know.
Therapist: Mhm.
Client: You're just kinda **floating**
Therapist: Kind of **in a canoe**? . . .
Client: No, **more like a great ole big barge**. . . .

Ferrara described other examples in which metaphors were less readily understood and the ensuing discussion focused on clarification rather than expansion. She did not report the relative frequency of each types of interaction, and research by Angus and Rennie (1988) suggests that collaborative use of metaphor may vary across therapists. Nonetheless, Ferrara's study strongly suggests that researchers should examine the entirety of a conversational interaction when investigating the role of metaphor and other figures of speech in affective communication.

The frequency of figurative language use in these studies suggests that metaphor plays an important role in communicating emotion. Research, however, has been limited to one context—client–therapist interaction—and there is limited knowledge of the generalizability of the findings. Furthermore, investigators have used a very broad definition of metaphor that includes idioms, similes, cliches, and so forth, and little effort has been made to distinguish among these linguistic devices in terms of their frequency and their communicative and therapeutic functions. Finally, because there are no independent measures of the emotional states speakers intend to communicate, there is no knowledge about the communicative effectiveness of metaphor. We turn to this issue in the next section.

FIGURATIVE LANGUAGE IN DESCRIPTIONS OF STANDARDIZED EMOTIONAL EXPERIENCES

The Case for Standardized Emotional Stimuli

Virtually all the studies reviewed above have examined figurative language in descriptions of autobiographical emotional states. Although a focus on people's descriptions of their own experiences may heighten the realism of the findings, this focus makes it difficult to identify relationships between the figure of speech speakers' use and the underlying emotional experiences they are intending to communicate. For example, it would be circular to assume that the metaphors produced to describe sadness in such studies as Karp (1996) and McMullen and

Conway (1996) are intended to describe the same underlying emotional state simply because of their uniformity. Several key questions with respect to a social-psycholinguistic theory of figurative language use cannot be adequately addressed without using a research paradigm in which the emotions being expressed can be measured independent of the language produced to describe them:[4]

(a)   To what extent do people produce similar expressions for similar underlying affective experiences?

(b)   How do figurative expressions for emotions relate to these underlying experiences?

(c)   How accurately can listeners identify the intended meaning of an emotional expression?

(d)   How does figurative language use vary with social factors such as speaker and listener gender?

Although some of these questions (b and c) might be addressed by developing independent measures of a person's affective experiences, others (a and d) can only be addressed by using an experimental design in which many people describe the *same* affective state.

The experimental paradigm we have been using to address these issues uses objective stimuli, namely, movie clips depicting characters undergoing emotional experiences. We believe that movie clips serve as excellent stimulus materials for studies of figurative language for several reasons: First, psycholinguistic research has shown that people mentally represent fictional characters' emotional states (e.g., Gernsbacher, Goldsmith, & Robertson, 1992; Gerrig, 1993; Miall, 1989); thus, if we are careful to ascertain beforehand that all viewers of a video clip will develop similar representations of a character's emotional state, we can study inter-speaker consistency in the type and content of figurative language used to express that emotional state. Second, if we have the emotional states depicted in video clips rated on a variety of dimensions (e.g., intensity, polarity), we can examine the effects of these dimensions on emotional language. Finally, because movies and other people's emotional states are common topics of everyday conversation (Fussell, unpublished data; Shimanoff, 1985), the task faced by speakers in a laboratory is natural and realistic, and the results should be generalizable to non-laboratory settings.

In each of the studies we describe below, speakers were shown video clips that their addressees had not seen. For each clip, their task was to describe a

---

[4]One attempt in this direction is found in the work of McMullen and her colleagues (McMullen & Conway, 1996), who link metaphor to the success of therapy as measured by objective outcome measures.

target character's emotional state so that the addressee could understand what the character was feeling. In all cases, we pretested the clips to ensure that they were interpreted similarly across viewers. There were no constraints on the types of messages speakers could create, and participants were unaware of our interest in figurative language.

In the remainder of this section we describe preliminary results from three studies we have conducted using movie clips as materials. Although we have not yet completed all analyses of the data, our results shed light on several issues, including the role of conversational interactivity in figurative language use, cross-individual consistency in figurative expressions for an affective experience, interactive construction of figurative expressions, and message comprehension. Our aim is to illustrate the types of questions that can be fruitfully addressed by using standardized emotional experiences as stimuli.

Using Figurative Language to Distinguish Between Different Emotions

In our first study using this paradigm (Fussell, Vallee, Stelmack, & Moss, 1994), we asked a small group of students to describe the emotional experiences of characters in three movie clips to a listener who had not seen the clips. The experiences in the clips can be roughly glossed as *panic*, *anger*, and *elation*. In this study, the listener was a female confederate who was instructed not to ask questions or to make comments during speakers' descriptions. On the basis of an earlier study of written descriptions of autobiographical emotional states (Fussell, 1992), we anticipated that the rate of figurative expressions would be higher for the two negative emotions (sadness and anxiety) than for the positive emotion (elation).

Participants' messages were transcribed and coded for the number of literal and figurative adjectives and phrases describing emotional states they contained. There was substantial agreement in the literal expressions that participants used to describe each emotional state (e.g., "agitated," "happy," "confused"). Consistent with Fainsilber and Ortony (1987), speakers also used conventional and idiosyncratic metaphors to describe the emotional experiences (e.g., "he felt like he was drowning"). On the whole, however, speakers used figurative language less often than we had anticipated, and generally for descriptions of negative emotional states.

Using Figurative Language to Differentiate
Variations of a Single Emotional State

The results of the previous study might be taken as evidence that the time pressures of face–to–face conversation reduce the frequency and rate of metaphor use relative to studies in which there is no addressee present. Another possible explanation for the findings, however, stems from speakers' communicative goals. In the autobiographical studies described earlier there were implicit or explicit instructions to describe a *specific* occasion on which a person has experienced a type of emotion. As Schwarz has pointed out (1994, 1996, 1998) participants approach experimental instructions as though they adhere to Gricean rules of conversation (Grice, 1975). In the autobiographical studies, the instructions might have led participants to believe that their descriptions should serve to distinguish the episode they were describing from other experiences of the *same* class of emotions. No such implicit instructions are likely to have been present in the preceding study.

Why should this difference in communicative goals matter in terms of figurative language use? One reason is that the conventional affective lexicon may not suffice for expressing the nuances of specific emotional experiences. Many affective terms, such as *depressed,* are used loosely and therefore may not have the precision speakers desire. Furthermore, as Jones and Martin (1992) observed, literal terms for emotions often have more than one conventional sense; thus, figurative language may be one way to reduce potential ambiguities in the conventional affective lexicon. This observation is consistent with Roberts and Kreuz's (1994) findings that people report using metaphors, similes, and idioms to clarify their meanings.

To examine whether the low rate of metaphor use in our first study (Fussell et al., 1994) was an artifact of the experimental instructions, we conducted two larger studies of figurative language use in which speakers' goals were to describe different instances of the *same* emotional state. We chose to focus on *depression–sadness* because research has shown that discussions of sadness are common in conversation (Shimanoff, 1985); because speakers have been shown to use figurative language when describing autobiographical feelings of sadness (Fainsilber & Ortony, 1987; Fussell, 1992; Karp, 1996; McMullen & Conway 1996; Spiegelman, 1990); and because the wide range of affective reactions that fall in this category (fleeting "down" feelings to clinical depression that can lead to hospitalization) may make it especially important for speakers to disambiguate their meanings when they use terms like *sad* or *depressed.*

The stimuli for both of our studies consisted of brief (2 to 3 minute) film clips in which a central character was shown experiencing a form of depression or sadness. The manifestations of sadness in the clips varied in intensity, in the manner in which they unfolded, and in their purity (for instance, whether anger or anxiety was also present). The five clips are summarized briefly in Table 6.3.[5]

---

[5]Note that these are not pure emotions, but feelings more realistic to everyday life, and it is the role of figurative language in everyday conversation that we are most interested in examining.

TABLE 6.3

Brief description of movie clips depicting sadness or depression

---

Clip 1: Prince of Tides.

A man sits in a hotel room talking to his wife over the phone. She is breaking up with him. He hangs up, and starts writing a letter to his wife. He expresses his dismay that can't express his love for her. He appears sad and extremely disappointed in himself.

Clip 2: Steel Magnolias.

A woman is coming back from a funeral, apparently in control of her emotions. She breaks down when asked how she is doing, and starts screaming that she's fine but that her daughter is dead and never had the chance to do the things that she, the mother, could do. She appears alternately sad and angry.

Clip 3: Finnegan Begin Again.

A man is sitting in a chair in a very messy house. A woman knocks at the door, but he doesn't answer. Eventually, he reluctantly lets her in, and they discuss the fact that his wife has had a stroke and that his son had died in an accident. He moves slowly, and appears to have no energy.

Clip 4: Winter People.

A woman comes into a family room from the snow, moving very, very slowly. Her family asks her about her son, but she doesn't respond at first. After a few moments, she breaks out in a wail of despair at the loss of her son. She seems to be in mental anguish.

Clip 5: The Fisher King.

A drunken man is sitting outside in the cold, talking to a small wooden doll about how awful his life has been. Towards the end, he gets up and moves toward the edge of a bridge with bricks tied to his feet. It appears that he is about to commit suicide.

In the first study (Moss & Fussell, 1995), 26 female students described the five depressed characters' emotional states to a female partner who had not seen the clip. In the second study, male and female speakers described the clips to either a male or female partner who had not seen them. The two studies generated a total of 86 conversations about each of the five video clips, which we transcribed in detail (including filled pauses, false starts, repetitions, etc.)

according to the notation of MacWhinney's CLAN system (1995). We then coded the transcripts for emotion-related content (affective, cognitive, behavioral, and/or bodily reactions) and for figurative language use.

TABLE 6.4

Figurative Expressions for Sadness or Depression Video Clips[*]

Winter People

in shock (6), in a shock (1), in a state of shock (3), in a very shocked state (1), shock (2), shocked (5)
comatosed (1), comatosed-type thing (2)
dazed (4), in a daze (2), in this daze (1)
drained (1), empty (3)
freaking out (1)
frozen (2), frigid (1)
in a trance (3)
in her own world (2) in her own little world (1)
out of it (3), out of this world (1)
not all there (1)
numb (1)
a zombie (1)

Steel Magnolias

airing her feelings out (1)
breaks down (4), broke down (2)
falling apart (1)
emotionally stricken (1)
go crazy (1)
goes on and on (1), goes through this phase (1),
going ballistic (1)
like a hot air balloon (1)
in denial (1)
let it [her emotions] out (3), putting [her feelings] out in the open (2)
hold in [her emotions] (1)
hold up (1), holding up (1)
mixed emotions (1)
pushes back (her emotions) (1)
her emotions ran the whole gamut (1)
woke up to reality (1)

---

[*]Values in parentheses denote number of speakers using each term in their descriptions.

We found that speakers used an abundance of figurative expressions when their task was to characterize distinct instances of *sadness*. Examples for two of the five clips (*Winter People* and *Steel Magnolias*) are shown in Table 6.4. As can be seen, the figurative language used for each clip appears to capture the nuances of the depicted state of depression. Although the literal expressions that speakers used were fairly similar across clips (e.g., *sad, angry, depressed*), their idioms and metaphors were tailored to specific clips and to specific points in the characters' emotional experiences. For example, the character in the scene from *Winter People* was described as "dazed," "shocked," "in a trance," whereas the character in *Steel Magnolias* was described in such terms as "breaking down," "going ballistic," and "going crazy." This pattern of results is consistent with the hypothesis that figurative language is used to differentiate among variations of a single emotional state rather than to differentiate one emotional state from another.

Cross-Individual Consistency in Figurative Language Use

Gibbs and his colleagues (Gibbs, 1994b; Nayak & Gibbs, 1990) reported consistent correspondences between the use of idioms expressing emotional states and the contextual factors that give rise to emotions. For example, Nayak and Gibbs (1990) found that participants judged "flipped his lid" to be a better completion than "got hot under the collar" to the statement, "When Billy told his father he had totaled his new Porsche, his father ___," although both idioms can be glossed as "became angry." If this finding generalizes to other types of figurative language, there should be significant uniformity in the figurative expressions that speakers use to describe specific instances of an emotional state. Because we have collected so many descriptions of the same emotional event, we can examine this hypothesis empirically.

As can be seen in Table 6.4 above, where the frequency with which each expression was produced is listed in parentheses, we found striking overlap between participants' use of figurative language to describe characters' emotional states. For the scene from *Winter People*, numerous expressions referr to the central character's lack of emotional responsiveness, including *shocked, dazed, comatosed, drained, empty, frozen, numb,* and *tranced.* In contrast, the expressions for *Steel Magnolias* tended to refer to the character's futile attempts to keep her emotions under control, as evidenced by the expressions that refer to either holding her feelings in or letting them out. In short, not only is figurative language common in emotional descriptions, even in conversational settings, but these expressions appear to be a conventional way of talking about affective experiences.

Relationships Between Literal and Figurative Speech.

Our transcripts showed that speakers did not use figurative expressions in lieu of literal ones but rather in addition to them. Every description in our corpus contained at least a few literal terms for sadness. Often, figurative expressions followed literal descriptions, an observation suggesting that figurative expressions might be intended as a clarification:[6]

"She would go from crying to screaming to crying to screaming. So she was kinda—**she wasn't all there**. . . . " [*Pair 4*]

"He has something annoying him. I mean, it's just like **eating away at him**." [*Pair 5*]

"Yeah, he was really depressed and just **screwed up**." [*Pair 9*]

"He don't care about anything, you know? He's kinda just **blown everything off**." [*Pair 15*]

"She was very hysterical, she just **lost it**." [*Pair 50*]

At other times, figurative expressions appeared to set the stage for later details:

"And she like **freaks out** at this point in time. She starts yelling and stuff." [Pair 27]

"And she just **loses it** and starts crying." [Pair 35]

"She was like on an **emotional rollercoaster**. She'd be **on like a high**. She was like mad. And then she would kind of calm from it. And then she'd get mad." [Pair 38]

"And so finally, she just **let all her feelings out** and it was like a rage, almost." [Pair 40]

Because our corpus contains multiple instances of the same figurative expression, we have been performing detailed analyses of the ways in which these expressions co-occur with literal terms for sadness and depression.[7] We are especially interested in the relationships between word combinations that include intensifiers and modifiers (e.g., *very very unhappy, sort of sad*) and figurative speech, as researchers have argued that intensifiers and modifiers play an important role in emotional communication (e.g., Capps & Ochs, 1995),

---

[6]Pair numbering in brackets indicate the transcript from which the example was drawn.

[7]One of the strengths of the CLAN program (MacWhinney, 1995) is that it can examine co-occurrence matrices of virtually any type within a user-defined span of words.

and, as discussed earlier, there is evidence that metaphor may in part serve to convey intensity (Fainsilber & Ortony, 1987; Fussell, 1992).

Relationships Between Properties of Emotional States and Figurative Language Use.

As we argued earlier, when each participant in an experiment describes an emotional event from his or her own experience, it is extremely difficult to analyze the relationships between the properties of this emotional event and the language used to describe it. In our research paradigm, we have collected independent ratings of the video clips on Osgood's Semantic Differential (Osgood, Suci, & Tannenbaum, 1957), and we can compare these ratings with the figurative language used to describe each emotional episode. By this process we may be able to identify important relationships between the dimensional structure of an affective experience and the metaphors, similes, idioms, and other expressions used to describe that experience. The scene from *Winter People*, for example, was rated "passive" and "bad," whereas the scene from *Steel Magnolias* was rated "active" and "bad." Although we have not yet quantified the relationship, it is likely that the semantic differences between the figurative expressions used to describe the two clips (see Table 6.4 above) are related to this difference along the active/passive dimension.

Our method also allows us to examine figurative language use as a function of the temporal unfolding of an emotional reaction (Fehr & Russell, 1984; Reiser, Black, & Lehnert 1985; Shaver, Schwartz, Kirson, & O'Connor, 1987). For example, in a bothersome situation, a person might begin feeling slightly annoyed and, as the eliciting event continues, become angrier and angrier until he or she is in an absolute rage.[8] Gibbs (1994b; Nayak & Gibbs, 1990) pointed out that idioms such as *hot under the collar*, *hit the ceiling*, and *flip one's lid*, appear to map onto this temporal unfolding of experience; people's judgments of the appropriateness of these expressions in specific contexts are consistent with the view that people have schematic knowledge of how others react when they are in particular situations and feeling particular emotions. In our transcripts, figurative expressions appear to be closely tied to the precise moment of the character's experience that speakers were describing. For example, although the expressions in Table 6.4 reflect descriptions of the character's emotional state at the beginning of the *Winter People* clip, these expressions were replaced in the final moments of the clip with others such as "in a meltdown," "going berserk,"

---

[8]Listeners in our studies often asked questions that indicated that they wanted to know the point in the experience the speaker was describing (e.g., "So she was angry but not to the point of violence?" "It was to the point to where he would commit suicide?").

"going crazy," "going insane," "losing it," "losing her mind," and "going to pieces."

The Role of Conversational Interactivity

In the first of our two studies (Moss & Fussell, 1995), we examined the impact of conversational interactivity on descriptions of emotional states by manipulating listener responsiveness. In half the pairs (the *interactive condition*), listeners were allowed to interact freely with the speaker—asking questions, making comments—whereas in the other half (the *non-interactive condition*) the listener was asked to listen silently to the descriptions. Because studies have indicated that nonliteral language can sometimes be difficult to interpret out of context (e.g., Gibbs, 1979), we hypothesized that speakers would use figurative expressions more frequently in interactive than in noninteractive settings because in the former case they could use listener's responses to monitor his or her comprehension.

As predicted, speakers in our study generated many more words of description when describing the video clips to an addressee who could participate in the discussion rather than one who sat silently. With respect to figurative language use, however, we found that although speakers in the interactive condition produced more metaphors and idioms overall, their rate of figurative language per total words spoken was not significantly different from speakers in the non-interactive condition. This finding is consistent with our view that speakers consider figurative expressions to be conventional and readily understood ways of describing emotional experiences.[9]

Figurative Language in the Interactive Construction of Messages

In addition to providing feedback about a listener's understanding of a message, conversational interaction also allows for collaboration in the construction of messages themselves (Clark & Wilkes-Gibbs, 1986; Sacks, Schegloff, & Jefferson, 1974). As discussed earlier, Ferrara (1994) found evidence of these collaborations (which she calls "joint productions") in therapeutic conversations. We likewise found numerous joint productions in our corpus, many of which contained figurative language. For example:[10]

---

[9]It is possible that because the dyads were seated face-to-face, speakers could have monitored their addressees' nonverbal behaviors for signs of comprehension.

[10]For expository purposes, we have simplified the transcriptions by eliminating filled pauses and false starts.

[Pair 10]
Describer: She was just kind of walking along, and then all of a sudden
Listener: just **let it out**.
Describer: she just **let it out**.

In other cases, the listener predicted the character's bodily or behavioral responses implied by a figurative expression:

[Pair 23]
Describer: And then finally she just **broke down** and
Listener: just started crying.
Describer: just started crying.

The presence of feedback also enabled speakers and hearers to ensure that terms and expressions having both literal and figurative interpretations were understood correctly, as in the following two examples:

[Pair 12]
Describer: Lost.
Listener: Lost? Literally lost?
Describer: No, not literally lost.

[Pair 1]
Describer: Okay, she looks like she's in shock or something.
Listener: like surprised or like medical shock? Heat stroke?
Describer: No, like she's done something.

Finally, listeners also commonly responded to a figurative expression with a reformulation in other figurative terms:

[Pair 10]
Describer: It's almost like he's **not even there**.
Listener: mhm. Like **in his own world** or?
Describer: Kind of.

[Pair 12]
Describer: and then she just **goes berserk**.
Listener: So she kind of was like **in a meltdown** or something . . .?

Or they suggested figurative paraphrases:

[Pair 12]
Describer: He was trying to basically just remove himself from the
                problem, trying to see how he got
Listener: **block it out**?
Describer: Yeah.

Although we have yet to analyze these joint constructions systematically, it is clear that figurative expressions generated by both speaker and addressee are important to conversations about emotional states.

Effects of Speaker and Listener Characteristics on Figurative Language Use.

With the exception of isolated studies such as McMullen and Conway (1996) and Williams-Whitney et al. (1992), research has tended to neglect the impact of speaker and listener characteristics on figurative language production. Yet there is reason to suspect that these factors affect emotional communication in general and the use of metaphors, idioms, and the like in particular. Tannen (1990), among others, has argued that men and women speak essentially different languages with respect to emotion, but to our knowledge, this hypothesis has not been tested in an experimental paradigm that uses objective events as stimuli and thus can disentangle two separate ways that personal and social characteristics might affect emotional communication—by influencing choices about *what* types of events or experiences are described and by influencing *how* those events or experienced are described. In our studies, we have found no effects of a speaker's gender on any message characteristics, including figurative language use.

As Rime and his colleagues (Rime, Mesquita, Philippot, and Boca, 1991) point out, the "social sharing" of an emotion requires its formulation in mutually understood terms to an explicit or implicit addressee—that is, emotional expression requires perspective-taking. Some clinicians have gone so far as to suggest that successful therapy can be provided only by therapists of the same gender as the client (e.g., Feldstein, 1979; Hill, 1975; Orlinsky & Howard, 1976; Persons, Persons & Newmark, 1974). Yet, with a few notable exceptions (e.g., Higgins & Rholes, 1978; McCann, Higgins, & Fondacaro, 1991), virtually all research in the perspective-taking tradition has focused on the creation of names and descriptions for more or less objective things like objects, landmarks, and public figures (for reviews of this literature see Krauss & Fussell, 1996; Schober, 1998).

In the second of our two studies of descriptions of sadness we examined perspective-taking in affective communication by asking male and female speakers to describe the film clips to male and female addressees. The total number of words, sentences, and speaking turns by both speaker and listener were computed using MacWhinney's (1995) CLAN program. The preliminary results showed that the amount of descriptive information provided for each clip varied substantially as a function of listener but not speaker gender: For all clips, both male and female speakers used significantly more words to describe a character's emotional state to a male as opposed to a female addressee. We are currently in the process of comparing the content of messages intended for male versus female listeners to determine whether this difference in amount of information extends to differences in the amount and type of figurative language. We are also examining how speaker and listener gender affect the dynamics of the conversation.

Comprehension and-or Interpretation.

As argued earlier, when each person describes his or her own emotional experiences, it is difficult to determine how well the description has been understood because there is no independent measure of the underlying emotional state. In our studies, we made a preliminary attempt to develop an independent measure of the to–be–expressed affective experience by using a version of Osgood et al.'s (1957) Semantic Differential. We chose this measure in part because of its long history in the nonverbal communication literature (e.g., Krauss, Apple, Morency, Wenzel, & Winton, 1981). We also selected this measure because it can tap dimensions of emotional meaning without using terms that are conventional parts of the affective lexicon. In each experiment, we first pretested the scenes to ensure that viewers rated them similarly on the Semantic Differential; then, we assumed that the extent to which speakers and addressees completed the scale in the same way after their conversations reflected the extent to which the description had been understood.

In retrospect, it is not clear that the Semantic Differential is the best way to measure comprehension of descriptions of emotional states, at least in a conversational setting. In all three studies we have described in this section, we have found high correlations between speaker and listener ratings on the Semantic Differential (generally .50 or better); but curiously, these correlations have been unrelated to any message characteristics we measured (e.g., length and number of utterances, figurative language) and unrelated to the gender composition of the dyad. Yet, the dialogues differed substantially in length and in the number and types of questions asked by addressees. To better understand how emotional messages are interpreted, we are currently focusing on the *processes* addressees used to understanding speakers' emotional messages rather than on the final correlations between speakers' and addressees' ratings.

SOME LIMITATIONS TO THE PARADIGM

In this chapter we have argued that by conducting experiments using standardized affective experiences as stimuli, researchers can gain new insights about the role of figurative language in descriptions of emotions. By using standardized stimuli, investigators can examine such issues as interpersonal consistency in figurative language use, relationships between stimulus properties and the ways they are expressed, and effects of speaker and listener characteristics on figurative language production and comprehension.

Of course, along with the benefits of our proposed research strategy, there are several costs. The most glaring omission from our research program to date is the study of other examples of sadness or depression or other emotional states such as happiness or anger. This limitation, however, can be overcome by further experimentation. Below we briefly describe some further limitations of our paradigm that suggest that more major changes to the methods researchers use to investigate the relationships between figurative language and emotion may be required.

Relationship Between Verbal and Nonverbal Communication of Emotion.

Considerable debate has surrounded the issue of the relative priority of verbal, vocal, and nonverbal channels in the communication of emotions (e.g., Ekman, Friesen, O'Sullivan, & Scherer, 1980; Gallois, 1994; Krauss et al., 1981; Trimboli & Walker, 1987, Walker & Trimboli, 1989). Because we did not videotape our participants' conversations, our results cannot help clarify relationships between the communicative functions of verbal and nonverbal sources of information about emotional states. Nonetheless, at several places in our transcripts it was apparent that speakers resorted to bodily representations of characters' facial expressions and postures. Often, they prefaced these nonverbal displays by saying something such as: "The best way for me to communicate this is to show you." It might be informative to examine the relationship between these nonverbal displays and the literal and figurative content of the surrounding messages by using video- rather than audio-recordings in future research.

Effects of Emotional State on Affective Communication.

Although our participants might have empathized with movie characters' experiences, they probably did not fully feel the emotion at the time of their descriptions. It is entirely plausible that how a person expresses an emotional state depends upon whether he or she is *feeling* that state at the time of its description (Bowers, Metts, & Duncanson, 1985; Fiehler, 1990), especially in view of the demonstrated effects of arousal on other aspects of cognitive processing such as memory and social judgment (e.g., Christianson, 1992; M. Clark & Fiske, 1982; Fiedler & Forgas, 1988; Mackie & Hamilton, 1993; Winograd & Neisser, 1992). Innovative paradigm creation is required to examine the effects of a person's own affective state on message production while retaining the criteria for standardized emotional stimuli that we have argued for throughout this chapter.

Effects of Social Relationships on Figurative Language Use.

In our experiments, dyads were unacquainted. In everyday life, not only do people report emotional experiences most often to close friends, spouses and partners, or other family members (Rime et al., 1991), but these emotional experiences may involve these friends and family members in diverse ways. As a result, emotional expression is likely to be tempered by face management concerns (Brown & Levinson, 1987; Goffman, 1959; Holtgraves, 1998) and by norms about self-disclosure of emotions (for reviews of this literature, see Gallois, 1994 & Winton, 1990).

Several studies have found results consistent with the hypothesis that social norms and face management concerns affect emotional expression. For instance, Thimm and Kruse (1993) found that students were less willing to share their emotions with those of higher status than with those of equal status; when they did express their emotions, they tended to hedge their expressions with softening or intensifying remarks (e.g., "relatively," "actually," "somewhat," "totally," "absolutely," etc.) or nonverbal or paralinguistic behaviors (e.g., giggles, laughes, pauses); Shimanoff (1985) found that speakers tended to talk about positive but not negative responses to their addressees' actions or remarks and about negative but not positive aspects of their own behaviors; and Collier (1985) found that speakers used more complex grammatical forms to describe their negative as opposed to positive emotional states, which, he argued, might serve to qualify or attenuate the message. To the extent that figures of speech can be used to convey negative feelings indirectly, the use of such expressions might be even more prevalent in real-life social situations than we have found in our laboratory studies.

CONCLUSION

We have argued that analyzing multiple descriptions of the same affective experiences can lead to a number of important insights into figurative language production and comprehension in conversational settings. But our own studies are clearly small steps in this direction; additional studies using a variety of conversational contexts, research paradigms, and stimuli are required. Even if such studies are conducted, however, we would argue that rapid advancement in the area of figurative language production is unlikely to happen until researchers of adult linguistic phenomena follow the lead of child language investigators (cf. MacWhinney, 1995) by making their tapes and transcripts available to the entire community of adult language researchers.[11] By making it possible to test new hypotheses across current linguistic corpuses as well as by collecting new data, researchers can truly make progress in understanding how topics of conversation, individual and cultural characteristics of speakers and hearers, social settings, and related factors influence the frequency, type, and interactional consequences of figurative language use.

ACKNOWLEDGMENTS

We would like to thank Mary Brown, Sam Glucksberg, Matt McGlone, and J. Chad Schrock for their helpful suggestions with respect to the design of one or more of the studies reported herein, and Roger J. Kreuz for his extensive comments on an earlier draft of this chapter. We would also like to thank Tara Broom, Rebecca Brackin, Kenneth Brad Carpenter, Amy Stelmack, Ron Vallee, and Amy Watkins for their help in running experiments. Finally, we must express our deep appreciation to Mark Wilner, Gregory Mochan, and, especially, Anna Ho, for their excellent jobs of transcribing and coding the hundreds of hours of audio tapes generated by our participants' conversations.

REFERENCES

Angus, L. E. (1996). An intensive analysis of metaphor themes in psychotherapy. In J. S. Mio & A. N. Katz (Eds.), *Metaphor: Implications and applications* (pp. 73–84). Mahwah, NJ: Lawrence Erlbaum Associates.

Angus, L., & Rennie, D. (1988). Therapist participation in metaphor generation: Collaborative and non-collaborative styles. *Psychotherapy, 25,* 552–560.

Asch, S. E. (1958). The metaphor: A psychological inquiry. In R. Tagiuri & L. Petrullo (Eds.), *Person perception and interpersonal behavior* (pp. 86–94). Stanford: Stanford University Press.

Bowers, J. W., Metts, S. M., & Duncanson, W. T. (1985). Emotion and interpersonal communication. In M. L. Knapp & G. R. Miller (Eds.), *Handbook of interpersonal communication* (pp. 500–550). Beverly Hills, CA: Sage.

Brown, P., & Levinson, S. C. (1987). *Politeness: Some universals in language usage.* Cambridge, England: Cambridge University Press.

---

[11]For more information on the CHILDES project and the CLAN program, contact the Web site at: http://psyscope.psy.cmu.edu/childes/childes.html.

Bush, L. E. (1973). Individual differences multidimensional scaling of adjectives denoting feelings. *Journal of Personality and Social Psychology, 25,* 50–57.

Cacciari, C., & Glucksberg, S. (1994). Understanding figurative language. In M. A. Gernsbacher (Ed.), *Handbook of psycholinguistics* (pp. 447–477). San Diego, CA: Academic Press.

Capps, L., & Ochs, E. (1995). *Constructing panic: The discourse of agoraphobia.* Cambridge, MA: Harvard University Press.

Christianson, S.-A. (Ed.). (1992). *The handbook of emotion and memory. Research and theory.* Hillsdale, NJ: Lawrence Erlbaum Associates.

Clark, H. H., & Wilkes-Gibbs, D. (1986). Referring as a collaborative process. *Cognition, 22,* 1–39.

Clark, M. S., & Fiske, S. T. (Eds.). (1982). *Affect and cognition.* Hillsdale, NJ: Lawrence Erlbaum Associates.

Clore, G. L., Ortony, A., & Foss, M. A. (1987). The psychological foundations of the affective lexicon. *Journal of Personality and Social Psychology, 53,* 751–766.

Cohen, T. (1979). Metaphor and the cultivation of intimacy. In S. Sacks (Ed.), *On metaphor* (pp. 1–10). Chicago: University of Chicago Press.

Collier, G. (1985). *Emotional expression.* Hillsdale, NJ: Lawrence Erlbaum Associates.

Davitz, J. R. (1969). *The language of emotion.* New York: Academic Press.

Davitz, J. R., & Mattis, S. (1964). The communication of emotional meaning by metaphor. In J. R. Davitz (Ed.), *The communication of emotional meaning* (pp. 157–176). Westport, CT: Greenwood Press.

Ekman, P., & Davidson, R. J. (Eds.). (1994). *The nature of emotion: Fundamental questions.* New York: Oxford University Press.

Ekman, P., Friesen, W. V., O'Sullivan, M., & Scherer, K. (1980). Relative importance of face, body and speech in judgments of personality and affect. *Journal of Personality and Social Psychology, 38,* 270–277.

Fainsilber, L., & Ortony, A. (1987). Metaphorical uses of language in the expression of emotions. *Metaphor and Symbolic Activity, 2,* 239–250.

Fehr, B., & Russell, J. A. (1984). Concept of emotion viewed from a prototype perspective. *Journal of Experimental Psychology: General, 113,* 464–486.

Feldstein, J. C. (1979). Effects of counselor sex and sex role and client sex on clients' perceptions and self-disclosure in a counseling analogue study. *Journal of Counseling Psychology, 26,* 437–443.

Ferrara, K. W. (1994). *Therapeutic ways with words.* New York: Oxford University Press.

Fiedler, K., & Forgas, J. (Eds.). (1988). *Affect, cognition and social behavior: New evidence and integrative attempts.* Toronto, Ontario: Hogrefe.

Fiehler, R. (1990) *Kommunikation und Emotion: Theoretische und empirische Untersuchungen zur Rolle von Emotionen in der verbalen Interaktion.* Amsterdam: Walter de Gruyter.

Fussell, S. R. (1992). *The use of metaphor in written descriptions of emotional states.* Unpublished manuscript, Carnegie Mellon University.

Fussell, S. R., Vallee, R., Stelmack, A., & Moss, M. M. (1994, November). *Content and communicative effectiveness of descriptions of emotional states.* Paper presented at the 35th annual meeting of The Psychonomic Society, St. Louis, MO.

Gallois, C. (1994). Group membership, social rules, and power: A social-psychological perspective on emotional communication. *Journal of Pragmatics, 22,* 301–324.

Gernsbacher, M., Goldsmith, H., & Robertson, R. (1992). Do readers mentally represent characters' emotional states? *Cognition and Emotion, 6,* 89–111.

Gerrig, R. J. (1993). *Experiencing narrative worlds: On the psychological activities of reading.* New Haven, CT: Yale University Press.

Gerrig, R., & Gibbs, R. (1988). Beyond the lexicon: Creativity in language production. *Metaphor and Symbolic Activity, 3,* 1–19.

Gibbs, R. W., Jr. (1979). Contextual effects in understanding indirect requests. *Discourse Processes, 2,* 1–10.

Gibbs, R. W., Jr. (1983). Do people always process the literal meanings of indirect requests? *Journal of Experimental Psychology: Learning, Memory and Cognition, 9,* 524–533.

Gibbs, R. W., Jr. (1986). Skating on thin ice: Literal meaning and understanding idioms in conversation. *Discourse Processes, 9,* 17–30.

Gibbs, R. W., Jr. (1994a). Figurative thought and figurative language. In M. A. Gernsbacher (Ed.), *Handbook of psycholinguistics* (pp. 411–446). San Diego, CA: Academic Press.

Gibbs, R. W., Jr. (1994b). *The poetics of mind: Figurative thought, language, and understanding.* New York: Cambridge University Press.

Gibbs, R. W., Jr. & O'Brien, J. E. (1990). Idioms and mental imagery: The metaphorical motivation for idiomatic meaning. *Cognition, 36,* 35–68.

Glucksberg, S., Gildea, P., & Bookin, H. B. (1982). On understanding nonliteral speech: Can people ignore metaphors? *Journal of Verbal Learning and Verbal Behavior, 21,* 85–98.

Goffman, E. (1959). *The presentation of self in everyday life.* Garden City, NY: Anchor Books.

Grice, H. (1975). Logic and conversation. In P. Cole & J. L. Morgan (Eds.), *Syntax and semantics: Vol. 3, Speech acts.* New York: Academic Press.

Higgins, E. T., & Rholes, W. J. (1978). "Saying is believing": Effects of message modification on memory and liking for the person described. *Journal of Experimental Social Psychology, 14,* 363–378.

Hill, C. E. (1975). Sex of client and sex and experience level of counselor. *Journal of Counseling Psychology, 22,* 6–11.

Holtgraves, T. M. (1998). Interpersonal foundations of conversational indirectness. In S. R. Fussell & R. J. Kreuz (Eds.), *Social and cognitive approaches to interpersonal communication.* Mahwah, NJ: Lawrence Erlbaum Associates.

Johnson-Laird, P. N., & Oatley, K. (1989). The language of emotions: An analysis of a semantic field. *Cognition and Emotion, 3,* 81–123.

Jones, G. V., & Martin, M. (1992). Conjunction in the language of emotions. *Cognition and Emotion, 6,* 369–386.

Karp, D. A. (1996). *Speaking of sadness: Depression, disconnection, and the meanings of illness.* New York: Oxford University Press.

Kovecses, Z. (1986). *Metaphors of anger, pride and love: A lexical approach to the structure of concepts.* Philadelphia, PA: John Benjamins.

Krauss, R. M., & Fussell, S. R. (1996). Social psychological models of interpersonal communication. In E. T. Higgins & A. Kruglanski (Eds.), *Social psychology: Handbook of basic principles* (pp. 655–701). New York: Guilford Press.

Krauss, R. M., Apple, W., Morency, N., Wenzel, C., & Winton, W. (1981). Verbal, vocal, and visible factors in judgments of another's affect. *Journal of Personality and Social Psychology, 40,* 312–320.

Kraut, R. E., Lewis, S. H., & Swezey, L. W. (1982). Listener responsiveness and the coordination of conversation. *Journal of Personality and Social Psychology, 43,* 718–731.

Kreuz, R. J., & Roberts, R. M. (1993). The empirical study of figurative language in literature. *Poetics, 22,* 151–169.

Kreuz, R. J., Roberts, R. M., Johnson, B. K., & Bertus, E. L. (1996). Figurative language occurrence and co-occurrence in contemporary literature. In R. J. Kreuz & M. S. MacNealy (Eds.), *Empirical approaches to literature and aesthetics* (pp. 83–97). New York: Ablex.

Labov, W., & Fanshel, D. (1977). *Therapeutic discourse: Psychotherapy as conversation.* New York: Academic Press.

Lakoff, G. (1987). *Women, fire, and dangerous things.* Chicago: University of Chicago Press.

Lakoff, G., & Johnson, M. (1980). *Metaphors we live by.* Chicago: University of Chicago Press.

Mackie, D. M., & Hamilton, D. L. (Eds.). (1993). *Affect, cognition, and stereotyping: Interactive processes in group perception.* San Diego, CA: Academic Press.

MacWhinney, B. (1995). *The CHILDES project: Tools for analyzing talk.* Hillsdale, NJ: Lawrence Erlbaum Associates.

McCann, C. D., Higgins, E. T., & Fondacaro, R. A. (1991). Primacy and recency in communication and self-persuasion: How successive audiences and multiple encodings influence subsequent evaluative judgments. *Social Cognition, 9,* 47–66.

McMullen, L. (1985). Methods for studying the use of novel figurative language in psychotherapy clients. *Psychotherapy, 22,* 610–619.

McMullen, L. (1989). Use of figurative language in successful and unsuccessful cases of psychotherapy: Three comparisons. *Metaphor and Symbolic Activity, 4,* 203–225.

McMullen, L., & Conway, J. (1994). Dominance and nurturance in the figurative expressions of psychotherapy clients. *Psychotherapy Research, 4,* 43–57.

McMullen, L., & Conway, J. (1996). Conceptualizing the figurative expressions of psychotherapy clients. In J. S. Mio & A. N. Katz (Eds.), *Metaphor: Implications and applications* (pp. 59–71). Mahwah, NJ: Lawrence Erlbaum Associates.

Miall, D. (1989). Beyond the schema given: affective comprehension of literary narratives. *Cognition and Emotion, 3,* 55–78.

Mio, J. S., & Katz, A. N. (Eds.). (1996). *Metaphor: Implications and applications.* Mahwah, NJ: Lawrence Erlbaum Associates.

Moss, M. M., & Fussell, S. R. (1995, March). *Interpersonal communication of emotional information.* Paper presented at the annual meeting of the Southeastern Psychological Association, Savannah, GA.

Nayak, N. P., & Gibbs, R. W., Jr. (1990). Conceptual knowledge in the interpretation of idioms. *Journal of Experimental Psychology: General, 116,* 315–330.

Orlinsky, D. E., & Howard, K. I. (1976). The effects of sex of therapist on the therapeutic experiences of women. *Psychotherapy: Theory, research, and practice, 13,* 82–88.

Ortony, A. (1975). Why metaphors are necessary and not just nice. *Educational Theory, 25,* 45–53.

Ortony, A., Clore, G. L., & Collins, A. (1988). *The cognitive structure of emotions.* Cambridge, England: Cambridge University Press.

Ortony, A., Clore, G. L., & Foss, M. A. (1987). The referential structure of the affective lexicon. *Cognitive Science, 11,* 341–364.

Osgood, C. E., Suci, G. J., & Tannenbaum, P. H. (1957). *The measurement of meaning.* Urbana: University of Illinois Press.

Persons, R. W., Persons, M. K., & Newmark, I. (1974). Perceived helpful therapists' characteristics, client improvements, and sex of therapist and client. *Psychotherapy: Theory, Research, and Practice, 11,* 63–65.

Planalp, S. (1993). Communication, cognition, and emotion. *Communication Monographs, 60,* 3–9.

Pollio, H., & Barlow, J. (1975). A behavioral analysis of figurative language in psychotherapy: One session in a single case study. *Language and Speech, 18,* 236–254.

Reiser, B. J., Black, J. B., & Lehnert, W. G. (1985). Thematic knowledge structures in the understanding and generation of narratives. *Discourse Processes, 8,* 357–389.

Rime, B., Mesquita, B., Philippot, P., & Boca, S. (1991). Beyond the emotional event: Six studies on the social sharing of emotion. *Cognition and Emotion, 5,* 435–465.

Roberts, J., & Wedell, D. (1994). Context effects on similarity judgments of multidimensional stimuli: Inferring the structure of the emotion space. *Journal of Experimental Social Psychology, 30,* 1–38.

Roberts, R. M., & Kreuz, R. J. (1994). Why do people use figurative language? *Psychological Science, 5,* 159–163.

Sacks, H., Schegloff, E. A., & Jefferson, G. (1974). A simplest systematics for the organization of turn-taking for conversation. *Language, 50,* 696–735.

Schober, M. F. (1998). Different kinds of conversational perspective-taking. In S. R. Fussell & R. J. Kreuz (Eds.), *Social and cognitive approaches to interpersonal communication.* Mahwah, NJ: Lawrence Erlbaum Associates.

Schwarz, N. (1994). Judgment in a social context: Biases, shortcomings, and the logic of conversation. In M. P. Zanna (Ed.), *Advances in experimental social psychology* (Vol. 26, pp. 123–162). San Diego, CA: Academic Press.

Schwarz, N. (1996). *Cognition and communication: Judgmental biases, research methods, and the logic of conversation.* Mahwah, NJ: Lawrence Erlbaum Associates.

Schwarz, N. (1998). Communication in Standardized Research Situations: A Gricean Perspective. In S. R. Fussell & R. J. Kreuz (Eds.), *Social and cognitive approaches to interpersonal communication.* Mahwah, NJ: Lawrence Erlbaum Associates.

Shaver, P., Schwartz, J., Kirson, D., & O'Connor, C. (1987). Emotional knowledge: Further exploration of a prototype approach. *Journal of Personality and Social Psychology, 52,* 1061–1086.

Shimanoff, S. B. (1985). Expressing emotions in words: Verbal patterns of interaction. *Journal of Communication, 35,* 16–31.

Siegelman, E. (1990). *Metaphor and meaning in psychotherapy.* New York: Guilford.

Tannen, D. (1990). *You just don't understand: Women and men in conversation.* New York: Ballantine Books.

Thimm, C., & Kruse, L. (1993). The power–emotion relationship in discourse: Spontaneous expression of emotions in asymmetric dialogue. *Journal of Language and Social Psychology, 12,* 81–102.

Trimboli, A., & Walker, M. B. (1987). Nonverbal dominance in the communication of affect: A myth? *Journal of Nonverbal Communication, 11,* 180–190.

Walker, M. B., & Trimboli, A. (1989). Communicating affect: The role of verbal and nonverbal content. *Journal of Language and Social Psychology, 8,* 229–248.

Williams-Whitney, D., Mio, J. S., & Whitney, P. (1992). Metaphor production in creative writing. *Journal of Psycholinguistic Research, 21,* 497–509.

Winograd, E., & Neisser, U. (Eds.). (1992). *Affect and accuracy in recall: Studies of "flashbulb" memories.* Cambridge, England: Cambridge University Press.

Winton, W. M. (1990). Language and emotion. In H. Giles & W. P. Robinson (Eds.), *Handbook of language and social psychology,* (pp. 33–49). Chichester, England: Wiley.

PART III

Perspective-Taking and Conversational Collaboration

— 7 —

Different Kinds of Conversational Perspective-Taking

Michael F. Schober

New School for Social Research

Consider this interchange between an interviewer(*I*) and respondent (*R*) in a major national survey (reported in Suchman & Jordan, 1991):[1]

I: Generally speaking, do you usually think of yourself as a
      Republican, Democrat, Independent, or what.
R: As a person.
I: As a Republican::
R: No.
I: Democrat::
R: No.
I: Independent or what.
R: Uhm:: I think of myself as a (pause) Christian.
I: OK. (Writing) But politically, would you have any
      particular::(inaudible)
R: I am one of Jehovah's Witnesses so, you know, when it comes to::
I: I see.
R: So I'm, I am acclimated toward government, but it is that of
      Jehovah God's kingdom.
I: Yes.

This interviewer and respondent are seriously obstructing each other, even though their conversation is orderly on its surface. The respondent—perhaps deliberately—takes the interviewer's question to be about self-concept rather than political affiliation. The interviewer, following her employers' instructions, keeps asking the same question after the respondent has already given evidence of being unwilling or unable to answer it on the survey's terms. The respondent and interviewer have different conceptions of what phrases like "or what" mean, different conversational agendas, and (most likely) different world views. In some

---

[1]In this excerpt, double colons indicate that speakers have lengthened words.

sense, they have such different perspectives on what is going on that they don't even seem to be engaged in the same activity.

An extreme example like this one shows just how important the coordination of perspectives is to successful communication. It also highlights the fact that many different kinds of perspective are simultaneously present in conversation. Conversational participants have their own world views, conversational agendas, and conceptions of how particular phrases are intended. They also have physical vantage points from which they speak. Differences in any of these perspectives can lead them to have trouble or to use extra effort in understanding each other.

Some researchers have explicitly or implicitly taken perspective-taking to be a (if not *the*) fundamental task of communication (see, e.g., Fisher & Ury, 1981; Flavell, Botkin, Fry, Wright, & Jarvis, 1968; Gottman, Notarius, Gonso, & Markman, 1976; Graumann, 1989; Graumann & Sommer, 1988; Krauss & Fussell, 1991; Piaget, 1959; Reithaug, 1984; Stein, Bernas, Calicchia, & Wright, 1996). In successful communication, according to this view, at least one party takes the other's perspective. Communication is unsuccessful when neither party manages to mentally "step into the other's shoes," to be non-egocentric. Both speakers and addressees can take each other's perspectives. When Madeline speaks to Dorothy, she can design her utterances to be understandable from Dorothy's point of view. When Dorothy understands what Madeline has said, Dorothy sees things from the perspective Madeline has taken, at least for the moment.

My aim here is to examine some of the different kinds of perspectives that can simultaneously be present in conversations. As I will propose, in taking the different kinds of perspectives conversational participants have different kinds of evidence available to them, some tangible and some tenuous. When the perspective-taking evidence is more tenuous, characterizing speakers' perspective options and certain other aspects of conversational coordination is more difficult. Perspective-taking in conversation turns out to be far more complicated than it at first appears.

DIFFERENT KINDS OF PERSPECTIVE

Theorists from different areas of psychology have had different notions of what a perspective is (for discussions, see Graumann, 1989; Krauss & Fussell, 1988). As Krauss and Fussell (1996) have pointed out, one can conceive of a person's perspective as encompassing just about any aspect of a person, from relatively stable features like beliefs and attitudes to changing features like physical vantage points and current states of comprehension. Here I will focus on four of the different ways that "perspective" has been used: (a) as a speaker's time, place and identity; (b) as a speaker's conceptualizations; (c) as a speaker's conversational agenda; and (d) as a speaker's knowledge. In describing all these phenomena as perspectives, I don't mean to suggest that this is the only way they can be conceived; they may well be separate phenomena, as many researchers in language and communication have assumed. Rather, I propose that because they have all been labeled *perspectives*, it is worth examining whether they are coordinated in conversation in the same ways.

Perspective as Speaker's Time, Place, and Identity

One major sort of perspective is the kind found in *deictic* . or *indexical* expressions. (Fillmore, 1977, 1982; Levelt, 1989), whose referents depend on their occasions of use. When speakers use deictic terms they express something about their identity, their location, and their time—their perspective on the world, at least for the moment. Terms like *I* and *you* usually show that the origin of the utterance is the current speaker. Deictic expressions of time like *now, then, today, yesterday, next year*, etc. usually indicate the moment or general time period that the speaker must be in. Similarly, deictic expressions of place usually indicate a speaker's physical location and vantage point. A speaker who uses *here, there, this, that, come*, or *go* is expressing his or her situatedness in a particular location.

Deictic expressions do not only specify the speaker's own time, place and identity. Speakers can use them to specify the identity and situation of other people too, as when they use *I* while quoting or reporting someone else's speech. And there are other ways they can use deictic expressions to take another person's point of view (see Brown & Levinson, 1987). For example, speakers who want to express solidarity sometimes switch "person-center," speaking as if they were the addressee—"Yes dear, it hurts terribly, I know," (Brown & Levinson, 1987). Speakers can shift to another time by using different verb tenses, as when they switch to the "vivid present" when telling stories—"And Mia says to Bill . . ." (see Wolfson, 1982). Speakers can shift place with demonstratives (using *here* rather than *there, this* rather than *that*) or with verbs of movement (*come* rather than *go, bring* rather than *take*).

One of the most well-studied kinds of deictic expression is the kind found in descriptions of locations or spatial relations, which almost always reflect particular vantage points on a scene. Different researchers have come up with different terminologies to categorize these perspectives, and they sometimes use the same terms to mean different things (see Levinson, 1996, for a discussion). To give an idea of the complications involved, some researchers (e.g., Levelt, 1989; Miller & Johnson-Laird, 1976) contrast the speaker's perspective (deictic) with all other perspectives (intrinsic, thus grouping the addressee's point of view with the point of view of any inanimate objects in the scene (intrinsic). Another set of researchers (e.g., Herskovits, 1986; Retz-Schmidt, 1988) contrast the perspective of all speakers in the conversation (deictic) with all other possible perspectives (intrinsic), thus classifying the point of view of the addressee with the speaker's (deictic).

To avoid this kind of confusion, I will use the terms I proposed in Schober (1995, in press). Imagine that Monica and Tom are conversing face to face in a room. A chair is between them, facing to Monica's left. Monica has many choices of frames of reference as she describes the location of a potted plant in the room. She could describe the plant's location from her own *speaker-centered* perspective as "on the right" (or as "on my right," if she wants to indicate the frame of reference explicitly). She could describe the same location from Tom's perspective, using an *addressee-centered* description like "on the left" (or "on your left"). She could describe the plant's location using an *object-centered* description that uses the chair's frame of reference—"behind the chair." Or she could describe the plant's location with an *environment-centered* description that reflects an external or "absolute" reference frame—"in the back of the room" or "at the north end."

There are other options as well. Each of these perspectives has subtypes. For example, Lang, Carstensen, and Simmons (1991) detail different kinds of object-centered perspectives; Levelt (1989) details different kinds of deictic perspectives. And descriptions can simultaneously reflect multiple perspectives. For example, if Monica's and Tom's vantage points are similar, the same plant could be located "on the left" (or "on our left"), reflecting one or the other or both of their perspectives. Or the plant "in back" could be both in back of the chair (object-centered) and at the back of the room (environment-centered) (see Schober, 1993, 1995). Finally, spatial descriptions like "between" and "near" are *neutral* with respect to perspective (even though they use objects as reference points): They do not reflect any coordinate system at all, because they hold no matter what the vantage points of any people or objects in the scene are, and no matter what coordinates the environment provides. Such descriptions have been called, variously, "local references without a coordinate system" (Levelt, 1989); descriptions "ohne erschliessbare Origobesetzung," that is, without a recoverable frame of reference (Herrmann, Dietrich, Egel, & Hornung, 1988); topological localizations (Egel & Carroll, 1988); descriptions in a "landmark" frame of reference (Craton, Elicker, Plumert, & Pick, 1990; Pick, Yonas, & Rieser, 1979); and neutral descriptions (Schober, 1995).

Perspective as Conceptualization

Another kind of perspective is what I will call conceptualization—the way a speaker characterizes the topic under discussion for the moment, as conventionally indicated by the linguistic form. Every choice of linguistic form reflects one take on the situation, event, object, or location it describes (see E. V. Clark, 1990, 1995) and limits the set of possible interpretations (H. H. Clark, 1991). Speakers' conceptualizations of the topic under discussion can be seen at several different levels—in the words they use, the propositions they use, and in their more extended discourse forms.

At the word level, different words presuppose different ways of conceiving of their referents (see E. V. Clark's [1987] principle of contrast; H. H. Clark & Schober, 1991; Ravn, 1987). This is true of all sorts of words. The same object can legitimately be referred to as "Boots," "that awful cat," and "my pet." The same set of more abstract entities can legitimately be called "the media," "those bloodsuckers," and "the voice of the people." The same action can reasonably be called "moving," "running," or "whizzing by." A location can be described as "to the left" or "on the left"; "*to* the left" presupposes an implicit path of motion, while "*on* the left" is a static conceptualization (see Talmy, 1975, 1983). (This last example highlights the fact that conceptualization differs from spatial perspective. These two descriptions differ in conceptualization, but they both reflect the same frame of reference.)

Conceptualizations can also be seen in speakers' choices of propositions. Like words, propositions also reflect one possible way of characterizing the event or state of affairs they describe, one way of breaking down the event or situation into component parts. Every time a speaker chooses one particular framing of an event or situation, she has chosen one possible perspective on it. To use H. H. Clark and E. V. Clark's (1977) term, speakers constantly solve the problem of "experiential chunking," that is, the problem of how to break down the events and experiences they want to talk about into units. Linda can describe Fred's act of locomotion with the utterance "Fred walked," but she can talk about exactly the same act very differently by chunking it into a set of component actions: "Fred lifted his left foot while swinging his right arm, brought down his weight on his left foot, and then lifted his right foot." These different descriptions characterize the action differently—they reflect different perspectives.

In a related vein, speakers describing spatial scenes have to choose how to "linearize" their descriptions—how to organize the 2- or 3-dimensional information present in the situation into the linear sequence that speaking requires. For example, speakers describing an apartment can take a mental tour of the apartment starting at the entrance and traveling room to room, or they can give a more hierarchical structural description, describing all the bedrooms before describing all the bathrooms (see Linde & Labov, 1975; Ullmer-Ehrich, 1982). As another example, speakers can localize an object by starting with local details and ending up with the global picture ("the vase on the table in the living room"), or they can start with the global picture and end with local details ("in the living room there's a table that has a vase on it") (Plumert, Carswell, De Vet, & Ihrig, 1995). In both examples, each alternate linearization reflects a different take on the situation—a different conceptualization or perspective.

These conceptualizations reflect what words and propositions *conventionally* indicate. Of course, neither words nor propositions reflect exactly the same perspectives across all contexts. "That awful cat" can be an epithet, a detached description, or a term of endearment. But such different uses of "that awful cat" are conceptually related in a way that alternative formulations are not. And even though alternate wordings can reflect similar attitudes or underlying intentions (*illocutionary forces*, to use the technical term), as when "my pet" and "that awful cat" are both used as endearments, they still differ conceptually.

Here is another level where one can see conceptualizations operating in propositions. Speakers can word the same message differently so as to highlight different thematic material (Fillmore, 1977; Levelt, 1989), and each wording reflects a different perspective. For example, when Betsy uses an active-voice sentence like "The cat swallowed the insect," she has foregrounded the agent of this action (*cat*), even though she could have foregrounded the patient (*insect*) with a passive-voice sentence like "The insect was swallowed by the cat." In addition to voice, speakers can use aspect, mood, and other linguistic devices to convey different perspectives (see E. V. Clark, 1990). Unlike the kinds of wording- and proposition-level perspectives I just described, these kinds of conceptualization have to do not with how the elements of the proposition are selected, but with how already-selected elements are expressed.

Conceptualizations can span units larger than the individual proposition. For Lakoff and Johnson (1980), for example, utterances reflect underlying conceptualizations (or "metaphors," in their terminology). Jenny's utterances "I am really drawn to Phil" and "There was real electricity between us" both reflect an underlying conceptualization of LOVE AS A PHYSICAL FORCE. This conceptualization differs from an alternative conceptualization of LOVE AS A JOURNEY, which can be seen in utterances like "We have come a long way together" and "We were stuck in a rut."

These various sorts of conceptual perspectives—word-level, proposition-level, metaphor-level—are interrelated. A speaker's word choices reflect conceptualizations, and these constrain the kinds of sentences the speaker utters. Sentence-level choices affect the global shape of the discourse. Similarly, global discourse-level perspective choices affect both the forms of sentence-level propositions and lexical choices.

Although these phenomena have all been called perspectives, I realize that I am traversing terrain that has also been named differently. Some researchers would call the conceptualization that a word implies the word's semantics or its entailments.[2] Other researchers have used "thematic structure" or even "grammatical structure" to indicate what I am calling the conceptualization implied by a proposition's organization (see Levelt, 1989). Again, my point is not that the only way to conceive of these phenomena is as perspectives. But I believe it is useful to consider them as perspectives so as to compare how the different kinds are coordinated conversationally.

Perspective as Conversational Agenda

Perspective has been used to describe what might be called the agendas, the underlying intentions, or the purposes behind utterances in conversation. The notions of intentionality and purpose are extremely tricky and raise unsolved (perhaps unsolvable) problems of definition (see, e.g., Ajzen, 1988; Craig, 1986, 1990; Davidson, 1980; Fishbein & Ajzen, 1975; Levelt, 1992). But they have nonetheless been invoked as perspectives that speakers take.

I mean this category to include not only the intentions underlying single utterances but also conversational agendas that stretch beyond single utterances. These agendas can take different forms. In the example at the start of this chapter, the interviewer's conversational agenda could be called "following the script in a standardized survey interview," while the respondent's agenda could not. To take another case, conversational participants can believe they are both engaged in small talk or in serious talk; when their agendas are mismatched, utterances like "How are you?" can be interpreted quite differently. Here are some other examples: Andrea's purpose can be to communicate in great detail, but Alex may be speaking in vague generalities (see Russell & Schober, 1997; Wilkes-Gibbs, 1986). Julie might mean "let's do lunch" as a serious invitation, but Paul might mistake it for a platitude (see Isaacs & H. H. Clark, 1990). Connie might mean "that adorable cat" quite earnestly, but Evan might mean it sarcastically under the agenda of engaging in insulting banter.

In what sense exactly do these speakers have different perspectives on these utterances? More traditional accounts would consider these speakers to have different plans, different discourse goals, or different indirect illocutionary intentions. As with my other perspective categories, I don't mean to suggest that considering them to be perspectives is the only possible analysis. Rather, I mean to be taking seriously a notion like that found in Keysar (1994): If an addressee (or a reader of a retrospective account of a conversational interchange) mistakenly takes the speaker's ironic banter as earnest, the addressee (or reader)

---

[2]In a way, saying that words imply different conceptualizations and that the same objects can be referred to differently is a restatement of the distinction between sense and reference. To use the classic example, both "the morning star" and "the evening star" refer to the same entity, but the phrases have different senses—what I would call different conventional conceptualizations.

has missed the speaker's perspective (Keysar, 1994). Under this notion, speakers who understand each other's agendas are aware of each other's perspectives.

Note that speakers can simultaneously have several underlying agendas, as when they intend the same utterance to have different forces for different listeners (H. H. Clark & Carlson, 1982), or when they intend their utterances to have equivocal implications (Bavelas, Black, Chovil, & Mullett, 1990). It is unclear whether one should say such speakers have several simultaneous perspectives or one perspective that is the sum of their different intentions.

Perspective as Knowledge

Perspective has also been conceived of as people's background beliefs and thoughts. Unlike the other three kinds of perspective I have described, which reflect the momentary stances people take, this kind of perspective is seen as a relatively stable feature of a person. A person's perspective on the world consists of the way he or she thinks and perceives—his or her knowledge, beliefs, opinions, attitudes, values, cognitive styles, etc. (see, e.g., Fisher & Ury, 1981; Gottman et al., 1976; Graumann, 1989; Hastorf & Cantril, 1954; Regan & Totten, 1975; Ross, 1977). For lack of one unifying term I will call this kind of perspective *knowledge*. But I mean this perspective to encompass beliefs and opinions and values, and I mean for it to range in scope from single pieces of knowledge to large-scale webs of belief or world views.

People's knowledge and world views motivate their choices of conceptualization (whether at the word or proposition level) and their agendas. Die-hard militarists are more likely than die-hard pacifists to refer to a weapon as a "peacekeeping device" (conceptualization) and to mean it earnestly (agenda). If pacifists use "peacekeeping device" at all, their agenda is more likely to be ironic. And people's choices of conceptualizations and agendas give evidence about their world views. A speaker whose vocabulary reflects highly specialized knowledge about opera is likely to be an opera specialist, or at least an opera buff. A speaker who consistently uses bigoted terms without apology is liable to be considered a bigot.

At first blush it might seem that knowledge is not a language-relevant perspective in the same way that conceptualization and agenda are. Rather, knowledge seems to supply the motive for producing utterances with particular conceptualizations and agendas. But this can't be quite right: At least on some occasions, knowledge must operate at a distinct level. This is because one's assessments of speakers' knowledge can form the basis of how one interprets speakers' agendas and conceptualizations. For example, one's interpretation of "that delightful cat" as ironic can convince one that a speaker shares one's knowledge that the cat has misbehaved, or one can interpret the phrase as ironic because one already knows the speaker knew about the cat's misbehavior.

On this view of perspective, Susan takes Harrison's perspective when Susan considers Harrison's group membership, character, or experiences as she speaks to him or interprets what he says. This is the view held by those who consider that speakers (or writers) are taking their addressees' (or readers') perspectives when they tailor their utterances for their addressees or readers—that is, when they follow a principle of audience design (e.g., Fussell & Krauss, 1989, 1992; Traxler & Gernsbacher, 1993). It is also the view held by those who say that people speaking at the appropriate level of expertise for their conversational partner are taking the partner's perspective (e.g., Isaacs & H. H. Clark, 1987; Shatz & Gelman, 1973).

HOW DO PEOPLE INFER EACH OTHER'S PERSPECTIVES IN CONVERSATION?

If perspective-taking is fundamental to communicating, then a basic question is how people know the perspectives of their conversational partners. People don't have direct access to each other's private thoughts and experiences, and they don't experience the world through other people's eyes. So perspective-taking is a matter of inference. As with all inferences, there is always the risk of being wrong, like Saki's character Francesca, who "prided herself on being able to see things from other people's points of view, which meant, as it usually does, that she could see her own point of view from various aspects." (Saki, 1912/1988, p. 587). And inferences can never access *all* aspects of another person's mental life. People have inexpressible experiences that they can't share and private thoughts that they choose to conceal.

But people do have grounds from which they can infer certain aspects of others' perspectives. At any moment in a conversation people have a great deal of evidence about their partners at their disposal (see Brennan, 1990; H. H. Clark & Marshall, 1981). Some of this evidence is solid, as it relies on what can be observed physically; some is more tenuous, as it relies on additional inferences and beliefs, which may or may not be justified. This evidence includes:

1. Immediate perceptions of the physical setting of the conversation. Perspectives can be inferred from what each conversational partner can perceive and from judgments of which parts of the perceptual environment are shared.

2. The utterances themselves. Perspectives can be inferred from the words and propositions in those utterances, in that they conventionally reflect particular conceptualizations, which in turn can give evidence about agendas and world views.

3. The history of what has been said—and understood—thus far in the conversation. The perspectives in the current utterance can be inferred from the perspectives that speakers have already used in previous utterances. The perspectives that have been "successful"—those underlying the utterances that both parties agree have been understood— are particularly informative. For example, if in earlier successful descriptions the speaker has taken the addressee's spatial perspective, the addressee might infer that the current description is also likely to reflect the addressee's perspective.

4. Beliefs about the conversational partner's group membership, expertise, etc. Perspectives can be inferred from the groups people believe their conversational partners belong to—their ethnic backgrounds, social classes, genders, sexual orientations, nationalities, schools, churches, professions, neighborhoods, families, marital statuses, and so forth. People who belong to the same groups can assume some shared knowledge, beliefs, and assumptions (what H. H. Clark and Marshall [1981] call *common ground* based on community co-membership) that non-members can't. They can sometimes assume shared goals or values. If Monica knows or assumes that Felix belongs to some of the same groups that she does, she can assume commonality around topics relevant to those groups, although it may be unwise to assume commonality on other topics. If Monica knows that on some dimension Felix belongs to a different group than she does, she can design what she says and can interpret what Felix says accordingly.

5. Beliefs about the conversational partner's unique experience. Perspectives can be inferred from more than just group membership. If Vicki knows particular facts about Nick as a person or knows of particular experiences Nick has had, she can take Nick's perspective, designing what she says for Nick and interpreting what Nick says accordingly.

Judging other people's perspectives from beliefs about their group membership and personal history is a tricky business. Sometimes it is straightforward. Piano tuners can reasonably assume that fellow piano tuners know certain facts about the art of piano tuning. People who love Viennese cuisine can be assumed to know what Wienerschnitzel tastes like. But beliefs about others' group membership and personal history can lead to unwarranted perspective inferences, as when people mistakenly believe they know their conversational partners' world views because of the partners' ethnic background, social class, or gender. Stereotypic beliefs about group membership are only relevant to some topics of discussion, and speakers can unwisely assume too much about their partners' knowledge.

Also, different kinds of perspective inferences may be warranted for different kinds of groups. Membership in some groups, but not all, is immediately apparent to other people. Some groups reflect pre-existing social categories, and some are ad hoc, forming on the fly during the course of a particular conversation (e.g., people with big feet who have trouble finding shoes that fit). Some groups are joined by choice and some are not. People can be deeply committed to some groups but not to others, and their commitments can waver. This is all complicated by the fact that people belong to many (sometimes incompatible) groups simultaneously (see H. H. Clark, 1996, for further discussion of group membership).

These different kinds of evidence all come into play as people take each other's knowledge, agendas, conceptualizations, and spatial perspectives into account. But they come into play differently because only the physical setting of the conversation and the words people use are immediately observable. The other kinds of evidence are less solid, because they rely on memories and inferences. How are the different kinds of evidence relevant for different kinds of perspective-taking?

Evidence in Spatial Perspective-Taking

In typical face-to-face conversations involving spatial descriptions, participants can immediately observe two concrete kinds of evidence of each other's perspectives: (a) the physical setting of the conversation, and (b) the words their partners use, words like *left* and *front*. The words themselves do not reflect unique perspectives: The term *left* could indicate the speaker's left, the addressee's left, an object's left, or the environment's left. Knowledge of the conventional meaning of *left* is of course necessary for inferring which spatial perspective the speaker has taken. But it is only when such knowledge is combined with knowledge of the physical setting of the conversation that an utterance of "left" can be seen to reflect one (or more than one) particular perspective.

The physical setting—the participants' viewpoints, the disparity in their viewpoints, and the arrangement of objects in the scene—is observable or directly inferable in at least three ways (Schober, 1995). First, it is *public*: Not only does each party know about the other's viewpoint and the arrangement of objects in the scene, but each knows that the other knows about them, and each knows that the other knows that the other knows, etc. This satisfies the technical requirements for truly mutual knowledge (see H. H. Clark & Carlson, 1981; H. H. Clark & Marshall, 1981; Schiffer, 1972). Second, it is *preset*: People's viewpoints and a scene with objects in it necessarily exist before a spatial description can be uttered or interpreted. And third, it is *fixed* as long as participants or objects in the scene don't move. If they do move, the newly emerging spatial perspective options will be immediately calculable because of the public nature of the relevant knowledge. (As I will argue, the evidence for conceptualizations, agendas, and world views is not public, fixed, or preset in the same way as the evidence for spatial perspectives.)[3]

The other kinds of evidence—conversational history and beliefs about the other person's group membership and experience—are less immediately observable, but they can be useful in spatial perspective-taking. Speakers can infer the spatial perspective of an utterance from the history of which spatial perspectives have already been used successfully in the conversation. In successive descriptions of locations on identical or similar displays for the same partner, speakers are extremely consistent in the proportions of different spatial perspectives they use (Schober, 1993, 1995). For example, a speaker who has taken the addressee's perspective in earlier location descriptions is highly likely to continue in the same vein in the next description, provided the addressee has given evidence of understanding the earlier descriptions.

People may also sometimes infer spatial perspectives from their beliefs about the partner's group membership or unique experience. As Graf (cited in Herrmann & Grabowski, 1994) has shown, students are more likely to take a professor's spatial perspective than a fellow student's, presumably because they want to be polite or deferential, and they are more likely to take a child's perspective than another student's, presumably because they believe the child is more likely to have difficulty understanding speaker-centered descriptions. Speakers who have evidence that their partners have poor spatial abilities take their partners' perspectives more often (Schober, 1997). In any of these cases, addressees who know what the speaker thinks of them may be able to infer which perspective the speaker has used. But, of course, this kind of inference is tenuous in a way that inferences based on more tangible evidence are not.

Evidence in Taking Conceptualizations

Conceptualizations operate differently than spatial perspectives. Conceptualizations are not generally visible from the partner's physical location and orientation, nor from the details of the physical situation the interlocutors find themselves in. Instead, people come to know each other's

---

[3]This is an oversimplified view of the role of physical evidence. Additional kinds of physical evidence can be important for spatial perspective-taking, as when people point overtly, glance in particular directions, and present each other with other kinds of direct visual evidence of understanding locations (see Brennan, 1990). And sometimes direct physical evidence is much less important, as when people give route directions over the telephone or in other situations where they or the scene they are describing is not mutually visible (see Taylor & Tversky, 1992, 1996).

conceptualizations through the words themselves—both through the words and linguistic constructions that are used and through the words and linguistic constructions that could *potentially* be used. Unlike with spatial perspectives, speakers may not be certain about their partners' conceptualizations of the topic under discussion until some words have been uttered.

For example, consider how a speaker might refer to a particular object in conversation: as a shoe, a penny loafer, a piece of footwear, etc. Before any words have been used to refer to the object in a conversation, both speakers know a range of possible terms that could be used, but neither is likely to know which particular conceptualization his or her partner prefers, unless they have particular shared expertise or experience. But once one speaker has used "penny loafer," his or her conversational partner now has evidence for the speaker's current conceptualization. The same goes for other linguistic constructions. Before either speaker has described an event (for example, Don pushing Alison in a stroller), neither has solid evidence for the other's chosen conceptualization. But once one speaker has described the event (for example, by using the passive form to focus on Alison—"Alison was being pushed in her stroller"), the other now has reliable evidence of how that speaker has chosen to characterize the event.

In one sense, conceptualizations are public, preset, and fixed even before a word has been uttered, because people within a linguistic community know which conceptualizations particular words or phrases conventionally indicate.[4] But in another sense, before a conversation has begun conceptualizations may not be public, preset, or fixed, because speakers may not know which conventional conceptualizations their conversational partners are likely to choose. So the potential conceptualizations in a linguistic community are public, but individual choices of conceptualization within a conversation are often unknown before they are uttered—perhaps even by the speaker. (Of course, whatever is uttered only gives evidence for what the speaker is willing to make public; speakers have private conceptions that they never share.)

Both kinds of evidence—pre-existing knowledge of the available conceptualizations and knowledge of which conceptualizations have been used in the current conversation—play a role in speakers' word choices (see H. H. Clark 1991). As Garrod and Anderson (1987) have shown, speakers tend to choose words that conform to the words their partners have chosen. In fact, speakers sometimes persist in using a word that has already been used successfully (say, "penny loafer" to pick out a shoe from among several), even when they no longer need to use such a precise word (say, if circumstances have changed so that now the pennyloafer is the only shoe, so that they could get by with using

---

[4]Note that this doesn't mean that meanings within a linguistic community are completely determinate; people regularly use words in novel ways (see H. H. Clark, 1991; H. H. Clark & Gerrig, 1983).

the basic-level word *shoe*) (Brennan & H. H. Clark, 1996). In other words, the history of what both parties agree has been said and understood thus far in the conversation—the common ground with the conversational partner—strongly affects current conceptualizations.

But actual and potential choices of linguistic construction are not the only possible ways to infer conceptualizations. People's physical vantage points can provide evidence for their conceptualizations in situations that satisfy these two conditions: Both partners' physical experience of the same object is different enough that it affects how each conceives of the object, and at least one partner is aware of the difference and how it might affect the other's conceptualization. For example, imagine that you see a brand new car with a dented door, but your partner sees only the unblemished side of the car. Your physical vantage point and your knowledge of what your partner can see provide evidence that may be relevant to your description of the car. Referring to the car as "the wreck" is unlikely to prove successful, because your partner's potential conceptualizations rely on different perceptual evidence than you have.

What addressees know of speakers' group memberships and unique experience can also give evidence about the speakers' potential and actual conceptualizations. Speakers of different dialects—say, American and British English—sometimes know enough about each other's dialects to know how their partner's range of options for a particular reference differs from theirs. Note that this cross-dialect case is comparable, but not identical, to the case within a single dialect where speakers, by virtue of knowledge or expertise (say as a plumber), can tailor their speech for their partners who have a different level of expertise.

Evidence in Taking Agendas

The evidence for inferring conversational agendas is often less solid than the evidence available for spatial perspectives or conceptualizations. Although some situations rigidly determine conversational agendas (think of official interactions in courtrooms, Departments of Motor Vehicles, classrooms), the agendas in many casual conversations aren't public, preset, or fixed. People often aren't fully aware of each other's agendas. They don't necessarily have predetermined agendas before the conversation starts; in fact, they may still be unsure of their own agendas during the conversation. And agendas are often unstable; they can change without fanfare or conversational disruption.

So how do people infer each other's agendas? Consider the situation of being asked for the time by a stranger in a bar. Among other things, this request could be a friendly conversation opener, a romantic advance, or a sincere request for the time (and only the time). What information do you have at your disposal?

You have the physical setting and the words themselves, but neither gives much information about the stranger's agenda. You can use your previous experience with people of the stranger's type (those who belong to the groups that you assess the stranger belongs to) to impute an agenda, but you may be wrong. The safe thing to do is to put off determining an agenda until more is said and the stranger's motives become clearer in subsequent conversation.

This is a reasonable strategy, but people don't necessarily follow it. In some experimental conversations, people seem to impute agendas to their conversational partners from the very beginning of the conversation, even if they don't strictly need to yet (Russell & Schober, 1997). In the absence of clear information to the contrary, people can mistakenly assume that others share their own agendas.

Of course, additional knowledge about a conversational partner's previous agendas and proclivities helps increase the likelihood of inferring an agenda appropriately. But, again, such evidence of speakers' likely agendas is far less solid than the immediate physical evidence for spatial perspectives or the immediate verbal evidence for conceptualizations. This tenuousness is troubling because of how important agendas may be to language understanding: Some theorists have argued that people can only produce and comprehend language because they have constraining beliefs about the current agenda or goals of the ongoing "language game" (Wittgenstein, 1958), social "frame" (Bateson, 1952/1972), or "activity type" (Levinson, 1979, 1981) in which they are engaged (see also Grice, 1975).

Evidence in Taking Others' Knowledge Into Account

The words that speakers use provide some evidence of their expertise—consider opera buffs who use technical terms in conversation. But this evidence is not entirely reliable. Opera buff James might seem to know more than he does by using jargon he doesn't really understand, or he might use nontechnical words that don't reflect his full knowledge because he intends to make himself understandable to his less knowledgeable addressees.

This is not to say that conversational partners can't be confident about their partners' knowledge. The relevant pieces of someone's knowledge *can* be public, preset, or fixed within a conversational interaction, but only if interlocutors know the right sort of information about each other. For example, a lawyer who knows that my legal knowledge comes largely from popular media and high school civics courses can infer that my knowledge about legal intricacies is lacking. This can affect the vocabulary he or she uses with me (he or she is likely to assume that my range of potential conceptualizations is restricted) and how he or she interprets my imprecise descriptions of a lawsuit.

So although prior knowledge about a partner can provide evidence of the partner's knowledge, this evidence rests on memories of previous inferences, rather than on immediate tangible evidence.

The evidence for larger scale kinds of knowledge like world views is even more tenuous. Although speakers' utterances may suggest that they have particular world views, it is extremely difficult to pin an entire world view on a speaker on the basis of one utterance or one conversation. Stereotypic knowledge about people's group memberships and knowledge about their personal experiences can also be useful in inferring their world views. But, of course, knowing someone's group memberships and personal experiences is not enough to guarantee accurate knowledge of his or her world view.

Individual pieces of knowledge and larger scale knowledge structures can be mutually known to conversational partners. And both parties can know that one has a particular kind of knowledge or world view and the other doesn't. But this kind of knowledge about another's knowledge rests on a far less solid base than does knowledge about spatial perspectives or conceptualizations.

HOW LESS TANGIBLE EVIDENCE MUDDIES THE WATERS

I have proposed that speakers' utterances reflect several perspectives simultaneously, and that the interpretation of these perspectives depends on different kinds of evidence, some tangible and some tenuous. When perspectives rest on less tangible evidence, they are harder to characterize in other ways too— both for conversational participants and for researchers. In particular, it is harder to characterize what speakers' perspective options are, and it is harder to characterize the collaborative effort involved in an utterance.

Perspective Options

For spatial perspectives, the repertoire of perspective options is well-defined (despite researchers' quarrels about classification schemes and terminology). Speakers' expressions can either be speaker-centered, addressee-centered, object-centered, environment-centered, or neutral. Or they can be ambiguous, as when they reflect multiple perspectives simultaneously (e.g., "on the left," where the description is true from both the speaker's and the addressee's perspectives). In the prototypical face-to-face conversation involving locations, a conversational participant—and an observing researcher—can tell which perspective options are available to a speaker.

The spatial perspective options are so well-defined because of the tangible evidence the scene provides. In the prototypical situation, both participants can see each other and they can see the various objects in the scene. This means that they necessarily know what the other's vantage point on the scene is, precisely what the disparity between their two vantage points is, if any, and what additional perspective options are afforded by the arrangement of the objects. For example, if the objects in a scene have their own intrinsic fronts and backs or lefts and rights, object-centered descriptions are afforded, but if the objects don't have such features—think of lamps and balls—object-centered descriptions aren't possible. Similarly, if the objects are arranged appropriately, neutral descriptions like "between the lamp and the ball" or "in the middle" are available.

The perspective options for conceptualizations are harder to characterize. Unlike spatial perspectives, which "belong" to particular people or objects, conceptualizations can only sometimes be attributed to one conversational partner and not the other. Consider when a militarist uses "peacekeeping device" to refer to a missile in a conversation with a pacifist. In this case, the conceptualization "peacekeeping device" reflects the militarist's views and can be said to "belong" to the militarist and not to the pacifist; the militarist has produced a speaker-centered utterance. Contrast this with a case where a shoe clerk uses "the loafer" to pick out a shoe for a new customer. Although this case is similar to the militarist–pacifist case, it seems odd to say that the clerk's utterance of "loafer" is speaker-centered. Unlike the pacifist, who thinks of missiles as death machines rather than as peacekeeping devices, the customer probably has no objection to conceiving of the shoe as a loafer and may have had that conception even before the clerk said anything.

What distinguishes the cases where conceptualizations can and can't be attributed to particular people? The crucial factor is evidence. Without evidence of their addressees' conceptualizations, speakers' options include the full range of conceptualizations that the language provides. The shoe clerk who has no evidence of how the customer is likely to conceive of a particular shoe can call it a "shoe," a "pennyloafer," a "brown shoe," a "piece of footwear," etc. When speakers have evidence that their partners hold or are likely to prefer particular conceptualizations (as in the militarist–pacifist case), then their perspective options are clearer—they can choose to take the other person's perspective or to introduce a different perspective.

The evidence that allows perspectives to be attributed to particular speakers (and thus limits speakers' conceptualization options) can be more or less solid:

(1) Tangible physical evidence, which is present even before a word is uttered, can clarify the perspective options in a few ways. One way is that it can provide evidence about what is mutually known and what isn't. Recall the earlier example where only one speaker can see the dent in the car; in such cases, a conceptualization like "the wreck" reflects the perspective of the speaker who can see the dent. Another way is that the nature of the physical scene itself— what potential alternative referents surround the target—can limit the options. Consider the shoe clerk again: If the shoe display contains only brown shoes,

"the brown shoe" is unlikely to be among the conceptualizations that could allow the customer to pick out the target shoe.

(2) Speakers' pre-existing beliefs about each other's world views, agendas, group membership, knowledge, etc. can also provide evidence that clarifies the perspective options, as in the militarist–pacifist example. As long as both know the relevant aspects of each other's world views, their conceptualizations can be attributed to one or the other. Of course, when speakers' beliefs about each other are wrong, the options are only well-defined from one person's point of view. If the militarist speaker mistakenly believes his or her militarist addressee is a pacifist, an attempt to take the partner's perspective by using "death machine" is an addressee-centered utterance only from the speaker's perspective. From the addressee's perspective, the conceptualization will probably be hard to classify.

(3) Conversational evidence—what has been said and understood successfully—can also clarify whose perspective is being used. For example, if the customer has already successfully used "loafer" to refer to the shoe, the clerk's current range of perspective options in referring to the same shoe has shifted. Now one particular perspective is marked as the one the customer proposed, and because the clerk understood the customer, this perspective is also marked as successful. The clerk's perspective options now include taking the perspective that the partner proposed or proposing a different perspective (say, "shoe"). Although it is common for speakers to use the terms that their partners have already proposed (Garrod & Anderson, 1987), sometimes people don't converge on the same terms, each using their own over the course of a conversation (see Brennan & H. H. Clark 1996).

So particular conceptualizations can become associated with particular people; as with spatial perspectives, the conceptualization options can include speaker-centered and addressee-centered conceptualizations (or, if both speaker and addressee subscribe to the same views, conceptualizations that are ambiguous—speaker-or-addressee-centered, that is, joint). To extend the analogy from the spatial case, are there neutral conceptualizations that don't reflect either person's point of view? In some cases, yes: The militarist and the pacifist can try to use less value-laden terms than "peacekeeping device" or "death machine"—for instance, "weapon." But whether more neutral conceptualizations that avoid taking either person's perspective are *always* available in conversation is an open question.

As for agendas and knowledge, which often rely on more tenuous evidence than conceptualizations, the perspective options are often even less well-defined. Only when agendas and knowledge are extremely explicit can utterances be attributed to one or the other person's agenda or world view. Tangible physical evidence and conversational evidence can limit speakers' beliefs about their partners' agendas and knowledge. But this is quite different from what happens in the spatial case, where the physical scene itself provides a clearcut set of perspective options. With agendas and knowledge, speakers' choices are much less clear. It is harder for them to know if they have stumbled upon mutually acceptable perspectives, or if they have blundered into deep misunderstandings because of mismatches in their agendas or world views.

Collaborative Effort

Another aspect of perspective-taking which is harder to characterize when evidence is less tangible is *collaborative effort*. This notion comes from H. H. Clark & Wilkes-Gibbs' (1986) seminal paper on conversational referring, which proposed that speakers do not merely minimize their own effort by using the shortest, simplest noun phrases that are sufficiently unambiguous for their addressees. Rather, speakers try to minimize collaborative effort—the effort that both parties ultimately will have undertaken by the time both parties have agreed the reference has been understood. This collaborative effort includes the individual mental effort involved in the speaker's production, the individual mental effort involved in the addressee's comprehension, and the collective effort (the number of words and conversational turns) involved for both parties to agree that the reference has been understood.

So, for example, speakers might use longer noun phrases to describe objects than many standard theories predict, because they believe that by putting in extra individual effort early on they will not have to refashion the description later so the addressee can get it. Alternatively, speakers might put in less individual effort at first, trading off such that the addressee or the pair must do more work later on. Speakers might do this for several reasons: First, they might not be able to design the ideal noun phrase in the time allowed. Second, the information they need to convey might be so complex that it can't easily be understood all at once. Third, speakers might not know enough about what their addressees are likely to accept for them to present the reference right the first time. H. H. Clark & Wilkes-Gibbs claim that the push to minimize collaborative effort leads to particular conversational moves, like presenting a noun phrase in installments or allowing addressees to refashion unsuccessful descriptions (H. H. Clark & Wilkes-Gibbs, 1986).

When the perspective-taking evidence is straightforward, as with spatial perspectives, complex judgments of individual and collective effort are feasible, and one can imagine how speakers might go about making them. Speakers have to judge: (a) how hard it will be to produce a spatial description from each available perspective; (b) how hard it will be for the addressee to comprehend a spatial description from each available perspective; (c) whose effort—their own or their addressee's—needs more minimizing; and (d) what the conversational consequences of using a particular perspective will be—that is, which perspectives will ultimately lead to efficient comprehension.

In prototypical situations involving spatial descriptions, such computations are feasible because the evidence is so tangible and because the amount of effort involved in an individual act of comprehension or production is determinable. Speakers find it easier to produce egocentric descriptions and harder to produce addressee-centered descriptions, especially when the speaker's and addressee's viewpoints are further offset (Bürkle, Nirmaier, & Herrmann, 1986). The same is true for comprehension: Addressees find addressee-centered descriptions easier to understand and speaker-centered descriptions harder to understand. So speaker- and addressee-centered descriptions lead to an imbalance: They make things easier for one party, but harder for the other.

Other spatial perspective options don't seem to create the same kind of imbalance. Object-centered descriptions seem to be of intermediate difficulty, somewhere between speaker- and addressee-centered (Miller & Johnson-Laird, 1976; Schober, 1996; Schober & Bloom, 1995). Neutral descriptions are easy to produce and comprehend, because they don't require either party to choose between two points of view (Schober, 1995). In fact, in one study (Schober, 1995), both parties in conversations about locations preferred neutral descriptions when their vantage points were offset, and they used more and more neutral descriptions over time; in some cases, 75% of speakers' location descriptions were neutral by the end of the conversation. This finding is consistent with the proposal that neutral descriptions resolve the imbalance and minimize effort for both parties.

So particular spatial perspectives are easier or harder for speakers to produce and for addressees to comprehend, and the amount of effort involved is measurable (see Carlson-Radvansky & Irwin, 1994, for another example of such a measurement: A spatial description like *above* is more quickly understood when it reflects more than one spatial perspective). Speakers can observe addressees' vantage points and compute which perspectives are likely to cause the addressee to put in more effort. These assessments can be refined by knowledge of their particular addressees' spatial abilities and conversational preferences. But my point is that each individual's mental effort and the pair's collective effort can be defined, and so speakers' judgments about least collaborative effort—as well as researchers' claims about least collaborative effort—can rest on solid footing, at least in principle.

Such definitions are much harder to ascertain for conceptualizations, even though it is in the domain of conceptualizations that the principle of least collaborative effort was proposed (H. H. Clark and Wilkes-Gibbs [1986] were examining conceptualizations underlying references to objects). The amount of collective effort that a pair undergoes in order to agree that a reference has been understood can be observed—when the pair takes longer and uses more words and turns to understand each other, they have put in greater effort. But the *individual* effort involved in the production and comprehension of particular words is only sometimes calculable—only in those situations where evidence is tangible or solid. Speakers and addressees can only be said to be following a principle of least collaborative effort if they have a metric by which to judge how easy or hard particular conceptualizations are to produce and comprehend. Such a metric may be available to speakers and addressees when evidence is tangible and conceptualizations can be attributed to one or the other party. For example, the shoe clerk who uses the customer's term *loafer* may have judged that taking the customer's perspective by using the customer's preferred term would be collaboratively efficient, perhaps more efficient than a term that the clerk might prefer. But when the evidence is less solid, computations of potential collaborative effort are on much shakier ground and may even be impossible.

How is collaborative effort determined for agendas and knowledge? Collaborative effort is relatively straightforward in situations where two people's knowledge (expertise) on a well-defined topic differs and both know it (see Isaacs & Clark, 1987). Even though it would be easiest for a New Yorker to refer to a particular building as the Chrysler Building, the New Yorker in conversation with a non-New Yorker knows that the non-New Yorker probably won't understand the reference. The New Yorker can minimize collaborative effort by avoiding words that reflect knowledge that only a New Yorker could have. But collaborative effort is difficult to determine for less clearcut cases, as when both parties do not know each other's relative expertise.

I have not mentioned conversational agendas and world views in discussing the principle of least collaborative effort. This is because they are not negotiated conversationally in the same way that spatial perspectives and conceptualizations are. I don't mean to imply that agendas and world views are not affected by collaborative processes in conversation, nor that misunderstandings don't sometimes result from lack of knowledge about agendas and world views. But agendas and world views are not "on the table" in the same way that spatial perspectives and conceptualizations are. That is, every spatial perspective or conceptualization is an explicit proposal that the addressee can accept or reject. In contrast, agendas are rarely proposed explicitly, and although they can be implicitly renegotiated in ongoing conversation, they must occasionally be stable if they are to affect what speakers say and addressees understand (Bratman, 1990; Russell & Schober, 1997). World views are even less likely to be negotiable in ongoing conversation. Thus computations of least collaborative effort come into play for spatial perspectives and conceptualizations in ways that they don't for agendas and world views.

COMPLICATIONS

Even when the evidence for inferring perspectives is tangible and solid, perspective-taking is more complicated than I have made it out to be. Here are three kinds of complications.

(1) Roles

Conversational participants play several roles simultaneously. In the most stable role, people maintain their identity as a person—*A* remains *A* throughout the course of a conversation. In a role that shifts often, *A* is sometimes a speaker and sometimes an addressee. In a role that shifts, but less often, *A* is sometimes a person who has something to say—a purveyor of information—and sometimes a person to whom something is being said. Note that *A* can shift between being speaker and addressee several times while maintaining the task role of information purveyor.

The complication this raises for conversational perspective-taking is that people could take another person's perspective for any of these roles. I have been classifying perspectives as speaker- and addressee-centered. But they could just as well be person-*A*-centered and person-*B*-centered, or information-purveyor-centered and information-gatherer-centered.

Most analyses of perspective-taking have not made this distinction, partly because the different roles aren't always easy to disentangle. I was able to disentangle them in one of my spatial perspective-taking studies (Schober, 1995). In the experiment, one person, the director, had a set of locations to describe for the other person, the matcher. After two rounds of conversation, the director and matcher switched task-level roles. Because they also alternated between being speaker and addressee often during the course of the conversations, I could determine for which role they were taking spatial perspectives. In this experiment they consistently took the perspective of the person who needed information, even as informational roles switched.

Less is known about the roles for which people take each other's conceptualizations. Often the first conceptualization that a speaker proposes persists in subsequent references by both parties, no matter who has the information-purveying role (Garrod & Anderson, 1987). But what really persists is the first conceptualization that both parties have agreed upon, even if that conceptualization was initially proposed by the person who needed information (Brennan & H. H. Clark, 1996; H. H. Clark & Wilkes-Gibbs, 1986; Schober & H. H. Clark, 1989). Even less is known about the roles for which people take each other's agendas or world views. Further disentangling needs to be done to clarify how roles and perspectives interact.

(2) Extra Levels of Perspective-Taking

I have argued that it is only sometimes possible to classify an utterance as speaker- or addressee-centered; it depends on how tangible and solid the evidence for the attribution is. But even in the most tangible cases, there seems to be an additional level at which researchers should consider utterances as speaker- or addressee-centered. Take a straightforward face-to-face encounter where a speaker's expression "on the left" definitely reflects his or her own frame of reference. From everything I have considered so far, the utterance should be classified as speaker-centered. But at another level, this might be wrong.

Imagine that the speaker isn't very good at imagining how things look from other points of view. Imagine further that the addressee is quite good at it, and each knows the other's propensities. After having weighed the options, the speaker might use the speaker-centered "on the left" because he or she judges this term to be most collaboratively efficient: The addressee probably will have less trouble comprehending the speaker-centered description than the speaker would have producing an addressee-centered description. The speaker has considered his or her own needs, the addressee's needs, and the pair's joint needs. Hasn't the speaker taken the addressee into account? Surely this speaker-centered utterance differs from one by a speaker who fails to consider his or her addressee's point of view at all—say, one of Piaget's egocentric children.

This less egocentric use of speaker-centered expressions is exactly what I observed in one of my studies of spatial perspective-taking (Schober, 1993). Speakers used speaker-centered descriptions more often when their addressees gave them license to, that is, when their addressees gave no evidence of any discomfort with understanding speaker-centered utterances. When their addressee couldn't give such evidence (e.g., the addressee was imaginary) or the addressee failed to understand speaker-centered descriptions, speakers used addressee-centered descriptions. Merely categorizing speakers' descriptions as speaker-centered doesn't show just how much they took their addressees into account.

The same goes for conceptualizations. If the militarist uses "peacekeeping device" with full knowledge that the pacifist will understand (though disagree heartily with the conceptualization), the speaker-centered utterance is less egocentric than if the militarist had not considered the pacifist at all. The point is that there is a level of perspective-taking that has to do with the degree to which a speaker has considered the partner's needs, and the categories I have laid out don't include this.

(3) What Does It Mean To *Take* A Perspective?

Taking another perspective isn't the same thing as giving up one's own, nor is it the same thing as agreeing with the accuracy or validity of that perspective.

One can understand what bigoted, ironic, or kind remarks mean without agreeing with the bigoted, ironic, or kind perspective underlying them. The trouble is that giving evidence that one has understood what someone says *does* suggest at least some agreement with his or her perspectives—at least sufficient willingness to consider matters from that point of view for the moment.

For example, if the shoe clerk uses "loafer," and the customer gives evidence of having understood what the shoe clerk said, the customer is showing that he or she has no objection, and the clerk has license to continue conceptualizing the item as a loafer. If Pat uses the speaker-centered "on my left" and Chris gives evidence of having understood what Pat said, Pat has license to continue speaking egocentrically. In a sense, every time speakers describe or refer to something, they are making invitations that their addressees can accept or reject (Graumann, 1989). If the addressees accept the offer, they not only imply that they can figure out what object the speakers intend to pick out, but also that they are willing to agree, for now, with the speakers' perspectives on it. Giving evidence of understanding does imply a kind of tacit approval of a speaker's perspective.

In many cases an addressee will have nothing to lose by accepting a speaker's description. But sometimes an addressee does *not* want to endorse the speaker's view, for example, when the speaker refers to the addressee's beloved pet as "that beast," or when the prosecutor has called the addressee's witness a murderer. More subtle versions of this phenomenon occur when speakers presuppose perspectives that addressees are unwilling to accept, but that aren't the focus of conversation. The addressees are given an unpleasant choice. They can either ignore the presupposition and pretend that it didn't happen, but this choice can license speakers to believe that addressees find the presupposition acceptable. Or they can disrupt the conversational flow and direct attention to the irksome perspective, risking the loss of the speaker's good will.

CONCLUSIONS

In examining spatial perspectives, conceptualizations, agendas, and knowledge, I have only looked at some of the perspectives that exist simultaneously in conversations. These different kinds of perspectives can operate quite independently. For example, the conceptualizations inherent in spatial descriptions (e.g., the difference between "on the left" and "toward the left") can have nothing to do with the spatial perspectives they reflect. When speaker Linda chooses whether to take her own perspective (her left) or her partner Don's (his right), it is unlikely that her choice is affected by whether she conceives of the locations as static (*on* the left or right) or pathlike (*toward* the left or right).

Not only can the different kinds of perspectives operate independently, but different mental processes seem to be involved in their use. For example, mental rotation processes (or something very much like them) come into play in spatial perspective-taking (see Bürkle et al., 1986; Herrmann & Grabowski, 1994), but mental rotation probably doesn't come into play much in the determination of conversational agendas or world views.

But the different kinds of perspectives *can* be related. Speakers' conceptualization choices can affect the spatial perspectives they use. For example, a speaker who conceptualizes a scene as corresponding to a clock face has different spatial perspectives available as options than does a speaker who conceives of a scene as a grid. With a clock face, a speaker has the option not only of using speaker-centered descriptions like "at 10 o'clock for me" but also of using neutral perspectives with expressions like "clockwise" and "counterclockwise." With a grid, a speaker has fewer neutral perspective options, but he or she has other person-centered options such as corners and quadrants. Speakers' conversational agendas can also affect their conceptualizations. To reuse an earlier example, speakers describe exactly the same layout using different conceptualizations (linearizations) when their purpose is to describe a location rather than give directions (Plumert et al., 1995). For other examples of how speakers' agendas affect the words they choose, see Ravn (1987).

Under what conditions the different perspectives affect one another remains unknown. In fact, many things about perspective-taking remain unknown. *Must* at least one party take the other's perspective? Or can both parties get along having what Piaget (1959) called "collective monologue"? What would this "getting along" mean? If a speaker happens to hit upon his or her addressee's favorite perspective, but never considered the addressee at all, should the speaker's mental processes be characterized as perspective-taking? The list of questions stretches on.

But I am convinced of two things. First, I believe that the evidence that conversational participants have for inferring each other's perspectives is an important part of the answer to many research questions about perspective-taking. Conceptualizations should operate like spatial perspectives, for example, to the extent that the evidence they rest on is the same kind of evidence. Second, perspective-taking can and should be studied empirically. The challenge is to provide convincing empirical demonstrations in situations where the evidence for inferring perspectives—both for conversational participants and for researchers—is less tangible than in concrete spatial cases.

ACKNOWLEDGMENTS

Many thanks to Susan Brennan, Fred Conrad, and Alex Russell for comments on earlier drafts of this chapter and to Herb and Eve Clark for stimulating discussions about perspective. This chapter was supported in part by NSF Grant

IRI-9402167. Any opinions, findings, and conclusions or recommendations expressed in this material are those of the author and do not necessarily reflect the views of the National Science Foundation.

REFERENCES

Ajzen, I. (1988). *Attitudes, personality and behavior.* Chicago: Dorsey Press.

Bateson, G. (1972). A theory of play and fantasy. In *Steps to an ecology of mind.* (pp. 177–193). Northvale, NJ: Jason Aronson Inc. (Reprinted from *Psychiatric Research Reports, no.* 2 [1955], pp. 39–51, American Psychiatric Association.)

Bavelas, J. B., Black, A., Chovil, N., & Mullett, J. (1990). Truth, lies, and equivocations: The effects of conflicting goals on discourse. *Journal of Language and Social Psychology, 9,* 135–161.

Bratman, M. E. (1990). What is intention? In P. R. Cohen, J. Morgan & M. E. Pollack (Eds.), *Intentions in communication* (pp. 15–31). Cambridge, MA: MIT Press.

Brennan, S. E. (1990). *Seeking and providing evidence for mutual understanding.* Unpublished doctoral dissertation, Stanford University, Stanford, CA.

Brennan, S. E., & Clark, H. H. (1996). Conceptual pacts and lexical choice in conversation. *Journal of Experimental Psychology: Learning, Memory and Cognition, 22,* 1482–2493.

Brown, P., & Levinson, S. C. (1987). *Politeness: Some universals in language usage.* Cambridge, England: Cambridge University Press.

Bürkle, B., Nirmaier, H., & Herrmann, T. (1986). *"Von dir aus . . .": Zur hörerbezogenen lokalen Referenz* ["From your point of view . . . ": On listener-oriented local reference] (Bericht Nr. 10). Mannheim, Germany: University of Mannheim, Forschergruppe "Sprechen und Sprachverstehen im sozialen Kontext."

Carlson-Radvansky, L. A., & Irwin, D. E. (1994). Reference frame activation during spatial term assignment. *Journal of Memory and Language, 33,* 646–671.

Clark, E. V. (1987). The principle of contrast: A constraint on language acquisition. In B. MacWhinney (Ed.), *Mechanisms of language acquisition* (pp. 1–33). Hillsdale, NJ: Lawrence Erlbaum Associates.

Clark, E. V. (1990). Speaker perspective in language acquisition. *Linguistics, 28,* 1201–1220.

Clark, E. V. (1995). Speaker perspective and lexical acquisition. In S. Gahl, A. Dolbey, & C. Johnson (Eds.), *Proceedings of the 20th Annual Meeting [1994], Berkeley Linguistics Society* (pp. 125–133). Berkeley, CA: Department of Linguistics, University of California at Berkeley.

Clark, H. H. (1991). Words, the world and their possibilities. In G. Lockhead & J. Pomerantz (Eds.), *The perception of structure* (pp. 263–277). Washington, D.C.: American Psychological Association.

Clark, H. H. (1996). *Using language.* Cambridge, England: Cambridge University Press.

Clark, H. H., & Carlson, T. B. (1981). Context for comprehension. In J. Long & A. Baddeley (Eds.), *Attention and performance IX* (pp. 313–330). Hillsdale, NJ: Lawrence Erlbaum Associates.

Clark., H. H., & Carlson, T. B. (1982). Hearers and speech acts. *Language, 58I,* 332–373.

Clark, H. H., & Clark, E. V. (1977). *Psychology and language: An introduction to psycholinguistics.* New York: Harcourt Brace Jovanovitch.

Clark, H. H., & Gerrig, R. J. (1983). Understanding old words with new meanings. *Journal of Verbal Learning and Verbal Behavior, 22,* 591–608.

Clark, H. H., & Marshall, C. R. (1981). Definite reference and mutual knowledge. In A. H. Joshi, B. Webber, & I. A. Sag (Eds.), *Elements of discourse understanding* (pp. 10–63). Cambridge, England: Cambridge University Press.

Clark, H. H., & Schober, M. F. (1991). Asking questions and influencing answers. In J. M. Tanur (Ed.), *Questions about questions: Inquiries into the cognitive bases of surveys* (pp. 15–48). New York: Russell Sage Foundation.

Clark, H. H., & Wilkes-Gibbs, D. (1986). Referring as a collaborative process. *Cognition, 22,* 1–39.

Craig. R. T. (1986). Goals in discourse. In D. G. Ellis & W. A. Donohue (Eds.), *Contemporary issues in language and discourse processes* (pp. 257–272). Hillsdale, NJ: Lawrence Erlbaum Associates.

Craig, R. T. (1990). Multiple goals in discourse: An epilogue. *Journal of Language and Social Psychology, 9,* 163–170.

Craton, L. G., Elicker, J., Plumert, J. M., & Pick, H. L., Jr. (1990). Children's use of frames of reference in communication of spatial location. *Child Development, 61,* 1528–1543.

Davidson, D. (1980). *Essays on actions and events.* New York: Oxford University Press.

Egel, H., & Carroll, M. (1988). *Überlegungen zur Entwicklung eines integrierten linguistischen und sprachpsychologischen Klassifikationssystem für sprachliche Lokalisationen* [Considerations for the development of an integrated linguistic and psycholinguistic classification system for verbal localizations] (Bericht Nr. 18). Mannheim, Germany: University of Mannheim, Forschergruppe "Sprechen und Sprachverstehen im sozialen Kontext."

Fillmore, C. J. (1977). The case for case re-opened. In P. Cole & J. M. Sadock (Eds.), *Syntax and semantics: Vol. 8, Grammatical relations* (pp. 59–81). New York: Academic Press.

Fillmore, C. J. (1982). Towards a descriptive framework for spatial deixis. In R. J. Jarvella & W. Klein (Eds.), *Speech, place, and action* (pp. 31–59). Chichester, England: Wiley.

Fishbein, M., & Ajzen, I. (1975). *Belief, attitude, intention and behavior: An introduction to theory and research.* Reading, MA: Addison-Wesley.

Fisher, R. D., & Ury, W. (1981). *Getting to yes: Negotiating agreement without giving in.* Boston: Houghton Mifflin.

Flavell, J. H., Botkin, P. T., Fry, C. L., Jr., Wright, J. W., & Jarvis, P. E. (1968). *The development of role-taking and communication skills in children.* New York: John Wiley.

Fussell, S. R., & Krauss, R. M. (1989). The effects of intended audience on message production and comprehension: Reference in a common ground framework. *Journal of Experimental Social Psychology, 25,* 203–219.

Fussell, S. R., & Krauss, R. M. (1992). Coordination of knowledge in communication: Effects of speakers' assumptions about what others know. *Journal of Personality and Social Psychology, 62,* 378–391.

Garrod, S., & Anderson, A. (1987). Saying what you mean in dialogue: A study in conceptual and semantic co-ordination. *Cognition, 27,* 181–218.

Gottman, J., Notarius, C., Gonso, J., & Markman, H. (1976). *A couple's guide to communication*. Champaign, IL: Research Press.

Graumann, C. F. (1989). Perspective setting and taking in verbal interaction. In R. Dietrich & C. F. Graumann (Eds.), *Language processing in social context* (pp. 95–122). North-Holland: Elsevier Science Publishers.

Graumann, C. F., & Sommer, C. M. (1988). Perspective structure in language production and comprehension. *Journal of Language and Social Psychology, 7,* 193–212.

Grice, H. P. (1975). Logic and conversation. In P. Cole, & J. L. Morgan (Eds.), *Syntax and semantics: Vol. 3, Speech acts* (pp. 225–242). New York: Academic Press.

Hastorf, A., & Cantril, H. (1954). They saw a game: A case study. *Journal of Abnormal and Social Psychology, 49,* 129–134.

Herrmann, T., Dietrich, S., Egel, H., & Hornung, A. (1988). *Lokalisationssequenzen, Sprecherziele und Partnermerkmale: Ein Erkundungs-experiment* [Localization sequences, speaker goals, and partner features: An exploratory study] (Bericht Nr. 12). Mannheim, Germany: University of Mannheim, Forschergruppe "Sprechen und Sprachverstehen im sozialen Kontext."

Herrmann, T., & Grabowski, J. (1994). *Sprechen: Psychologie der Sprachproduktion* [Speaking: Psychology of speech production]. Heidelberg: Spektrum Akademischer Verlag.

Herskovits, A. (1986). *Language and spatial cognition: An interdisciplinary study of the prepositions in English.* Cambridge, England: Cambridge University Press.

Isaacs, E. A., & Clark, H. H. (1987). References in conversation between experts and novices. *Journal of Experimental Psychology: General, 116,* 26–37.

Isaacs, E. A., & Clark, H. H. (1990). Ostensible invitations. *Language in Society, 19,* 493–509.

Keysar, B. (1994). The illusory transparency of intention: Linguistic perspective taking in text. *Cognitive Psychology, 26,* 165–208.

Krauss, R. M., & Fussell, S. R. (1988). Other-relatedness in language processing: Discussion and comments. *Journal of Language and Social Psychology, 7,* 263–279.

Krauss, R. M., & Fussell, S. R. (1991). Perspective-taking in communication: Representations of others' knowledge in reference. *Social Cognition, 9,* 2–24.

Krauss, R. M., & Fussell, S. R. (1996). Social psychological models of interpersonal communication. In E. T. Higgins & A. Kruglanski (Eds.), *Social psychology: Handbook of basic principles* (pp. 655–701). New York: Guilford Press.

Lakoff, G., & Johnson, M. (1980). *Metaphors we live by.* Chicago: University of Chicago Press.

Lang, E., Carstensen, K.-U., & Simmons, G. (1991). *Modeling spatial knowledge on a linguistic basis* (Lecture Notes in Computer Science, Vol. 481). Berlin: Springer-Verlag.

Levelt, W. J. M. (1989). *Speaking: From intention to articulation.* Cambridge, MA: MIT Press.

Levelt, W. J. M. (1992). Fairness in reviewing: A reply to O'Connell. *Journal of Psycholinguistic Research, 21,* 401–403.

Levinson, S. C. (1979). Activity types and language. *Linguistics, 17,* 356–399.

Levinson, S. C. (1981). Some pre-observations on the modeling of dialogue. *Discourse Processes, 4,* 93–116.

Levinson, S. C. (1996). Frames of reference and Molyneux's question: Cross-linguistic evidence. In P. Bloom, M. A. Peterson, L. Nadel, & M. F. Garrett (Eds.), *Space and language,* (pp. 109–169). Cambridge, MA: MIT Press.

Linde, C., & Labov, W. (1975). Spatial networks as a site for the study of language and thought. *Language, 51,* 924–939.

Miller, G. A., & Johnson-Laird, P. N. (1976). *Language and perception.* Cambridge, MA: Harvard University Press.

Piaget, J. (1959). *The language and thought of the child.* New York: Harcourt, Brace.

Pick, H. L., Yonas, A., & Rieser, J. J. (1979). Spatial reference systems in perceptual development. In M. H. Bornstein & W. Kessen (Eds.), *Psychological development from infancy* (pp. 115–145). Hillsdale, NJ: Lawrence Erlbaum Associates.

Plumert, J. M., Carswell, C., De Vet, K., & Ihrig, D. (1995). The content and organization of communication about object locations. *Journal of Memory and Language, 34,* 477–498.

Ravn, K. (1987). *On calling things names.* Unpublished doctoral dissertation, Stanford University, Stanford, CA.

Regan, D., & Totten, J. (1975). Empathy and attribution: Turning observers into actors. *Journal of Personality and Social Psychology, 32,* 850–856.

Reithaug, T. (1984). Context effects on children's use of language. *Scandinavian Journal of Educational Research, 29,* 43–56.

Retz-Schmidt, G. (1988). Various views on spatial prepositions. *AI Magazine, 9,* 95–105.

Ross, L. (1977). The intuitive psychologist and his shortcomings: Distortions in the attribution process. In L. Berkowitz (Ed.), *Advances in experimental social psychology.* (Vol. 10, pp. 173–220). New York: Academic Press.

Russell, A. W., & Schober, M. F. (In press). How beliefs about a partner's goals affect referring in goal-discrepant conversations. *Discourse Processes.*

Saki (H. H. Munro) (1988). The unbearable Bassington. In *The complete works of Saki,* (pp. 569–687). New York: Dorset Press. (Reprinted from Saki [1912] *The unbearable Bassington.* London, England: The Bodley Head.)

Schiffer, S. R. (1972). *Meaning.* Oxford, England: Oxford University Press.

Schober, M. F. (1993). Spatial perspective-taking in conversation. *Cognition, 47,* 1–24.

Schober, M. F. (1995). Speakers, addressees, and frames of reference: Whose effort is minimized in conversations about locations? *Discourse Processes, 20,* 219–247.

Schober, M. F. (1997). How partners with high and low spatial ability choose perspectives in conversation. Manuscript in preparation.

Schober, M.F. (1996). Addressee- and object-centered frames of reference in spatial descriptions. *In P. L. Olivie, (Ed.), Cognitive and computational models of spatial representation: Papers from the 1996 AAAI Spring Symposium,* (pp. 92–100). Menlo Park, CA: The AAAI Press.

Schober, M.F. (in press). How addressees affect spatial perspective choice in dialogue. In P. L. Olivier & K.-P. Gapp, (Eds.), *Representation and processing of spatial expressions.* Mahwah, NJ: Lawrence Erlbaum Associates.

Schober, M. F., & Bloom, J. E. (1995, November). *The relative ease of producing egocentric, addressee-centered, and object-centered spatial descriptions*. Poster session presented at the 36th Annual Meeting of the Psychonomic Society, Los Angeles, CA.

Schober, M. F., & Clark, H. H. (1989). Understanding by addressees and overhearers. *Cognitive Psychology, 21,* 211–232.

Shatz, M., & Gelman, R. (1973). The development of communication skills: Modifications in the speech of young children as a function of the listener. *Monographs of the Society for Research in Child Development, 38,* 1–38.

Stein, N. L., Bernas, R. S., Calicchia, D. J., & Wright, A. (1996). Understanding and resolving arguments: The dynamics of negotiation. In B. K. Britton & A. G. Graesser (Eds.), *Models of understanding text* (pp. 257–287). Mahwah, NJ: Lawrence Erlbaum Associates.

Suchman, L., & Jordan, B. (1991). Validity and the collaborative construction of meaning in face-to-face surveys. In J. M. Tanur (Ed.), *Questions about questions: Inquiries into the cognitive bases of surveys* (pp. 241–267). New York: Russell Sage Foundation.

Talmy, L. (1975). Semantics and syntax of motion. In J. P. Kimball (Ed.), *Syntax and semantics*, (Vol. 4, pp. 181–238). New York: Academic Press.

Talmy, L. (1983). How language structures space. In H. L. Pick, Jr. & L. P. Acredolo (Eds.), *Spatial orientation: Theory, research, and application* (pp. 225–282). New York: Plenum Press.

Taylor, H. A., & Tversky, B. (1992). Spatial mental models derived from survey and route descriptions. *Journal of Memory and Language, 31,* 261–292.

Taylor, H.A., & Tversky, B. (1996). Perspective in spatial descriptions. *Journal of Memory and Language, 35,* 371–391.

Traxler, M. J., & Gernsbacher, M. A. (1993). Improving written communication through perspective-taking. *Language and Cognitive Processes, 8,* 311–334.

Ullmer-Ehrich, V., (1982). The structure of living space descriptions. In R. J. Jarvella & W. Klein (Eds.), *Speech, place, and action* (pp. 219–249). Chichester, England: Wiley.

Wilkes-Gibbs, D. (1986). *Collaborative processes of language use in conversation*. Unpublished doctoral dissertation, Stanford University, Stanford, CA.

Wittgenstein, L. (1958). *Philosophical investigations*. Oxford, England: Blackwell.

Wolfson, N. (1982). *CHP: The conversational historical present in American English*. Dordrecht, Netherlands: Foris.

— 8 —

Language Users as Problem Solvers: Just What Ambiguity Problem Do They Solve?

Boaz Keysar

University of Chicago

Everyone who uses language knows that it is ambiguous. Consider this excerpt from a recommendation letter: "Anybody who will get this fellow to work for him would indeed be fortunate." The writer might be either congratulating or warning future employers. Typically, the inherent ambiguity of language gets in the way of successful communication, or at least, it gets in the way of those who attempt to explain how communication succeeds even though language has such high potential for ambiguity.

Ambiguity abounds in all levels of language, from the pragmatic down to the phonological level. As Nusbaum and Henly (in press) observed, there is no one-to-one mapping between the linguistic stimulus and the intended meaning at any level of linguistic analysis. Consequently, theories of language must explain how language users overcome this problem. How do they typically arrive at a unique interpretation of a potentially multiple-meaning linguistic stimulus? In this chapter I briefly describe the major traditional theoretical solution to this problem at the semantic–pragmatic level and illustrate the theoretical and empirical problems associated with this solution.

I talk about "language users" in general but mainly focus on the problem that addressees, readers, and overhearers solve in interpreting utterances. Speakers face a similar problem when they attempt to construct utterances to be interpreted unambiguously by their addressees, but although the problem is similar, it is not obvious that the solution is the same. I discuss speakers' solutions briefly at the end of this chapter.

My main argument is that language users actually attempt to solve a problem different from the one that has traditionally been assumed. Therefore, the traditional approach is wrong in its assumption about the ambiguity problem that addressees solve. The traditional approach assumes that addressees solve the following problem: In view of the semantics of a sentence, or the literal meaning of an utterance, what is a speaker's intention? Of the different speech acts that a sentence can convey, which one does a speaker actually intend to convey? I argue that addressees do not attempt to solve this problem. Instead, they attempt to solve the following problem: In view of the meaning of this utterance from my perspective, or given the intention this utterance conveys when interpreted from my perspective, what did the speaker actually intend?

THE PERSPECTIVE–FREE APPROACH

Linguistic theory and philosophy of language have provided a clean, elegant solution to the ambiguity problem in language by proposing that people use *literal meaning* as an anchor. Literal meaning has received bad press in psycholinguistics during the last 10 years, but the basic idea is both highly attractive theoretically and intuitively appealing. The traditional theory assumes that sentences have a meaning that is context independent, a meaning that any competent language user can compose from knowledge of the meaning of words and rules of composition (e.g., Katz & Fodor, 1963). One way to "identify" literal meaning is with the "anonymous letter criterion"—a sentence's meaning that a person arrives at when given the sentence with no context whatsoever (Katz, 1972). This notion is attractive because it sounds intuitively right. People feel as if they know the literal meaning of "the cat is on the mat." More important, this idea simplifies theories, and ties them to a long tradition in philosophy of mind, a tradition that developed a logic to represent semantic relations giving rise to literal meaning (Ayer, 1936; Carnap, 1956). This notion also provides a simple starting point for computer simulations of language use, and it draws a clear line between meaning and actual language use. If meaning is anchored in literal meanings, then all that is left to explain is how people use meaning to convey intentions.

What is the Problem that Language Users Solve? Language users must solve the many-to-many mapping between utterances and intentions (Nusbaum & Henly, in press). In the literal-meaning tradition, the anchor of linguistic computation is the literal meaning. Therefore, the problem of an addressee in this tradition is construed as "In view of the literal meaning of an utterance, what did the speaker intend?" In Grice's (1968) terms, the problem is to get from what a speaker said to what that speaker intended, or to the "speaker meaning." The traditional solution is Grice's important insight: Because linguistic communication is a cooperative behavior, language users observe norms of cooperation. When a sentence meaning seems to violate these norms, the speaker's meaning is different from the sentence meaning (Grice, 1975). In an analogous solution proposed by Searle (1975) as part of Speech Act theory, literal meaning is the basis for computation of intention. When a literal meaning conflicts with a context, an indirect speech act is computed as the speaker's intention.

Evaluation of the Traditional Solution

The traditional solution has been extremely influential and is taken for granted across the board in cognitive science disciplines. Yet in the last 15 years, research in psycholinguistics has tended to undermine some assumptions of this solution. Gibbs (1984, 1994) argues strongly against the very concept of literal meaning; he suggests that literal meaning is an ill-defined concept and that many utterances do not have a unique, identifiable literal meaning. Gibbs also challenges the context-free aspect of literal meaning, which he finds both conceptually and psychologically inadequate concept.

Further, the assumptions of the traditional view did not hold under empirical investigation. The stage model implied by Searle and certain interpretations of Grice's theories assume that a nonliteral meaning is computed only when a literal meaning is rejected. This assumption, which predicts that nonliteral meaning should take longer to comprehend than does literal meaning, has been refuted by several studies demonstrating that, with appropriate context, figurative language such as metaphors and idioms as well as indirect speech acts do not take longer to understand than does literal meaning (e.g., Gerrig, 1989; Gibbs, 1979, 1983, 1984; Ortony, Schallert, Reynolds, & Antos, 1978). The only exception to these results is the finding that a metaphorical reference takes longer to determine than does a literal reference (Gibbs, 1990), but so far it is unclear why referential metaphors show delayed comprehension when comparable nominative metaphors do not (Onishi & Murphy, 1993). Empirical research has also refuted the traditional assumption that comprehension of nonliteral language requires the literal meaning to be anomalous. Glucksberg, Gildea, and Bookin (1982) demonstrated that familiar metaphors are understood automatically, and Keysar (1989) showed that this understanding occurs whether the sentence has a semantically adequate or anomalous literal meaning.

The traditional approach assumes that language users make inferences when they attribute intentions to speakers, but such inferences are supposed to take place only when a meaning diverges from the literal meaning. Language users supposedly attribute a literal meaning to a speaker if the literal meaning makes sense; but when they attribute a nonliteral meaning to a speaker they make an inference about the status of the literal meaning. In contrast, experiments that I have conducted suggest that inferences about a speaker's intended meaning occur in a much more symmetrical manner than has been previously assumed (Keysar, 1994a; Keysar & Glucksberg, 1993). The experiments demonstrate that under some conditions readers follow the inference assumed by traditional theories: Readers infer a metaphorical interpretation because they reject a potential literal interpretation. Yet the experiments also demonstrate that under the same conditions readers do the same thing when they arrive at a *literal* interpretation:

Readers infer a literal interpretation because they reject a potential metaphorical interpretation.

This symmetry of inference is embodied in an example from Kosinski's 1971 book *Being There*. At a certain point in the book, the President of the United States deplored the economic situation and then turned to a Mr. Gardiner for his opinion. Mr. Gardiner responded: "In a garden [. . .] growth has its season. There are spring and summer, but there are also fall and winter. And then spring and summer again. As long as the roots are not severed, all is well and all will be well" (p. 45). The President was supposed to follow the traditional inference and probably inferred that Mr. Gardiner must have been speaking metaphorically. In contrast, readers who know that the speaker is a gardener who knows about nothing else make the mirror image inference: They infer that Mr. Gardiner was speaking literally.

The symmetry between the comprehension of literal and nonliteral utterances goes even further. Glucksberg and Keysar (1990) demonstrated that a metaphorical sentence of the form "An A is a B," which has been traditionally thought of as an implicit comparison ("An A is (like) a B"), is actually understood as a true class-inclusion statement. So when people understand "A cigarette is a time bomb," they understand it as categorizing a cigarette in the superordinate category that borrows the name "time bomb." Moreover, Gernsbacher and Keysar (1995) demonstrated that the same comprehension mechanisms underlying comprehension in general and language comprehension in particular operate in exactly the same way in the comprehension of metaphorical sentences.

Despite the lack of empirical support for the traditional view, the issue is by no means resolved and is still under lively debate. The assumptions of literal meaning still implicitly and sometimes explicitly pervade theories of language use (e.g., Dascal, 1987). In light of this perplexing situation, researchers have hypothesized the existence of "anchors," which might serve as alternatives to literal meaning. One such suggestion has been extensively developed by Raymond Gibbs in his 1994 book *The Poetics of Mind*. In contrast to the traditional assumption about the primacy of literal meaning, Gibbs suggests that the human mind is based on nonliteral principles. He argues that human thought is metaphorical and metonymic and that language reflects these basic conceptual relations (cf. Lakoff, 1987; Lakoff & Johnson, 1980). Gibbs supports his argument in favor of a conceptual metaphor-based approach with a variety of empirical findings (Gibbs, 1992; Gibbs & Nayak, 1991; Gibbs & O'Brien, 1990). As a whole, Gibbs' ideas have the potential to challenge basic principles in cognitive science (Keysar, 1996), but it is still too soon to determine the extent to which this approach can account for actual language use (Keysar & Bly, in press). Specifically, before accepting this conceptual metaphor approach, researchers must answer strong objections raised by Gregory Murphy, who argues that the current version of a conceptual metaphor theory is not theoretically coherent and that the supporting data can be better accounted for by an alternative view (Murphy, 1996).

PROPOSING AN ALTERNATIVE: A PERSPECTIVE-DEPENDENT APPROACH

I propose that the crux of what is wrong with the traditional approach is the way it construes the problem that an addressee attempts to solve in interpreting an utterance. The traditional assumption is that the addressee solves the problem of a speaker's intention in view of the literal meaning of an utterance. This solution assumes an anchor that is context-free and perspective-free. In other words, the literal meaning of an utterance does not depend on a speaker's or addressee's perspective but is "given" in the language. Research in psycholinguistics has provided a compelling case against the assumption of context-free computation. In fact, experimental evidence has demonstrated that addressees use context incrementally to create temporary interpretations as utterances unfold (Tanenhaus, Spivey-Knowlton, Eberhard & Sedivy, 1995). Because addressees use context to constrain potential interpretation, what interpretation problem do they solve? I propose a new explanation for the interpretation problem.

What *is* the Problem that Language Users Solve?

I propose that the interpretation problem is a function of perspective. The notion of perspective has been extensively investigated in the social sciences and consequently, like the notion of meaning, has too many different meanings (e.g., Anderson & Pichert, 1978; Cox, 1977; Graumann, 1989; Graumann & Herrmann, 1988; Krauss & Fussell, 1988; Long & Andrews, 1990; Mead, 1934; Piaget & Inhelder, 1956; Rommetveit, 1974; Schober, 1993; Traxler & Gernsbacher, 1993; Yaniv & Shatz, 1990). Krauss and Fussell (1996) provide a comprehensive review of the literature on perspective-taking in the context of models of communication. As Krauss and Fussell (1996) point out, most research on perspective-taking in communication focuses on the way that speakers attempt to take the perspective of addressees. Consequently, little is known about the way addressees, readers, and overhearers take the perspectives of speakers and writers. My proposal is targeted at understanding the interpretation problem that addressees solve in terms of perspective.

I use the term *perspective* to refer to access to information. An addressee's perspective is the information that the addressee has access to. Similarly, a speaker's perspective defines the information to which the speaker has access. The interaction between different perspectives in discourse can be considered in the following way: An addressee has a perspective, a speaker has a perspective, and these perspectives might overlap. To the extent that the perspective overlap is mutually known to speaker and addressee, this overlap constitutes mutual knowledge (Clark & Marshall, 1981) or part of the common ground between them (Clark, Schreuder, & Buttrick, 1983). In other words, if both speaker and addressee know that they mutually share information, this information is their mutual perspective. When addressees interpret utterances, they can in principle use one of the three perspectives: (a) They can use their own perspectives to arrive at an interpretation that uses egocentric information; (b) they can use a speaker's perspective; or (c) they can use the common perspective, their mutual knowledge.

Together with students in my laboratory (Keysar, Barr, Balin, & Paek, 1997), I have proposed that addressees follow the first interpretation strategy: They interpret utterances in a context-sensitive manner, but the context is their own, given by their own perspective and insensitive to what they know about the speaker's perspective. This interpretation strategy sometimes leads them astray, especially when a speaker's meaning depends on the mutuality of perspective. With this model in mind, I propose that the problem that an addressee solves is the following: In view of the interpretation from my perspective, what did the speaker intend? In other words, did the speaker intend the (egocentrically) computed intention, or could the speaker have had a different intention in mind? To solve this problem, our model assumes an adjusting correction mechanism that attempts to take into account the common perspective whenever the interpretation from an addressee's own perspective fails. Hence the model is named the *Perspective Adjustment Model*.

The proposed model (Keysar et al., 1997) makes the following assumptions about the two different processes. The process that generates an interpretation from an addressee's perspective is what the "comprehension system" knows how to do best; it is quick, efficient and relatively automatic. In contrast, the adjustment process that incorporates a speaker's perspective is relatively slow and dependent on available resources. This process attempts to implement what addressees know they "should" do. Addressees believe that they should take the speaker's perspective, that they should use the mutual perspective, and so on. This intuitive theory that addressees hold about communication is high-level knowledge that prescribes behavior. By using this intuitive theory, addressees attempt to be in line with normative rules of cooperative behavior.

The model does not make a strong assumption about serial versus parallel processing. There is no reason to assume that the "check" for violation of mutual perspective must be initiated only after an interpretation process is completed. Therefore, the two processes might be operating in parallel. We do not make an assumption of serial processing and it is possible that the time course of the two processes is different. Consequently, the faster, "egocentric" process is more likely to quickly constrain the interpretation and to result in a need for a correction whenever a check for violation of mutual perspective detects that addressees used information they "should" not have.

How is this model different from the traditional model? Apart from the obvious differences, the model assumes a different building block for interpretation, a contextualized, computed intention instead of a "context free" literal meaning. Also, instead of a perspective-free basic meaning, it assumes that even the basic computation is perspective-bound. An addressee's perspective determines the context used for the computation. The resulting interpretation from an addressee's perspective, then, is an intention: a particular speech act. By using their own perspectives as the basis for interpretation, addressees face a simpler ambiguity problem because their perspectives put constraints on the possible meanings that each utterance can convey. Therefore, the problem of the inherent ambiguity of language is sharply reduced: Even though each utterance can in principle have a large number of interpretations, addressees are not typically faced with all these potential interpretations, only with the interpretations specific to their perspective.

The general approach and the model I have described give rise to a variety of interesting predictions. In the rest of this chapter, I will review empirical studies that support implications of the perspective-bound approach.

ARE LANGUAGE USERS PERSPECTIVE–BOUND?

Illusion of Transparency

In general, the perspective-bound approach implies that language users perceive language as relatively unambiguous because they do not perceive utterances but perceive perspective-bound interpreted utterances. That is, they perceive utterances as "carrying" a *particular,* and often unique intention, even when the same utterance can convey other intentions. When Terry Gross interviewed Peter O'Toole on National Public Radio, the actor explained that he had been spending much of his time on writing his memoirs.

> *Terry*:   So how much are you acting now?
> *Peter*:   I am not acting at all [pause] . . . I am just sitting here
>   with the headphones on trying to answer your questions.

Both interlocutors seem to have had a particular interpretation for the ambiguous utterance "How much are you acting now?" The miscommunication resulted because both considered only their own interpretations and did not take into account alternative interpretations of the ambiguous utterance.[1] Each seems to have thought the meaning to be relatively transparent or as adequate to the utterance. In my model, interpretations or perceived intended meanings generally *seem* relatively transparent to language users: Once an ambiguous utterance is interpreted in a unique way, the interpretation seems more adequate than possible alternative interpretations. Therefore, to the extent that utterances are ambiguous, their potential ambiguity should be underestimated, and the extent to which a particular utterance seems to carry an intention should be overestimated. This implication derives from the model's assumption that a language user's own perspective is the basis for disambiguating utterances. I review several experiments that reveal different facets of such illusion of transparency in language.

Overestimation of the Transparency of Idiomatic Meaning. Idioms are by definition expressions whose meanings are not a compositional function of their words. In the prototypically opaque idiom "to kick the bucket," the connection of the expression to its meaning (to die) is not at all transparent. Yet many idioms seem relatively transparent to native speakers of a language. For example, native English speakers think that "to go against the wind" is transparent: It apparently makes sense to them that the idiom means to do something the hard way. For instance, walking against the direction of the wind is harder than walking in the same direction because of the wind's resistance. Together with Bridget Bly, I investigated this subjective feeling of transparency. We hypothesized that native speakers of a language perceive such idioms as more transparent than they actually are (Keysar & Bly, 1995, in press).

Our argument was that once language users know the actual meaning of the idiom and once it makes sense to them, they discount the possibility that alternative meanings could make just as much sense. They also discount the possibility that the actual meaning would not make as much sense as it does had they not learned it as the idiomatic meaning of the expression. This argument is counterintuitive: If "to go against the wind" meant to do something with greater ease, then this hypothetical meaning would make a lot of sense and its opposite meaning (to do something the hard way) would be perceived as less transparent.

To investigate our hypothesis, we used archaic English idioms that are no longer in common use, such as "the goose hangs high." We taught participants that the idiom meant either that the future is highly promising (the original meaning) or that the future is very gloomy. We demonstrated that once people learn a meaning for the idiom, they perceive this meaning as relatively transparent—a reaction that did not depend on whether they learned the real, original meaning of the idiom or its conceptual opposite.

---

[1]It is also possible that O'Toole was joking and only pretended to misunderstand Terry Gross.

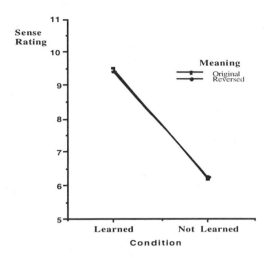

FIG. 8.1. Ratings of the extent to which idioms make sense as a measure of perceived transparency. Both the original and the reversed meanings were perceived as more transparent than their opposite meaning when they were learned as the "true" meaning of the idiom (From "Intuitions of the Transparency of Idioms," by B. Keysar & B. Bly, 1995, *Journal of Memory and Language, 34,* p.101.) Copyright 1995. Reprinted with permission).

The illusion of transparency was revealed in two ways. First, we reasoned that if participants think that one meaning of the idiom makes more sense than another, they should believe that an uninformed person would agree on the idiom's meaning. Indeed, once they learned a particular meaning they did think that an uninformed individual would be more likely to think that the idiom meant what they believed it to mean than they would the opposite meaning. We also directly tested how transparent a learned meaning becomes by asking participants to rate how much sense each meaning makes, and a learned meaning was perceived as much more sensible than its opposite (Figure 8.1). Moreover, the more they used the idiom with the learned meaning in mind, the less sense the alternative meaning made to them. These findings suggest that our participants thought the meaning they learned was "carried" by the expression and was more transparent than the alternative meaning. Furthermore, the feeling of transparency is to a large extent a function of the belief that the idiom has a particular meaning and of the effort involved in making sense of that meaning.

Perhaps our results could not possibly be generalized from unused, archaic idioms to those that are used in current language; perhaps the example of "to go against the wind" is strong counterevidence. No native English speakers in their right minds would believe that had the idiom meant doing something with relative ease, this meaning would have made sense. Indeed, any idiom dictionary reveals numerous idioms of the form "to (verb) against (noun)," as in "to go against the grain," and all these idioms refer to an activity done the hard way. Such an objection, however, reflects the presence of the intuition of inflated transparency that we are arguing about. As an exercise, try to imagine a situation in which going against the wind is actually easier than going with it. Pilots know that a head wind facilitates takeoff and the same is true for trying to fly a kite. After this exercise, the alternative meaning makes a bit more sense. A hard-core skeptic might still argue that if this meaning makes sense, then there would be examples of such idioms in the language. In fact, there is at least one such example, in which an expression of the form "to (verb) against (noun)" is used to convey ease of movement. Commuters want to travel against traffic; the idea makes sense.

Transparency of Intentions. Our findings with idiom transparency reflect the way human minds attempt to make sense of linguistic expressions that result in overestimation of transparency of meaning. But this overestimation should not affect communication among native speakers of a language because the meanings of idioms are highly conventional. Most native speakers of English know the meaning of "to go against the wind," and consequently they share the meaning's sense of transparency. But when a native speaker speaking to a non-native speaker of English chooses to use an idiom, the speaker might expect that the other person understands the idiom because of the false sense of transparency. Yet the issue of overestimated transparency might be much more pervasive than in the relatively constrained case of idiomatic meaning. Pragmatic intentions are generally expected to be perceived as relatively transparent. Because every utterance can convey more than one speech act, the illusion of transparency of intention should be fairly pervasive, if we are correct.

In a study demonstrating that young children behave as if speakers' intentions are relatively transparent, Olson (1991; Olson & Torrance, 1987) described a situation in which experimenters told 5- to 8-year-old children a story about Lucy. Lucy has two pairs of red shoes, one old and one new. She wanted Linus to bring her the new shoes but asked him for her "red shoes." Even though the reference is ambiguous, the children tended to believe that the expression actually referred to the intended pair of shoes, as if they took the expression to be transparent vis-à-vis the actual *intention* of the speaker.

Of course, such a result can also be explained in other ways. The experiment might reveal nothing about overestimation of the transparency of intentions; instead it might reveal young children's confusion about who knows what.

They might have difficulty keeping track of what character in a story has access to what information, as much research on the development of theory of mind has suggested (e.g., Astington, Harris, & Olson, 1988; Perner, Leekam, & Wimmer, 1987; Wellman, 1990). Although this explanation is possible, I argue that this finding actually points to a fundamental aspect of language use, which extends beyond young children and holds for adults as well (Keysar, 1993). I argue that adults and children alike tend to perceive intentions as relatively transparent and by doing so underestimate the ambiguity of utterances. Adults and children differ, of course, but the main difference is that adults have acquired strategies to compensate for this basic tendency. Part of becoming a competent user of a language involves learning strategies to adjust from a relatively egocentric perspective and to correct for the perspective of others. I describe adults' basic illusion of transparency and then turn to the hypothesized adjustment processes.

What would it mean for adults to overestimate the transparency of intentions? Imagine the following situation: Jane and John go to a movie that is supposed to be fairly good. Both hate the movie because they think it pretentious and boring. As they leave the theater they spot a mutual friend, Mary, who is about to go to the next showing. John then comments to Mary, with a straight face and flat intonation, "You are just going to love this movie." John is being sarcastic, but, as the utterance was ambiguous, does Mary perceive the intended sarcasm? From Mary's perspective, because she does not know whether Jane and John actually liked the movie, both sarcastic and nonsarcastic interpretations are possible. Jane knows that Mary does not know John's true opinion of the movie. This situation is analogous to the young child's position, when the child knows that Linus does not know which shoes Lucy is asking for. My prediction is that Jane would underestimate the ambiguity of John's utterance because she knows what he intended. In this case, Jane knows that John was being sarcastic; thus she would tend to overestimate the extent to which Mary would be able to perceive his intended meaning.

I have documented this phenomenon in a variety of studies (Keysar, 1994b, 1995). In a typical experiment participants read scenarios such as this (for more examples see the appendix in Keysar, 1994b):

Mark asked his office mate, June, to recommend a restaurant; his parents were in town, and he wanted to take them to a good place. "I strongly recommend this new Italian place, called Venezia. I just had dinner there last night and it was marvelous. Let me know how you all enjoy it." That evening, Mark and his parents ate there; the food was unimpressive and the service was mediocre. The next morning, Mark said to her: "You wanted to know about the restaurant, well, marvelous, just marvelous."

In this scenario, the participants knew that Mark was being sarcastic because they knew that he did not enjoy the dinner. In a comparison scenario, the information was identical, except that Mark enjoyed the dinner. In this case, participants typically thought that Mark was not being sarcastic.

The participants' main task was to evaluate the addressee's perspective. In this case, they decided whether June would perceive Mark's message as sarcastic or sincere. In principle, if participants evaluate the utterance and whatever contextual information June might have, they should provide the same answer in both cases. Their evaluation of June's interpretation should not be affected by their privileged information about the valence of Mark's experience (positive or negative) or about what Mark actually intended. In contrast, if they take the utterance as less ambiguous after they know what Mark intended, then they should conclude that June will be more likely to perceive sarcasm when Mark actually intended it than when he did not. This is precisely what happened. In several experiments, participants tended to perceive the intended meaning as relatively transparent and to believe that addressees would be more likely to perceive it than an alternative meaning (Figure 8.2). The measure of transparency is the *difference* between the two conditions, not the absolute number: The phenomenon is demonstrated by the fact that with negative event information participants attribute *more* perception of sarcasm to an addressee than they do with positive event information.

There is one caveat here. I could explain the results differently by assuming that participants inferred that Mark conveyed the sarcasm with his intonation. If he did, then the results should depend on the fact that Mark said the utterance. To test this possibility we compared the same two conditions with an additional change: Instead of "telling" June that the dinner was marvelous, Mark left her a note. The results were identical. The phenomenon (i.e., the difference between the negative and positive information) was the same regardless of the modality of Mark's utterance. Therefore it is safe to conclude that these results genuinely reflect an illusion of transparency of intentions.

This conclusion led us to explore an even more radical possibility. Perhaps the illusion of transparency of intentions originates from a speaker's communicative intentions, or what Grice (1968) termed m-intention: an intention which is supposed to have its effect on an addressee by virtue of the addressee's realizing that the speaker wanted him or her to perceive this intention. For example, if I would like my 3-year-old to eat an apple, I could tell him, "Please eat the apple." My m-intention is fairly clear; I want him to realize that I would like him to eat the apple. Because he probably would not eat the apple under these circumstances, I might get him to do so by saying instead, "This apple is for me." In both cases I had an intention to get him to eat the apple, but only in the first case was the intention also an m-intention. In the experiment, Mark's sarcasm was a communicative intention. It is possible,

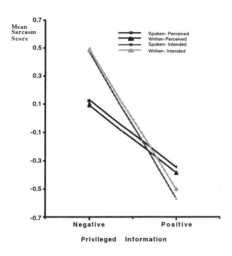

FIG. 8.2. Ratings of intended and perceived sarcasm. The intended meaning ratings indicate that speakers were perceived as more sarcastic when an event was negative than when it was positive. The perceived meaning ratings indicate that participants attributed to uninformed addressees the perception of sarcasm more when the event was negative then when it was positive—both when the message was spoken and when it was written. (From "The Illusory Transparency of Intention," by B. Keysar [1994], *Cognitive Psychology, 26,* p. 183. Copyright 1994. Reprinted with permission.)

then, that participants perceived Mark's sarcastic intention as transparent because it was an m-intention.

To test this hypothesis we separated the intended meaning from the information itself (Keysar, 1995). Recall the restaurant story. In addition to the two cases where the event was either positive or negative, we added a condition in which the event was negative: Mark hated the restaurant, but "Mark did not want June to feel bad." Mark had a bad experience, but his utterance, "Marvelous, just marvelous," was no longer sarcastic. Instead of a sarcastic m-intention, he was telling a white lie. When Mark attempted to conceal the way he really felt, his m-intention conveyed a sincere gratitude. As we expected, when we eliminated the sarcastic m-intention, there was no longer a difference in participants' attribution of perceived intention to the addressee (Figure 8.3). Even though the privileged information was negative, participants did not use it when taking the addressee's perspective. Instead, they relied on the inferred communicative intention. Because the m-intention was the same with the positive event as with the white lie, they attributed the same perceived intention to the addressee. Perhaps, then, Gricean m-intentions are at the core of the illusion of transparency of intentions.

In a pilot study, we also demonstrated that the phenomenon generalizes to other speech acts. For example, in one scenario a speaker said, "I haven't seen Donald for ages." The speaker was either making an informative statement or an indirect request to be invited to a dinner with Donald. Overall, participants tended to attribute to the addressee the perception of the speaker's actual intention, which was privileged to them.

But, a skeptic might say, perhaps the participants are simply confused about who knows what. If this is the case, then there is no illusion of transparency of intention, but instead participants have difficulty keeping track of who has access to what information. I propose that this is an unlikely explanation for the findings in the studies I mentioned. There are two main reasons to doubt it. First, Graesser, Bowers, Bayen, and Hu (in press) found that readers are very good at keeping track of who knows what and rarely confuse protagonists' accessibility to information. Their findings suggest that people have the tools to identify who has access to what information and are able to keep this information in memory. What our findings suggest is that people do not *use* this information when they evaluate the interpretation of an utterance from the perspective of a protagonist. They do not discount the information privileged to

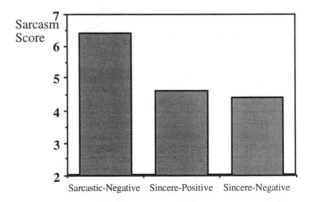

FIG. 8.3. Ratings of perceived sarcasm by addressee. The higher the number, the more participants thought that the addressee perceives sarcasm. Attribution of perception of sarcasm was a function of the speaker's m-intention (sarcasm or sincerity), not a function of the event's valence.

them, information that they know the protagonist does not know. Why? The reason, I suggest, is that they use their privileged information to disambiguate the speaker's utterance; afterward, the intention seems relatively transparent to them. The other reason to doubt this alternative explanation is that the phenomenon seems to be tightly related to inferred m-intentions, not simply to the privileged information about facts (e.g., good or bad experience at the restaurant). As Figure 8.3 illustrates, when Mark attempts to conceal the facts, participants no longer attribute the perception of sarcasm to the addressee. If they were simply confused about who knows what, their knowledge about the negative experience at the restaurant should have caused the same effect regardless of Mark's m-intention; in other words, the white lie condition and the negative information condition should have yielded similar results.

These findings support one aspect of the proposed model: They demonstrate that there is a general tendency to underestimate the ambiguity of utterances once the intended meaning is computed. Consequently, language users experience an illusion of transparency of intention.

Perspective Adjustments

Language users do know about perspective differences. They have metaknowledge about knowledge. Such metaknowledge includes knowledge about who knows what. They also know that they should not use information that is inaccessible to an addressee when taking the perspective of such addressee. In the model that we have proposed (Keysar, et al., 1997), we assume that language users make allowances for others' perspectives. In the case of addressees, whenever their perspectives diverge from a speaker's, then egocentric interpretation is adjusted. Overhearers, as in our sarcasm experiments, adjust to approximate the perspective of the addressee to evaluate the intention that the addressee would perceive. In general, we hypothesized an adjustment process that uses metaknowledge to compensate for perspective differences. In this sense, language users arrive at a mutual perspective only via a corrective process. The correction is a function of language users' application of normative knowledge about how communication takes place.

If language users make adjustments for perspective, why then do we find a relatively egocentric attribution of intended meaning in the sarcasm experiments? If they know that June does not know how much Mark enjoyed the dinner, the adjustment to June's perspective should lead them to the same answer when he liked the dinner and when he did not. The only way the model can explain the fact that we did find a difference between the two cases is by assuming that the adjustment was incomplete. Such incomplete adjustment processes have been demonstrated for a variety of judgment tasks (Tversky & Kahneman, 1974). In general, people's estimate of a particular value could be anchored even in relatively irrelevant value information. In our case, we expected a person's own perspective to act as an effective anchor and we evaluated this possibility with the following assumptions: The adjustment process is relatively slow and cognitively-taxing whereas an egocentric interpretation of a speaker's intent is relatively quick and easy. If this assumption is correct, perspective-taking under pressure should affect the adjustment process and result in greater underadjustment than when participants perform the task without pressure.

To test this hypothesis we replicated the same experiment with the scenarios that had either negative or positive event information—Mark had either a good or a bad dinner experience. The crucial addition to the design was a manipulation of pressure to respond. In one case, participants were instructed to take their time and ponder their answer. In the other case they were required to answer as quickly as they could. As the model predicts, when participants were under time pressure to respond, the effect was much larger than when they responded at their leisure (Keysar, 1995). We interpreted this pattern to mean that under pressure, a participant is more likely to fall back on his or her own interpretation and attribute the perception of that interpretation to the addressee. This idea suggests that the perspective of the addressee was indeed considered only as part of a correction process. The time course of the speeded participants provided another piece of evidence. In the case when Mark hated the restaurant and left a sarcastic note, a participant might answer that June would perceive sarcasm or that she would not. According to the model, only the second answer (no sarcasm would be perceived) is the result of an adjustment, and so this answer should take longer than a response that does not require an adjustment. Indeed, responses that the model assumes are the result of adjustment took longer than responses that are less likely to be the result of such an adjustment process.

Do Addressees Adjust? Once we discovered that readers and observers follow the Perspective Adjustment model we were intrigued by the possibility that the model is a general model of linguistic perspective-taking. If so, addressees should follow the same course: They should construct interpretations that are perspective-bound, but should also use their metaknowledge to adjust to a speaker's or their mutual perspective.

Consider the way addressees disambiguate referential expressions: John welcomes his daughter's friend Mary into the house, and Mary says, "Is she ready?" How does John identify a referent for the pronoun *she*? In virtually any theory of pronoun resolution (e.g., Gernsbacher, 1989, 1990; McKoon, Ward, & Ratcliff, 1993), he searches his memory for potential female referents and selects his daughter, whom he knows is preparing to go out. But suppose that he also knows that his wife is getting ready to go out with him, and he knows that Mary does not know this. Clearly, Mary could not have referred to John's wife because she does not have access to the information that the wife is getting ready at the same time. If John searches for potential referents of the speaker, his wife should not be in the referent set. In contrast, the Perspective Adjustment model makes the counterintuitive prediction that he might actually consider his wife as a potential referent of the pronoun *she*. In this case, the expression "Is she ready?" is ambiguous from John's perspective because it could refer either to his wife or to his daughter. The model also predicts that he will make allowances for Mary's perspective and eventually arrive at the intended referent, his daughter, via a correction process. If so, then the very presence of the information about his wife should result in interference.

These results occurred in an experiment reported in Keysar, et al. (1997). We modeled an experiment after the situation with John's wife and daughter and demonstrated that when privileged information provides a potential referent for a pronoun, addressees are slower to respond correctly and they make more errors than when the privileged information does not include a potential referent for the pronoun. This finding strongly suggests that addressees interpret utterances without regard to a speaker's perspective, but make adjustments when they are needed.

When People Speak. Research on language production has reported that speakers tailor their utterances to addressees (e.g., Clark & Marshall, 1981; Clark & Murphy, 1982; Krauss & Fussell, 1991; Levelt, 1989). For example, Krauss and Fussell (1991) discuss several experiments showing that speakers produce different descriptions depending on their intended addressees, and that intended addressees understand these utterances better than do nonintended addressees. Although current research demonstrates that speakers can take their addressees' perspective into account, it has not shown how they do it. In general, process models of production (e.g., Bock, 1995; Fromkin, 1971; Garrett, 1988; Levelt, 1989) have identified a variety of processes. Researchers have agreed that some processes are involved in conceptually designing an utterance, some in putting it in linguistic form, and some in monitoring and revising utterance plans. Speakers could use their addressees' perspectives or mutual perspectives when they design their utterances. In contrast, it is possible that speakers incorporate their addressees' perspective only as part of a correction mechanism. Because utterance production need not be a mirror image of utterance comprehension, both are viable options. Horton and Keysar (1996) hypothesized that when speakers plan their utterances, these plans are not audience-sensitive; they are not designed for specific addressees in a way that takes into account their mutual perspective. We also argued that as part of utterance monitoring, speakers detect and correct utterances that violate principles of audience design (Clark & Murphy, 1982). This "monitoring and adjustment" model, then, assumes that speakers take into account their addressees' perspectives only as part of the monitoring process.

To investigate the predictions of the model, Horton and Keysar (1996) asked people to describe simple shapes for addressees. The shapes appeared in a context that was either privileged to the speakers or shared with the addressees. For example, people described a circle in the context of a larger circle, and the context circle was either seen by both speaker and addressee or only by the speaker. We measured the extent to which the speakers relied on context by looking at the adjectives they used. In this case, referring to the circle as "small" indicated use of context. Overall, speakers relied on shared context more than they relied on privileged context. This fact is not surprising because they knew that the privileged context was inaccessible to their addressees. The question is, how did speakers incorporate this perspective information?

On the basis of our model, the difference between the shared and privileged context conditions is due to the monitoring function. Therefore, the model predicts that under pressure to initiate an utterance, speakers would be less able to monitor and that consequently they would not adjust for their addressees' perspectives. Indeed, when we asked speakers to initiate their utterances within 1.5 seconds the differences between context conditions disappeared. Speakers relied on shared and privileged contexts to the same degree (See Figure 8.4). We interpreted this finding to mean that under pressure, speakers produce an utterance that is a closer reflection of the utterance plan. This utterance plan does not take into account another's perspective. Only when speakers monitor do they detect cases that require adjustment and correct for perspective discrepancies. We presented evidence for pre-articulatory monitoring and correction, but it is possible that overt repairs function similarly.

Perspective Adjustment and Collaboration. The study of conversation has given rise to what Krauss and Fussell (1996) call "dialogic models" (e.g., Clark & Schaefer, 1989; Clark & Wilkes-Gibbs, 1986; Wilkes-Gibbs & Clark, 1992). Such models focus on the collaborative nature of a conversational interchange. By analyzing conversations, these researchers have demonstrated the ways that participants collaborate to arrive at a successful interaction. For example, Clark and Schaefer (1989) showed that conversations are composed of units of presentation and acceptance, where one party presents an utterance to the other and the conversation progresses only after the other party signals that he or she understands and therefore accepts the presentation. Wilkes-Gibbs and Clark (1992) further demonstrated that interlocutors are sensitive to their party's knowledge of referents: They provide longer descriptions of referents when their addressee is new to the conversation than when they had already conversed with the addressee about the topic.

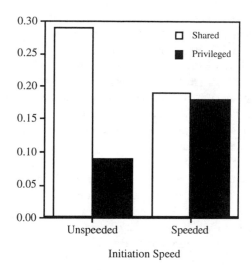

FIG. 8.4. Mean ratio of context-related adjectives to the total number of adjectives plus nouns per description as an index of reliance on context. Although speakers relied on shared context more than on privileged context when not speeded, they relied on shared and privileged context to the same degree when speeded in initiating their utterances. (From "When do Speakers Take Into Account Common Ground," by W. S. Horton & B. Keysar [1996], *Cognition, 59*, p. 108. Copyright 1996. Reprinted with permission.)

These findings or this approach may seem inconsistent with the model I have proposed because conversation appears to be geared toward shared meaning and interlocutors seem to be sensitive to the knowledge of their conversational partners. Such an interpretation is misguided. The fact that interlocutors collaborate is completely consistent with the Perspective Adjustment model. When an addressee interprets an utterance, the model assumes an egocentric interpretation, but also assumes a check vis-à-vis the knowledge of a speaker. If such a check either detects a violation of common ground or the check is uncertain about the validity of the interpretation, then the addressee pursues the path described by the Collaboration model—he or she asks questions of clarification. Similarly with speakers: They may monitor an utterance and realize that they are not sure about an addressee's ability to comprehend it. Then they may inquire, as the Collaboration model suggests. The main difference between the Perspective Adjustment model and the Collaboration model is in the level of analysis. The Perspective Adjustment model describes cognitive processes whereas the Collaboration model describes higher level, interpersonal moves.

Evidence presented in support of the Collaboration model is also consistent with the Perspective Adjustment model, for instance, Wilkes-Gibbs and Clark's (1992) report that interlocutors are sensitive to another's perspective. Our model can explain the results as a function of speakers' monitoring. As in Horton and Keysar's (1996) study, although speakers showed sensitivity to their addressees' perspectives, they did so only as part of monitoring, not as part of their utterance planning. They used their intuitive theory of conversation to guide them in evaluating their utterances and in correcting them when needed. This result could have occurred in the Wilkes-Gibbs and Clark (1992) study, although this conclusion is uncertain because their study focused on final products, on the conversation itself. If we can investigate the cognitive processes underlying the conversation in the Wilkes-Gibbs and Clark experiment, we might be able to determine the extent to which sensitivity to addressees guides a speaker's very production or acts only as a corrective measure.

Dialogic models bring up an important issue that I do not address in this paper, namely, the role of feedback and the functioning of comprehension mechanisms in an ongoing dynamic conversation. To date, this question is interesting, yet open. How do feedback and the possibility of feedback affect comprehension processes? Would addressees engage in adjustment processes, as we found in our experiments, if they are part of an ongoing conversation? Would they anchor on egocentric interpretations as we found in our studies? It would be interesting to investigate the extent to which comprehension is sensitive to situational demands such as the possibility of feedback. We know of only one piece of evidence related to this issue, but it is about production, not comprehension. Schober (1993) found that speakers provide more egocentric spatial descriptions when they speak to a *real* addressee than to an imaginary one. Perhaps speakers might "relax" their laborious monitoring when they have a real addressee. Real addressees can give them feedback when they do not understand; therefore, speakers need not be too vigilant about monitoring for common ground. Consequently, their utterances are more likely to reflect their inherently egocentric plans.

CONCLUSIONS

The experiments reviewed here suggest that two major processes are involved in language comprehension. Addressees, as well as observers and readers, quickly interpret utterances in a way that is contextualized but bound by the perspective of the comprehender. They also adjust to another's perspective by using metaknowledge about what is mutually known. An analogous model holds for speakers as well: They only take into account their addressees' perspectives when they monitor utterances, and correct them if needed.

This model could be refuted and counterevidence could be provided by showing that mutual perspective guides comprehension so that no egocentric interpretation takes place. To date, there is little direct evidence for the claim that comprehenders use mutual knowledge to interpret utterances, because studies investigating common ground and mutual knowledge *confound* mutual knowledge with self-knowledge. A typical experiment has attempted to demonstrate that an addressee used common ground by showing that the addressee used mutually known information. For example, participants were presented with a picture of flowers with a prominent flower at the center. The experimenters then asked an ambiguous question, "How would you describe the color of this flower?" (Clark, Schreuder, & Buttrick, 1983). Although a definite reference requires a unique referent, participants had no problem identifying "the flower" uniquely as the most salient flower. These results could be interpreted in terms of mutual perspective: Perhaps because participants knew that the flower is mutually salient, they were able to understand the question as referring to this flower. Alhough this interpretation is appealing, it is unwarranted by the data (Keysar, in press); a simpler theory that does not assume the use of mutual perspective can account for the data as well. Participants possibly interpreted the utterance egocentrically; because the flower was salient to them, they arrived at a unique interpretation. In other words, it is not sufficient to demonstrate that a comprehender used mutual knowledge to argue that mutual perspective guided the interpretation or that the information was used because it was mutual. Because every mutually known fact is also by definition known to an individual addressee, the addressee might have used the information because it was known to him or her, not because it was mutual. So this inherent conceptual confound must first be resolved to provide evidence relevant to the issue of common ground or common perspective.

There is a second reason why demonstrating that mutual knowledge is insufficient to refute the proposed model. Even if mutual knowledge is used because it is mutual, it is still consistent with our Perspective Adjustment model. The model does not assume that interlocutors do not use this metaknowledge; instead, it describes the processes underlying such use and the conditions under which these processes occur. The model assumes that an addressee uses mutual perspective but only as a corrective measure. To refute the model, the mutual perspective must be shown to play any other role, for example, to guide or restrict the very interpretation so that no correction is needed.

This account does not describe how language users arrive at the interpretation that I claim to be the basic building block. True, our model does not attempt to answer the question, "How do addressees create interpretations from their own perspective?" Such an account is not very easy to construct. One possibility is Sperber and Wilson's theory of relevance (Sperber & Wilson, 1982, 1986), but the exact predictions of relevance theory are still to be spelled out and tested in this context (see the debate in Sperber & Wilson, 1987). My current attempt is simply to suggest that perceived intentions are a basic building block of language use. This notion is a particular interpretation of Clark's (1992) assumption that "in language use, speaker's meaning is primary, and word or sentence meaning are derivative" (p. xv). We assume that computing a speaker's intention is what the comprehension system does well and fast. Although the system computes intentions, this computation does not involve considerations of mutual knowledge: Instead, it does the computation from the perspective of an addressee. The system also does not, as the traditional approach suggests, compute decontextualized meanings, literal meanings, or otherwise perspective-free meanings.

I propose that such quick and efficient computation of intention is one important way that our comprehension system tackles the inherent problem of ambiguity. People are basically insensitive to the extent of ambiguity because they comprehend utterances from their own perspectives. Consequently, intentions seem relatively transparent and utterances seem less ambiguous than they really are. The illusion of transparency that I have described is a natural outcome of the way the comprehension system works to reduce ambiguity. Using a personal perspective does not always eliminate ambiguity completely, but it reduces it drastically and makes the interpretation process feasible.

Language users could have reduced ambiguity differently; they could have arrived at intentions by using other perspectives. For example, addressees might use speakers' perspectives, their mutual perspectives, or mutual knowledge to interpret utterances. The Perspective Adjustment model and our data (Keysar et al., 1997) suggest that addressees do not. Comprehenders do not use speakers' or mutual perspectives to restrict ambiguity and arrive at intended meaning. The model assumes that they do use mutual perspective, but only when there is a need. They use it as a corrective measure.

Perceiving intentions as transparent seems to be part of acquiring language, as Olson and Torrance's (1987) young participants demonstrated. Adults might be perceiving Lucy's request for her "red shoes" as relatively unambiguous as well, because they know her intent. But, because they know that Linus does not know her actual intention, they know that from his perspective the utterance is actually ambiguous, and they make allowances for the perspective discrepancy. Therefore, I propose that language users solve a different problem from the one that the traditional theory assumes. Language users do not solve the problem, "How does literal meaning relate to speaker's meaning?" Instead, they solve the problem, "How does the contextualized computed intention relate to the speaker's actual intent?" Typically, the "transparent" intention is identical to the speaker's actual intent; sometimes it is not. When an interpretation is erroneous and comprehenders detect the error, they adjust.

ACKNOWLEDGMENTS

The preparation of this paper was supported by Public Health Service, grant R29 MH49685, to the University of Chicago, Boaz Keysar, Principal Investigator. I am grateful to Public Health Service for this support. I am indebted to Linda Ginzel and William Horton for thoughtful comments on earlier drafts and to my graduate students and research assistants who helped me think about these issues.

REFERENCES

Anderson, R. C., & Pichert, J. W. (1978). Recall of previously unrecallable information following a shift in perspective. *Journal of Verbal Learning and Verbal Behavior, 17,* 1–12.

Astington, J., Harris, P., & Olson, D. (Eds.) (1988). *Developing theories of mind.* New York: Cambridge University Press.

Ayer, A. (1936). *Language, truth and logic.* London: Gollancz.

Bock, K. (1995). Sentence production: From mind to mouth. In J. Miller & P. Eimas (Eds.), *Handbook of perception and cognition: Speech, language, and communication.* San Diego, CA: Academic Press.

Carnap, R. (1956). *Meaning and necessity (2nd ed.).* Chicago: Chicago University Press.

Clark, H. H. (1992). *Arenas of language use.* Chicago: University of Chicago Press.

Clark, H. H., & Marshall, C. R. (1981). Definite reference and mutual knowledge. In A. H. Joshi, B. Webber, & I. A. Sag (Eds.), *Elements of discourse understanding.* Cambridge, England: Cambridge University Press.

Clark, H. H., & Murphy, G. L. (1982). Audience design in meaning and reference. In J. F. Le Ny & W. Kintsch (Eds.), *Language and comprehension.* Amsterdam, Netherlands: North-Holland.

Clark, H. H., & Schaefer, E. F. (1989). Contributing to discourse. *Cognitive Science, 13,* 259–294.

Clark, H. H., Schreuder, R., & Buttrick, S. (1983). Common ground and the understanding of demonstrative reference. *Journal of Verbal Learning and Verbal Behavior, 22,* 245–258.

Clark, H. H., & Wilkes-Gibbs, D. (1986). Referring as a collaborative process. *Cognition, 22,* 1–39.

Cox, M. V. (1977). Perspective ability: The relative difficulty of the other observer's viewpoints. *Journal of Experimental Child Psychology, 24,* 254–259.

Dascal, M. (1987). Defending literal meaning. *Cognitive Science, 11,* 259–281.

Fromkin, V. (1971). The nonanomalous nature of anomalous utterances. *Language, 47,* 27–52.

Garrett, M. F. (1988). Processes in language production. In F. J. Newmeyer (Ed.), *Linguistics: The Cambridge survey, Vol. 3, Language: Psychological and biological aspects.* Cambridge, England: Cambridge University Press.

Gernsbacher, M. A. (1989). Mechanisms that improve referential access. *Cognition, 32,* 99–156.

Gernsbacher, M. A. (1990). *Language comprehension as structure building.* Hillsdale, NJ: Lawrence Erlbaum Associates.

Gernsbacher, M. A., & Keysar, B. (1995, November). *The role of suppression in metaphor interpretation.* Paper presented at the 36th annual meeting of the Psychonomic Society. Los Angeles, CA.

Gerrig, R. J. (1989). Empirical constraints on computational theories of metaphor: Comments on Indurkhya. *Cognitive Science, 13,* 235–241.

Gibbs, R. (1979). Contextual effects in understanding indirect requests. *Discourse Processes, 2,* 1–10.

Gibbs, R. W. (1983). Do people always process the literal meanings of indirect requests? *Journal of Experimental Psychology: Learning, Memory and Cognition, 9,* 524–533.

Gibbs, R. W. (1984). Literal meaning and psychological theory. *Cognitive Science, 8,* 275–304.

Gibbs, R. W. (1990). Comprehending figurative referential descriptions. *Journal of Experimental Psychology: Learning, Memory and Cognition, 16,* 56–66.

Gibbs, R. W. (1992). What do idioms really mean? *Journal of Memory and Language, 31,* 485–506.

Gibbs, R. W. (1994). *The poetics of mind.* Cambridge, England: Cambridge University Press.

Gibbs, R. W., & Nayak, N. P. (1991). Why idioms mean what they do. *Journal of Experimental Psychology: General, 120,* 93–95.

Gibbs, R. W., & O'Brien, J. E. (1990). Idioms and mental imagery: The metaphorical motivation for idiomatic meaning. *Cognition, 36,* 35–68.

Glucksberg, S., Gildea, P., & Bookin, H. (1982). On understanding nonliteral speech: Can people ignore metaphors? *Journal of Verbal Learning and Verbal Behavior, 21,* 85–98.

Glucksberg, S., & Keysar, B. (1990). Understanding metaphorical comparisons: Beyond similarity. *Psychological Review, 97,* 3–18.

Graesser, A. C., Bowers, C., Bayen, U. J., & Hu, X. (in press). Who said what? Who knows what? Tracking speakers and knowledge in narrative. In W. van Peer, E. Andriga, D. Schram, & E. Tan (Eds.), *Narrative perspective: Cognition and emotion.*

Graumann, C. F. (1989). Perspective setting and taking in verbal interaction. In R. Dietrich & C. F. Graumann (Eds.), *Language processing in social context.* Amsterdam, Netherlands: Elsevier Science.

Graumann, C. F., & Herrmann, T. (1988). Other-relatedness in language processing. *Journal of Language and Social Psychology, 7,* 159–168.

Grice, H. P. (1968). Utterer's meaning, sentence meaning, and word meaning. *Foundations of Language, 4,* 225–242.

Grice, H. P. (1975). Logic and conversation. In P. Cole & J. Morgan (Eds.), *Syntax and semantics: Vol. 3, Speech acts.* New York: Academic Press.

Horton, W. S., & Keysar, B. (1996). When do speakers take into account common ground? *Cognition, 59,* 91–117.

Katz, J. (1972). *Semantic theory.* New York: Harper & Row.

Katz, J., & Fodor, J. (1963). The structure of semantic theory. *Language, 56*, 170–210.

Keysar, B. (1989). On the functional equivalence of literal and metaphorical interpretations in discourse. *Journal of Memory and Language, 28*, 375–385.

Keysar, B. (1993). Common sense and adult theory of communication. *Behavioral and Brain Sciences, 16*, 54.

Keysar, B. (1994a). Discourse context effects: Metaphorical and literal interpretations. *Discourse Processes, 18*, 247–269.

Keysar, B. (1994b). The illusory transparency of intention: Linguistic perspective taking in text. *Cognitive Psychology, 26*, 165–208.

Keysar, B. (1995). *Exploring linguistic perspective taking.* Unpublished manuscript, University of Chicago.

Keysar, B. (1996). From figures of speech to figments of thought. [Review of the book: *The poetics of mind: Figurative thought, language, and understanding.*] *Contemporary Psychology, 41*, 222-223.

Keysar, B. (in press). Unconfounding common ground. *Discourse Processes.*

Keysar, B., Barr, D. J., Balin, J. A., and Paek, T. (1997). *Definite reference and mutual knowledge: A processing model of common ground in comprehension.* Manuscript submitted for publication.

Keysar, B., & Bly, B. (1995). Intuitions of the transparency of idioms: Can one keep a secret by spilling the beans? *Journal of Memory and Language, 34*, 89–109.

Keysar, B. & Bly, B. (in press). Swimming against the current: Do idioms reflect conceptual structure? *Journal of Pragmatics.*

Keysar, B., & Glucksberg, S. (1993). Metaphor and communication. *Poetics Today, 13*, 633–658.

Kosinski, J. (1971). *Being there.* New York: Bantam Books.

Krauss, R. M., & Fussell, S. R. (1988). Other-relatedness in language processing: Discussion and comments. *Journal of Language and Social Psychology, 7*, 263–279.

Krauss, R. M., & Fussell, S. R. (1991). Perspective-taking in communication: Representations of others' knowledge in reference. *Social Cognition, 9*, 2–24.

Krauss, R. M., & Fussell, S. R. (1996). Social psychological models of interpersonal communication. In E. T. Higgins & A. Kruglanski (Eds.), *Social psychology: Handbook of basic principles.* (pp. 655–701). New York: Guilford Press.

Lakoff, G. (1987). *Women, fire, and dangerous things.* Chicago: University of Chicago Press.

Lakoff, G., & Johnson, M. (1980). *Metaphors we live by.* Chicago: University of Chicago Press.

Levelt, W. J. M. (1989). *Speaking: From intention to articulation.* Cambridge, MA: MIT Press.

Long, E. C. J., & Andrews, D. W. (1990). Perspective taking as a predictor of marital adjustment. *Journal of Personality and Social Psychology, 59*, 126–131.

McKoon, G., Ward, G., & Ratcliff, R. (1993). Morphosyntactic and pragmatic factors affecting the accessibility of discourse entities. *Journal of Memory and Language, 32*, 56–75.

Mead, G. H. (1934). *Mind, self and society.* Chicago: University of Chicago Press.

Murphy, G. L. (in press). On metaphoric representations. *Cognition, 60*, 173–204.

Nusbaum, H. C., & Henly, A. S. (in press). Understanding speech perception from the perspective of cognitive psychology. In J. Charles-Luce, P. A. Luce, & J. R. Sawusch (Eds.), *Spoken language processing.* Ablex.

Olson, D. R. (1991). Children's understanding of interpretation and the autonomy of written texts. *Text, 11,* 3–23.

Olson, D. R., & Torrance, N. (1987). Language, literacy, and mental states. *Discourse Processes, 10,* 157–168.

Onishi, K. H., & Murphy, G. L. (1993). Metaphoric reference: When metaphors are not understood as easily as literal expressions. *Memory & Cognition, 21,* 763–772.

Ortony, A., Schallert, D. L., Reynolds, R. E., & Antos, S. J. (1978). Interpreting metaphors and idioms: Some effects of context on comprehension. *Journal of Verbal Learning and Verbal Behavior, 17,* 465–477.

Perner, J., Leekam, S., & Wimmer, H. (1987). Three-year-olds' difficulty with false belief: The case for a conceptual deficit. *British Journal of Developmental Psychology, 5,* 125–137.

Piaget, J., & Inhelder, B. (1956). *The child's conception of space.* New York: Norton.

Rommetveit, R. (1974). *On message structure: A framework for the study of language and communication.* New York: Wiley.

Schober, M. F. (1993). Spatial perspective-taking in conversation. *Cognition, 47,* 1–24.

Searle, J. R. (1975). Indirect speech acts. In P. Cole & J. L. Morgan (Eds.), *Syntax and semantics: Vol. 3, Speech acts.* New York: Academic Press.

Sperber, D., & Wilson, D. (1982). Mutual knowledge and relevance in theories of comprehension. In N. Smith (Ed.), *Mutual knowledge.* London: Academic Press.

Sperber, D., & Wilson, D. (1986). *Relevance: Communication and cognition.* Cambridge, MA: Harvard University Press.

Sperber, D., & Wilson, D. (1987). Precis of relevance: Communication and cognition. *Behavioral and Brain Sciences, 10,* 697–754.

Tanenhaus, M. K., Spivey-Knowlton, M. J., Eberhard, K., & Sedivy, J. C. (1995). Integration of visual and linguistic information in spoken language comprehension. *Science, 268,* 1632–1634.

Traxler, M. J., & Gernsbacher, M. A. (1993). Improving written communication through perspective-taking. *Language and Cognitive Processes, 8,* 311–334.

Tversky, A., & Kahneman, D. (1974). Judgment under uncertainty: Heuristics and biases. *Science, 185,* 1124–1131.

Wellman, H. M. (1990). *The child's theory of mind.* Cambridge, MA: MIT Press.

Wilkes-Gibbs, D., & Clark, H. H. (1992). Coordinating beliefs in conversation. *Journal of Memory and Language, 31,* 183–194.

Yaniv, I., & Shatz, M. (1990). Heuristics of reasoning and analogy in children's visual perspective taking. *Child Development, 61,* 1491-1501.

— 9 —

The Grounding Problem in Conversations
With and Through Computers

Susan E. Brennan

State University of New York, Stony Brook

In this chapter I look at human–computer interaction as a kind of coordinated action that bears many similarities to conversational interaction. In human–computer interaction, a computer can be both a medium to communicate *through* and a partner to communicate *with*. I consider how people coordinate their activities with other people electronically, over time and distance, as well as how they communicate with computers as interactive partners, regardless of whether the currency of interaction is icons, text, or speech. The problem is that electronic contexts are often impoverished ones. Many of the errors that occur in human–computer interaction can be explained as failures of *grounding*, in which users and systems lack enough evidence to coordinate their distinct knowledge states. Understanding the grounding process provides not only a systematic framework for interface designers who want to understand and improve human–computer interaction, but also a testbed for cognitive and social psychologists who seek to model the effects of different contexts and media upon language use.

Conversations *Through* Computers

To communicate successfully, two people need to coordinate not only the content of what they say, but also the process of saying it. Consider Don, sitting in his office early one morning, typing an email message to Michael, whose office is in another building. If Don wants to get Michael to join him for lunch at a particular restaurant, he cannot simply write, "Let's meet at Arizona at 1:00." There are many points at which something could go wrong. Don needs to be confident that Michael is able to receive the message (is his computer on?), is attentive enough to know there is a message (or is he playing Tetris again?), has received the message (or is his mail server down?), knows that the message is from Don (and not someone else), can figure out what Don means (Arizona is that restaurant with the great desserts on Manhattan's Upper East Side), and is willing and able to commit himself to the action it proposes (and does not have an impending deadline or early afternoon meeting). So after sending his invitation, Don awaits evidence that Michael has received, understood, and committed to the invitation. Meanwhile, Michael does not begin hunting for a cab as soon as he gets Don's message, but sends an email reply. If their electronic connection is unreliable, or if Michael needs to further clarify or modify their plans, they may exchange still more email before they consider their plan to meet at the restaurant to be common ground. Depending on time and other pressures, Don may opt to telephone Michael if an email response is not forthcoming. In this way, Don and Michael engage in the process of *grounding* in order to come to the mutual belief that they understand one another sufficiently well for the purpose at hand.

The grounding process has been described within a framework that views communication as a form of collaborative action (Brennan, 1990a; Clark, 1996; Clark & Brennan, 1991; Clark & Schaefer, 1989; Clark & Wilkes-Gibbs, 1986; Isaacs & Clark, 1987; Schober & Clark, 1989). According to this view, for a speaker (take Don, in this example) to contribute to a conversation, it is not sufficient for him simply to produce an utterance. He must also acquire sufficient evidence that the utterance has been heard and understood as intended. But how he grounds the utterance will vary, depending on several factors. One kind of factor involves Don's current purposes; if he really hates being stood up in public places, then he will require strong evidence that Michael is coming before concluding that the two of them have a lunch appointment. On the other hand, if Don will be hanging out at the restaurant bar anyway and it is not so important that Michael show up on time, then he will require less evidence. Depending on their purposes, a speaker and an addressee adjust their *grounding criteria* to seek and provide more or less evidence that an utterance presented by the speaker has been accepted by the addressee (Clark & Schaefer, 1989; Clark & Wilkes-Gibbs, 1986; Wilkes-Gibbs, 1986).

Another factor that affects how grounding takes place is the communication medium itself. Depending on whether the medium is face to face, telephone, email, text teleconferencing, video teleconferencing, fax, or postal mail, different constraints are placed on the exchange of evidence (Brennan, 1990a; Clark & Brennan, 1991). For instance, the immediacy with which two people can exchange evidence is critical. If Don and Michael are able to produce and receive a rapid succession of turns—for instance, if they are using an interactive electronic "chat" program where they can simultaneously type and see what the other is typing, or even better, if they are talking on the phone, or best of all, if they are talking face to face—then it is much faster and easier for them to reach the mutual belief that they understand one another than if they are sending email messages or faxes or even worse, postal mail. This is true because producing an utterance, knowing whether an addressee has attended to it, and turning over the conversational floor to that addressee for a response cost relatively less in time and effort in a medium in which two people can be temporally co-present than in one in which they cannot. In media where people are not co-present (in the same place, at the same time) and utterances are not ephemeral, such as with email, faxes, and postal letters, people tend to ground larger installments than in spoken conversation. In these ways, the affordances of a medium impose particular costs on the grounding process and on how grounding shapes the conversations conducted over that medium (Clark & Brennan, 1991).

Many studies have described how the form of communication differs across media (Cohen, 1984; Ochsman & Chapanis, 1974). Grounding provides a useful framework with which to predict and explain these differences (Clark & Brennan, 1991; Whittaker, Brennan, & Clark, 1991).

Conversations *With* Computers

The grounding process is useful as well in understanding what happens when the interactive partner is a computer. Consider what happens when Don returns from lunch and logs in to his computer. He means to copy some files into a public directory so that his supervisor can review them. He types, "copy report.97 public." The system returns a prompt. Then he copies another file by typing, "copy budget.97 public." Again, a prompt. Later, he is surprised to discover that *public* does not contain his two intended files after all. It turns out that he had forgotten to create a *directory* called "public" before trying to copy his files, and instead he wrote the files, one after another, into a *file* named "public," the second file overwriting the first. Many DOS and UNIX®[1] users have experienced this kind of mishap. They soon learn to check to see whether their commands have had the desired effect; for instance, after copying, moving, or deleting a file, they may list the contents of a directory to discover whether all is as expected. Such checking behavior is a way of grounding with an uncooperative operating system.

Seeking evidence that things are on track is not unique to situations that involve communication. Many other sorts of activities require people to express their intentions as action sequences and then to evaluate the results of their actions against their intentions (Hutchins, Hollan, & Norman, 1986; Norman, 1990). Experience with the physical properties of the world, with cause–and–effect sequences, and with perceptual feedback can make this process fairly straightforward for adults dealing with physical objects. Many objects have obvious affordances that enable people to recognize what they are for and how to use them (Norman, 1990; see also Gibson, 1977). In the physical world, actions often result in incremental perceptual feedback that people can use to evaluate their progress toward a goal. But this is not always the case in an electronic world; affordances and the results of actions are often not represented explicitly.

---

[1] UNIX is a registered trademark in the United States and other countries, licensed exclusively through X/Open Company Limited.

Human conversation and human–computer interaction are both coordinated activities. In both, people need to be able to seek evidence that they have been understood and to provide evidence about their own intentions. However, unless a system's designers have been attentive to the system's user interface, or unless the user is an expert, the evidence needed for grounding can be very difficult to get, and errors can be very difficult to recognize. It often falls to users to put in the extra effort needed to try to keep things on track. This is what I call *the grounding problem in human–computer interaction.* This problem exists in conversations both with and through computers—that is, whether the computer is primarily an object to interact with (in the case of single-user applications like word processors, database query programs, spreadsheets, or autonomous software agents) or a medium for interacting with other people (in the case of email or teleconferencing programs). Next, I present some background about how computers evolved into interactive partners. Then I consider how the grounding problem has been addressed or ignored in different kinds of human–computer dialogs, both graphical and language-based. Finally, I discuss how electronic interfaces could better support users' grounding activities with spoken dialog systems.

THE EVOLUTION OF HUMAN–COMPUTER INTERACTION

To consider how support has evolved for enabling people to ground their activities with computers, it is necessary to consider how computers evolved to be interactive in the first place.[2] In the early days of computing, people did not "interact" with computers. In the 1940s, engineers instructed Eniac, the first general-purpose electronic computer, by rewiring it. By the 1950s, programmers were able to control Univac with typewritten commands rather than with dials and switches. Batch processing was yet another advance, one that made computers available to many more users. Users scripted out every instruction in advance and represented the instructions by punching tiny square holes in precise locations on cardboard cards. Then they carefully transported their huge stacks of cards to the local computing center, waited a day or so, and then returned with the hope that none of their cards had been mispunched or misordered. As often as not, one card would have been out of order or mispunched, and then users were faced with the nightmarish task of trying to figure out what was wrong (or simply starting over). The prevailing metaphor for a computer was a giant calculator, not an interactive partner.

---

[2]For a comprehensive and entertaining history, see Howard Rheingold's (1985) book, *Tools for thought: The people and ideas behind the next computer revolution.* This is that rare account with which the computer scientists described in its pages actually concur.

By the late 1950s, PDP-1 computers became available; these so-called *minicomputers* were the size of only two refrigerators. A PDP-1 could be controlled by a high-speed paper tape as well as by punched cards, and the tapes could be changed while the machine was running. So, in a crude fashion, the computer operator could interact with the computer. An experimental psychologist named J. C. R. Licklider envisioned future possibilities for interacting with such machines (Licklider, 1960, as quoted in Rheingold, 1985, p. 40):

> The equipment will answer questions. It will simulate the mechanisms and models, carry out the procedures, and display the results to the operator. It will transform data, plot graphs (. . . in whatever way the human operator specified, or in several alternative ways if the human operator is not sure what he wants).

During the 1950s, an electrical engineer named Doug Engelbart suggested that keyboards could be hooked up to computers, users could be taught to type, and computers could display information on cathode-ray screens. This was considered a crazy idea by his colleagues in academia and industry, but he eventually received a small amount of funding from the Air Force to pursue it. He also proposed that computers could be used for text editing and, in the mid 1960s, constructed the first mouse input device (Rheingold, 1985). These ideas were important in enabling the kind of human–computer interaction we take for granted today.

The First Conversational Computer. In 1963, Ivan Sutherland presented the world with what is widely acknowledged to be the first human–computer interface to support real-time graphical human–computer interaction. His *Sketchpad* system included a display, tablet, stylus, and graphical elements that behaved like physical objects and enabled a user and a system "to converse rapidly through the medium of line drawing" (Sutherland, 1963). Users conversed with Sketchpad by pointing and drawing. The system responded by updating the drawing immediately, so that the relationship between the user's action and the graphical result was clear. Interestingly enough, Sketchpad launched not one but two of the most influential metaphors that have been developed for computing. First, even though Sketchpad was primarily graphical, Sutherland saw it as *conversational*. That is, it was highly responsive; feedback was so timely and relevant that it could be considered analogous to backchannels in human conversation (these include timely responses such as acknowledgments, nods, and eye contact; see Yngve, 1970). The second metaphor grew out of the feeling users had of directly manipulating graphical objects. Sketchpad launched a style of human–computer interaction that has been labeled *direct manipulation* (Shneiderman, 1982, 1983) and with it, the gradual but profound revolution in the design and usability of computers that has led to today's desktop and windows-based systems.

Conversation Versus Direct Manipulation

From the late 1970s until the early 1980s (and much later for some), users typically interacted with computer systems through a teletype (TTY) interface. The user would type a command and then receive a text response printed on the screen, along with a prompt signaling that the system was ready for the next command. Some applications, as well as operating systems such as VMS, DOS, and UNIX, still offer this type of interface. Such command-style interfaces are often categorized together with interfaces that rely on a *natural language* such as English (e.g., Schneiderman, 1992). Such interfaces are primarily language-based as opposed to graphical; they linearize human–computer interaction as a series of alternating turns; and they sometimes act as an agent or intermediary between users and their goals (see, e.g., Brennan, 1990b; Laurel, 1990). Sometimes these so-called "conversational" interfaces are contrasted with direct manipulation interfaces, as if they represent two distinct styles of interaction (Sutherland's early insights notwithstanding). For instance, Shneiderman (1992, 1993) has claimed that direct manipulation interfaces are superior to language-based interfaces. But I argue here that the features of direct manipulation interfaces that make them so usable are the very features that work so well in human conversation.

Direct manipulation interfaces provide excellent support for grounding. The objects of interest are continuously represented, actions are incremental, reversible, and physical (rather than syntactically complex), and there is immediate visual feedback about the effects of actions (Hutchins et al., 1986; Schneiderman, 1982). These interfaces are relatively easy for novices to learn to use and for occasional users to remember. The prevailing metaphor for computing is as a set of tools and objects with predictable uses and characteristics.

In contrast, with a language-based interface, the dominant metaphor is that of a more or less intelligent *agent*, a process to whom the user can delegate actions. Unfortunately, command language and query language interfaces can be difficult for novices and occasional users because they are underdetermined; that is, they require users to remember a set of commands and precise syntax, know exactly how to refer to the information and objects in a domain, and keep track of the current context. Schneiderman (1992), who classifies natural language and speech interfaces in the same general category as command and query language interfaces, points out that with natural language, users aren't burdened with learning and remembering special syntax; but for him, this advantage does not outweigh disadvantages such as unpredictability. Schneiderman (1986) argues:

> . . . human–human interaction is not necessarily an appropriate model for human operation of computers. Since computers can display information 1,000 times faster than people can enter commands, it seems advantageous to use the computer to display large amounts of information and allow novice and intermittent users simply to choose among the items.

The problems with direct manipulation dialogs include the possibility for users to become overloaded, as well as the difficulty of visibly representing complex queries and relationships among objects. To the extent that software is predictable and consistent, a tool metaphor works well; but as soon as the tool is expected to do any sophisticated processing, or if it breaks down or needs more information, or if what is going on cannot be visually represented, then it is more like an agent, with whom people must coordinate and communicate. The advantages of language-based interfaces over direct manipulation typically include the ability to use negation and quantification in queries, distinguish individuals from kinds, search very large databases, issue commands over sets, filter and request information in novel ways, and perform actions that are not in the here and now. Spoken input, although it can lead to recognition errors, has additional advantages: It does not rely on the user's hands or eyes, and it can work at a distance, over the phone, and in the dark.

Although speech and natural language technology has advanced considerably over the past couple of decades, the potential that many researchers have foreseen for these technologies in the human–computer interface has yet to be realized. Relatively few users depend on speech and natural language to interact with their computers. This is because simply having language as the currency of interaction is not enough to make an interface conversational. There are virtually no speech or natural language systems where as much theory and systematic effort has been devoted to the design of the dialog model as to the underlying signal processing or syntactic parsing mechanisms.

The relative success of direct manipulation interfaces, I believe, is not due to their literal resemblance to tools or to any particular "naturalness"; even a tool must be mastered, and graphical representations can be just as arbitrary or convention-based as linguistic ones. I argue that it is not whether the metaphor is a tool or an agent that makes or breaks an interface, but the extent to which the interface supports the grounding process. It just so happens that the architecture of a direct manipulation interface is more likely to support the grounding process than is the sometimes ad hoc feedback provided in a language-based system.

GROUNDING IN HUMAN–COMPUTER INTERACTION

Conversations with other people are rarely fluent and without mishap, and people do not expect them to be. Yet some human–computer interfaces are designed as if people rarely make errors (Lewis & Norman, 1986). In this section I discuss some of the ways in which computer interfaces help or hinder users in grounding their actions by providing feedback, representing shared context, enabling referring, and supporting incremental actions. Most of these examples are drawn from the experiences of college students trying to use popular applications and systems.

Feedback

One major problem with older command line interfaces to operating systems like VMS, DOS, and UNIX is that they often fail to provide appropriate feedback, apart from a bare prompt when ready for input. To discover whether a command has had a particular effect, users may need to search for evidence, as Don had to when he copied his UNIX files. Information about the status of an application is a powerful kind of evidence with which users can ground their activities. Sometimes this evidence is fortuitous, such as the whirring of a hard drive, a symptom that it is working. Sometimes status information is provided more explicitly by a software or hardware designer, such as the lights on a disk drive that borrow convention from traffic lights and flash green, yellow, or red. In the early 1980s, twinkling *run bars* in the bottom margin of windows containing interpreted Lisp code provided reassurance that a user's programs had not yet crashed, and command line systems sometimes produced a row of elliptical dots, showing that a command was in the process of being executed. Such features were strikingly innovative back then and are now commonplace. Many applications now provide static status information in the form of cursors that change to clocks or hourglasses or other symbols of waiting, or dynamic status information (time-elapsed or time-remaining) in the form of rectangles that fill slowly as a file is loaded or converted or saved.

Although these status messages do not exactly mimic what people do in conversation (imagine asking a hard question of someone who responded by turning over an hourglass!), they mimic human feedback behavior in spirit. Not only do people in conversation provide backchannel responses (Yngve, 1970), but they have other ways of signaling their metacognitive states in conversation, such as by filling a pause before an answer with "um" or "uh" (Brennan & Williams, 1995; Smith & Clark, 1993). If a speaker were to hesitate silently before answering a question, this pause would license unwanted implicatures; fillers such as *um* and *uh* display the fact that the speaker is working on producing an utterance. Hearers can use this information (the presence or absence of fillers) to make accurate inferences about the speaker's commitment to an answer based on the display that precedes the answer (Brennan & Williams, 1995). An unexpected delay licenses the inference that a conversational partner is having difficulty. Consider this example from a conversation between two people who were discussing objects in a laboratory experiment by Brennan and Clark (1996):

D:	number 3 is a, a car.
	(pause)
	did you get that?
M:	yes

After the pause, D explicitly elicited evidence from M. Typically in a task like this, M will acknowledge D's utterance as soon as possible with "mm hm" or "okay." An immediate acknowledgment saves a conversational turn; when D expects an acknowledgment and does not get one, she will probably infer that M has a problem. If M puts in the minimal effort required to provide a timely acknowledgment now, then M and D won't need to put in more effort to repair the problem later. In this way, both M and D share the responsibility for getting utterances understood, and this process is governed by a principle that Clark and Wilkes-Gibbs have called *least collaborative effort* (1986).

Although status indicators provide feedback that saves users the effort of hunting for evidence about what the system is up to, many interface functions are not designed with least collaborative effort in mind. As with human partners, the timing of feedback is critical in grounding with a computer, although the consequences of delayed feedback differ from context to context. If a system is slow to provide feedback, users may assume their inputs have not been received and may continue to click the mouse button or hit the carriage return. This practice can queue up unintended inputs that cause the wrong window to be selected or the wrong file to be opened. Or, in the absence of any expectations, users may simply wait, as did one novice who typed a query to a library database program. After 5 minutes with no feedback, he asked an expert, who reminded him to hit the carriage return.

Because of the obvious asymmetries in the capabilities of human and computer partners, most of the responsibility for coordinating joint activities with systems and for minimizing effort falls on users. At the same time, systems that provide feedback only about how commands have failed rather than about how they have been processed do not give users enough evidence to ground their actions. In these cases, users are forced to search for positive evidence, not only that their commands were executed, but that they were executed as intended. Mishaps such as copying several files over a single file (instead of moving them all to a directory) would be avoidable if the system's response to the user's move command were to include the name of the target file as positive evidence of how the command was interpreted or if potentially destructive commands were to require confirmation. For instance, in recent versions of DOS, as Don tried to copy his second file, he would have received a request for confirmation such as "Overwrite file: public?" This message contains at least two clues that something unexpected is about to happen: *Overwrite* describes a destructive action, and *file: public* tells Don that what he thought was a directory is really a file. If Don is paying attention (and does not just respond with an automatic "yes"), then he can compare the evidence with his goal and avoid the error.[3] Note that the system would not recognize any problem with this sequence of commands, because they are perfectly legal; it is up to the user to identify the error. For this to happen, the user needs to have not only evidence about system errors, but also evidence about successful actions.

Shared Context and Referring

In conversation, people construct and maintain discourse models that represent the entities under discussion as well as the relevant relationships between these entities. As two people in a conversation accumulate *common ground*, they presumably construct discourse models more similar to each other's, containing information that both believe to be shared. They rely on their common ground in referring to objects (Clark & Marshall, 1981); referring expressions become more efficient over repeated use (Krauss & Weinheimer, 1966) and reflect jointly achieved perspectives that may not be understood by third parties who have not participated in the conversations (Clark & Wilkes-Gibbs, 1986; Schober & Clark, 1989; Wilkes-Gibbs & Clark, 1992). During the process of grounding, people exchange evidence until they reach the mutual belief that they are talking about the same thing (Brennan, 1990a; Clark & Schaefer, 1987, 1989). Even people with very different language abilities (such as native and non-native speakers of English) rely on the process of grounding (Bortfeld & Brennan, 1997).

Because many interfaces do not maintain and use explicit discourse models, problems arise when users transfer their expectations about shared context from

---

[3]This kind of feature has been called a forcing function (see Norman, 1990). Forcing functions are safety nets that are provided wherever people meet technology (e.g., not only in human-computer interfaces but also in appliances, architecture, automobiles, etc.); they make it difficult or impossible to commit an error, and to that extent, they are enormously useful in enabling people to ground their actions with objects. Forcing functions have two major limitations: they typically prevent common errors that have been foreseen in advance, and they can sometimes be unnecessary and therefore annoying, which causes people to find ways to defeat them (such as ignoring a warning message or responding automatically to a request for confirmation).

their conversations with other people to their interactions with computers. People expect natural language interfaces to be able to handle ellipsis and pronominal references to previously mentioned entities, just as they expect human partners to do these things (Brennan, 1991). So errors occur when natural language interfaces treat each query in a dialog as an independent event. Another source of problems is that applications are often not presented as coherent interactive partners, with respect to their output messages. Consider this example in which an undergraduate tried to use the command interface to a library database:

System:	PLEASE SELECT COMMAND MODE
User:	>Please find an author named Octavia Butler.
System:	INVALID FOLIO COMMAND: PLEASE

Here, gratuitous user friendliness in the form of the word *please* led this user astray. In a study by Brennan & Ohaeri (1994), users of natural language interfaces tended to use more indirect language with computer partners that used indirect language. This was probably less a matter of saving face (see Brown & Levinson, 1987; Holtgraves, 1997) than simply adopting the kinds of phrasings that the partner used. Whether people are communicating with other people or with computer partners, and whether they use speech or text, they tend to converge with their partners in the terms they use (Brennan, 1996, in press). By using the same expression, two partners in conversation mark the mutual belief that they are referring to the same object (Brennan & Clark, 1996). As in the library database example, some speech- and language-based interfaces do not behave this way; their output messages are inconsistent with the input they can handle (Brennan, 1988, 1991).

Most direct manipulation interfaces do a better job of representing and sharing context[4] than do most language-based interfaces, because the objects of interest (such as icons) are continuously represented on the screen (Hutchins et al., 1986). What a direct manipulation interface displays on the screen amounts to the current state of its discourse model (Brennan, 1990b); what is on the screen is also a good estimate of the context it shares with a user. What is highlighted at any moment denotes what the system estimates to be the shared focus of attention. Of course, the user may be attending to something off the screen; some research prototypes have actually attempted to explicitly establish

---

[4]By *shared context*, I mean something akin to common ground. However, in order to avoid anthropomorphizing computer systems and to acknowledge the basic asymmetry between the partners in any human-computer dialog, I will reserve the term *common ground* for interactions between human beings, who have the capability to be mutually aware that they share knowledge.

co-presence by modeling the user's position and orientation in an office (e.g., Schmandt, Arons, & Simmons, 1985).

Referring is relatively straightforward in a direct manipulation interface because discourse entities are embodied in graphical icons and the same icons can serve as inputs to and outputs from commands (Draper, 1986). For instance, to ask about what files are contained in a folder, a user of the Macintosh[5] operating system need only double-click on the folder and the folder will flip open to display its files. Then the user can refer to any visible file by clicking on it; one additional gesture, such as another click or dragging, initiates a command with respect to that object. Cursors change location to represent attentional shifts on the screen; they change shape to represent larger context (or *mode*) shifts (Reichman, 1986). Transitions between system states can be expressed explicitly by animation; for example, when a folder is opened, its icon changes to show a transition to its open state.

Not all so-called direct manipulation interfaces enable grounding equally well. On Macintosh-style interfaces (including Microsoft's Windows 95[6]), objects of the same types are represented as icons that look alike, and applications look different from documents. There is a consistent spatial metaphor for referring; objects of all sorts can be moved around by the user, and they stay put when they are moved. This is not the case in Microsoft's Windows 3.1® and its predecessors, often considered a poor excuse for a direct manipulation interface. In Windows 3.1, applications are typically represented by identical icons (only the labels are different), documents are not even visible, and although objects can be moved, they return to their old locations when the system is rebooted (unless the user evokes an additional command), a violation of the spatial metaphor.

Although the graphical feedback used in some desktop and window-style interfaces to represent and update shared context works well for users with a bit of experience, it may not work for novices. Even the Macintosh desktop, the gold standard of direct manipulation interfaces, depends on feedback conventions that must be learned. For instance, on the Macintosh desktop (and its imitators), the window that receives input is typically the one that appears to be on top of the others; it is also highlighted with darker borders. If users are unaware of this convention, their input may go to an unintended window. UNIX window managers, on the other hand, are often customizable and can therefore rely on different conventions; some do not use highlighting to show which window is the current one, and some enable typing wherever the mouse cursor appears, even on windows that are partly occluded. And in direct manipulation interfaces, referring to objects can become complicated by *aliases*, pointers to objects (such

---

[5]Macintosh is a registered trademark of Apple Computer, Inc.

[6]Windows 3.1 and Windows 95 are registered trademarks of Microsoft Corporation.

as applications or folders) that resemble the actual object, but do not always behave the same. On the Macintosh, an alias has an italicized label and looks slightly different from a regular icon. Aliases are convenient for those in the know, but as conventions that depart from the spatial metaphor, they can be confusing.[7] Once learned, these conventions seem so natural that experts find it inconceivable that they could be opaque to novices.

Errors can result from combinations of inadequate feedback and failure to model context. For example, a common problem for novices is when newly saved files appear to be lost. In most Macintosh applications, a dialog window appears when "Save" is selected for a new file and the user is prompted to name the file by a cursor that appears in a slot labeled "Save Current Document as." However, above this slot is a scrolling window and pull-down menu that displays the folder in which the file will be saved, an important piece of information. Sometimes this folder coincides with what the user would consider to be the current context, and so there is no problem; the file gets saved right where the user expects it to be. But often, the default location happens to be the one where the application program is located or where files were saved the last time the application was used. This situation leads to confusion when the user is unaware of this convention or fails to notice where the file is going. The problem is that the destination is not labeled as such—it is labeled with only the name of the default current folder, next to a small triangle pointing down. The triangle is a convention indicating that the label is really a pull-down menu. To novices, who may not even notice the tiny triangle, nothing in this representation says that (a) the label shows the current context, according to the machine, and (b) this context can be reset by pulling down the menu and stepping up the hierarchy of folders in order to reach the desired folder. Novices, for whom this error is common, panic when they cannot find their files where they thought they left them. Experienced users make this error too, especially if they are in a hurry and ignore the default folder; for them it is only a minor annoyance (but an annoyance nevertheless) to hunt down the file using the "Find" command and move it to the right location. This error could be prevented if the destination were saliently labeled as such or if saving a file required confirmation of the destination, especially the first time the application is opened, when the context is especially likely to be ambiguous.

Grounding Incrementally

The grounding process requires that partners be able to seek incremental evidence of each other's understanding, as well as provide such incremental evidence about their own understanding. Such evidence may be either positive

---

[7] I thank Susan Fussell for bringing this example to my attention.

(evidence that a speaker believes everything is on track) or negative (evidence that a speaker has detected a problem). In the next example, speaker *B* arrives at an interpretation of speaker *A*'s first utterance that *A* did not intend:

A: You don't have any nails, do you?
B: *<pause>*
              Fingernails?
A: No, nails to nail into the wall.
              <pause>
              When I get bored here I'm going to go put up those
              pictures.
B: No.

Clarification subdialogs (see Jefferson, 1972) enable people in conversation to coordinate their individual knowledge states. In this example, before *B* understands and answers *A*'s question, she initiates a clarification subdialog that nests within the question and its answer. Although clarification subdialogs are relatively simple to manage in human conversation, this is often not the case with computers. Consider a user who evokes on-line help in the middle of trying to accomplish some task. Many help systems are not context-sensitive; they begin by presenting a long index of available topics, regardless of what the user and application are in the middle of doing. This would be like *A* responding to *B*'s request for clarification by ignoring its content and simply providing a long list of all the terms that *A* knows for *B* to select from.

In human conversation, grounding is frequently done in small increments, as when speakers give a telephone number three or four digits at a time, waiting for acknowledgments from addressees after each installment (Clark & Schaefer, 1987). Speakers trade off the costs of grounding with the benefits; exchanging evidence of understanding is harder in some communication media than in others, and this fact affects the strategies and techniques people choose for grounding (Clark & Brennan, 1991). Speakers are more likely to break a contribution up into installments when they have a high grounding criterion (such as when it is important that an addressee understand an utterance verbatim) or when they use media in which utterances are ephemeral and the costs of changing speakers are relatively low (such as telephone conversations, as compared to email).

Many direct manipulation interfaces support grounding rather well, with immediate visual feedback and incremental, reversible actions (Schneiderman, 1982). However, incremental grounding is not well supported in the on-line help of some applications. A user who is fortunate enough to find the answer to a question must absorb it all at once, because in order to return to the application's window, he or she must exit help (and the help window will not stay open when it is exited). This situation is particularly aggravating when the answer involves a long sequence of instructions. If the user wants to use this information step by step, she or he must repeatedly evoke and exit the help system, or else write it down or print it for later reference (which of course defeats the purpose of having an on-line help system). The solution to this problem is very simple: Enable the help window to stay open while the user returns to the application window.

MODELING HUMAN–COMPUTER INTERACTION AS JOINTLY ACHIEVED CONTRIBUTIONS

Contributions to human conversations are collective acts; that is, an utterance presented by a speaker is not part of the conversation's common ground until it has been accepted by an addressee (Clark & Schaefer, 1987, 1989; Clark & Wilkes-Gibbs, 1986). This acceptance happens through the systematic exchange of evidence during the grounding process. However, the situation is quite different in human–computer interaction. In direct manipulation interfaces, grounding often happens serendipitously, when the relevant objects are represented on the screen and are thus shared with users. In interfaces that are less graphical or entirely linguistic, shared context is much poorer unless system designers allow for appropriate feedback messages. Without systematic support for determining what kinds of messages to provide and when to provide them, the exchange of evidence is ad hoc at best. In this section I describe Clark & Schaefer's formal model of jointly achieved contributions in conversation. Then I describe proposals for incorporating these ideas into human–computer dialog (Brennan & Hulteen, 1995; Cahn & Brennan, 1997), in an attempt to solve the grounding problem in human–computer interaction.

The Contribution Model

According to the model proposed by Clark and Schaefer (1987, 1989), contributions have a *presentation phase*, in which the speaker produces an utterance addressed to a conversational partner, followed by an *acceptance phase*, in which the partner may explicitly acknowledge the utterance, modify it, clarify it, or implicitly accept it by continuing with the next relevant utterance. A particular utterance may present a contribution at the same time that it fulfills the acceptance phase for a previous contribution. Contributions may be nested within other contributions as parts of clarification subdialogs. Because an utterance presented by one partner does not become a contribution until it has been accepted by the other, both speakers and addressees are responsible for what is contributed.

Consider A's utterance from an earlier example, "You do not have any nails, do you?" Clark and Schaefer (1987, 1989) described four possible states that an addressee, B, can be in, with respect to such an utterance, u', by a speaker, A:

State 0: B did not notice that A uttered any u'.
State 1: B noticed that A uttered some u' (but was not in State 2).
State 2: B correctly heard u' (but was not in State 3).
State 3: B understood what A meant by u'.

In conversation, the addressee's response helps the speaker diagnose which of these states the addressee is in. According to Clark & Schaefer (1987, 1989), some utterances provide stronger evidence than others. For example, B may respond by repeating part or all of what he or she takes A to mean (strong, explicit evidence), or he or she may respond with an acknowledgment (somewhat weaker explicit evidence), or B may simply continue with what he or she takes to be a relevant next utterance (implicit evidence). We (Brennan & Hulteen, 1995) have extended these states in order to enable a system that uses natural language or speech to systematically provide context-appropriate feedback so that users can more easily identify the system's state with respect to a particular utterance.

Adapting the System's Feedback to its State of Understanding

As an example, consider a remote speech interface used over a telephone. Instead of direct manipulation, the paradigm is one of delegation to an agent. The problem is that after the user speaks, even the smallest of delays can be ambiguous. Has the system heard the utterance? Was the utterance interpretable? Or is the system still processing it? Alternatively, is it taking time for the application to carry out the command? In the face of so many possible attributions, users adopt various strategies such as repeating the utterance, hyperarticulating, shouting, or rephrasing. Some of these strategies, although they work in human conversation, may make matters worse with a speech recognizer. For instance, when people hyperarticulate, they pronounce commands in an exaggerated form that is unlike the tokens that the system was trained with, and so successful recognition is less likely than with commands pronounced naturally.

The Need for Context-Sensitive Feedback. In order to enable a user to coordinate his or her behavior with the many possible states a system can be in, the system needs to provide enough feedback for the user to recognize its state. For instance, a system can echo the user's utterance once it has been received:

User:	Read email messages.
System:	I heard you say *Read email messages.*

This kind of response provides the user with positive evidence that the system has attended to, heard, and interpreted the utterance. But consider the case when the evidence is negative:

User:	Read email messages.
System:	What was that again?

At this point, the user can tell that the system was attending and heard something, but was not able to interpret the utterance. Other negative evidence is possible when input is misrecognized:

User:	Read email messages.
System:	I heard you say *Delete email messages.*

Here, it is ambiguous whether the user will be able to interrupt the system in time to intercept this destructive command. When there is a high cost to misunderstanding, it is safer to respond with a request for confirmation.

User:	Read email messages.
System:	Do you want to *Delete email messages?*
User:	No! Read email messages.
System:	I heard you say *Read email messages.*

A request for confirmation lets the user intervene after a system's interpretation, before it acts on the command. Echoing an utterance and requesting confirmation both provide good evidence of whether the speech recognizer has heard the user's input. However, having to confirm each command is tiresome, especially when speech recognition performance is accurate. So it is also desirable for a system to adjust the feedback it provides depending on the dialog history; that is, if the recognition rate is high so far (the evidence being that the user has not had to initiate repairs), then the system could stop echoing all the user's commands and instead provide feedback at a higher, task level.

User:	Read email messages.
System:	You have five new email messages . . .

We have proposed that the feedback a system provides should be adapted to several factors: (a) the particular state the system has reached with respect to the user's utterance; (b) the likely costs of misunderstanding; (c) the dialog history so far; and (d) the ambient noise level in the user's environment (Brennan & Hulteen, 1995).

Grounding With a Spoken Dialog System. When a user delegates actions to a computer, things can go wrong in a wide variety of ways, especially when the interface acts as an intermediary between the user and one or more applications. With this in mind, we have extended Clark and Schaefer's (1989) model to cover the states that a computer system may be in with respect to a user's command (Brennan & Hulteen, 1995). From the user's perspective, these states are:

State 0:   **Not attending**. The system is not able to receive input from the user.

State 1:   **Attending**. The system is able to receive input (but is not yet receiving any).

State 2:   **Receiving**. The system is receiving input (but the input is not yet recognized as well formed).

State 3:   **Recognizing**. The system recognizes the input as well formed (but has not yet mapped it onto any plausible interpretation).

State 4:   **Interpreting**. The system has reached an interpretation (but has not mapped the utterance onto an application command).

State 5:   **Intending**. The system has mapped the user's input onto a command in its application domain (but has not yet acted).

State 6:   **Acting**. The system attempts to carry out the command (an attempt that may or may not turn out to be successful).

State 7:   **Reporting**. The system has attempted to carry out the command, and reports to the user any relevant evidence from the application domain.

In our model, States 0 to 2 follow Clark and Schaefer's, and their State 3 has been expanded into two states. States 5 to 7 are necessary extensions for dialogs that delegate actions to an agent. For some kinds of systems, the distinctions between these states may not be meaningful (that is, certain kinds of errors may not be possible); for others, it may be appropriate to divide these states into further stages. For instance, State 2 (receiving) errors are common in speech recognition interfaces where input may be heard but not parsed; they happen in text-based natural language interfaces when a word is misspelled, an unknown word is used, or keyboard input is noisy. But a speech recognition interface without a parser (one that maps a whole utterance onto a command without analyzing its constituents) would not need to distinguish between States 2, 3, and 4.

Coordinating Two Distinct Knowledge States

Misunderstandings cannot be repaired unless they can be recognized (Cahn & Brennan, 1997; Lewis & Norman, 1986; Luperfoy & Duff, 1996). Even though two people in conversation build shared representations, there is always some asymmetry; one person invariably recognizes a problem before the other one does. In order for a problem to be recognized, each partner needs to provide feedback not only when there is a problem, but also when the partner believes there is *not* a problem. A common assumption in human–computer dialog design, however, is that a system need provide only negative evidence (i.e., an error message) when it is unable to complete processing at a particular stage. To make this assumption is to minimize the opportunities for users to recognize problems that the system cannot recognize. By the same token, there is typically no provision in the interface for a *user* to provide a *system* with negative evidence. Both of these inadequacies need to be addressed in order to support grounding in human–computer interaction.

Positive Evidence From Systems. A system should at least be able to give the user positive evidence at each meaningful point where it could break down, where meaningful is defined as wherever the user could take some action to repair or prevent a problem. Many kinds of positive evidence are possible, such as these examples:

State 1:	"I'm listening."
State 2:	"I heard something."
State 3:	"I heard you say *Read email messages.*"
State 4:	"Do you want me to *Read email messages?*"
State 5:	"OK, I'll *Read email messages.*"
State 6:	(*system reads email messages aloud*)
State 7:	"That's all."

Obviously, the system should not provide feedback at *all* of these states, for that would be both tedious and redundant. Our proposal (Brennan & Hulteen, 1995) is that the system should provide negative evidence about the first state in which processing cannot be completed. For risky commands, the system should provide positive evidence at the state before which the risk occurs (here, at State 4, in the form of a request for confirmation). Positive evidence about having reached a particular state should also be provided whenever the system has recorded recent failures to reach that state or if the user has recently indicated to the system that it was in error about reaching a particular state. For instance, with a history of such problems at State 3, the system should echo the user's utterances until there is sufficient evidence (in the form of a series of successful recognitions) that these problems no longer exist. This approach assumes that evidence should be provided about the highest state at which the system has either *completed* or *attempted* processing, because reaching a particular state presumes that the system has successfully completed processing at lower-numbered states.[8] More details and examples of adaptive feedback are provided in Brennan and Hulteen (1995).

Negative Evidence From Users. In addition to enabling systems to provide positive evidence to users (Brennan & Hulteen, 1995), we have proposed that users be able to provide negative evidence to systems (Cahn & Brennan, 1997). Systems typically do not provide users with any way at all to signal that they are unhappy with a particular response; users are expected to just take what they can get and go on with the next query or command. A notable exception is work by Moore (1989, 1995) which enabled users to request explanations or express a vague but perfectly valid need for more information by responding with "huh?" If the user had the ability to respond to the system with "ok" (either to explicitly accept the response or to implicitly accept it by just going on with the next query), "huh?" (to request an explanation), "no, I meant" (to initiate a repair of the last contribution), and "never mind" (to abort), this would provide a beginning for the user to negotiate acceptance of the system's responses. The system would keep a structured dialog history in the form of jointly produced contributions (Cahn & Brennan, 1997). Information presumed by the system to be in common ground would be extracted from successful contributions (those with completed acceptance phases) and represented in the dialog history, while "huh" and "no, I meant" would evoke context-sensitive subdialogs in which the content of a contribution would not be added to the dialog history until the user and system repaired the problem at hand. If they were unable to do so, the user could simply abort the contribution. Throughout this process, the dialog history would keep track of how smooth or effortful an interaction was. More detail about this proposed architecture for explicitly supporting and modeling grounding using Clark and Schaefer–style contribution trees is provided in Cahn and Brennan (1997).

---

[8]Exceptions to this assumption are possible when two partners are capable of indirect communication—for instance, A may recognize B's intention without hearing exactly what B said.

CONCLUSION

In this chapter, I have discussed the grounding process and how it enables people to coordinate their distinct knowledge states, whether they are conversing face to face or electronically. I have argued that grounding is important to consider in human–*computer* dialog as well, and that many of the problems that arise when people try to use computers can be explained by inadequate feedback and impoverished context. Direct-manipulation-style interfaces that use desktop or tool-based metaphors for computing are common in today's computer systems; they tend to be easy to use because they support grounding by providing consistent and concrete representations of data, operations, and system states. Direct manipulation interfaces typically provide clear options for what a user can do next (thus bridging what Hutchins et al. [1986], termed the *gulf of execution* that exists between users and their goals), as well as feedback about a command's success or failure (bridging Hutchins et al.'s [1986] *gulf of evaluation*). By contrast, natural language and speech interfaces to applications are still relatively rare; even though speech and language technologies have improved rapidly, interfaces that depend on these technologies are typically underdetermined and often provide no explicit support for recovering from errors. This combination can be enough to make a speech or language interface unusable.

Communicating With Interface Agents

Computer interfaces are performing more and more complex tasks, such as enabling users to write programs, advising them, guiding them through simulation environments, filtering their email, teaching them, reminding them, traversing the Internet to search for specific information in their behalf, and scheduling their appointments by communicating with other users' calendars. Such applications take on more initiative than do text editors, spreadsheets, and drawing programs, and so they do not lend themselves as easily to tool metaphors; instead, they are more like coaches or assistants. As interfaces manage more complex tasks, become more "intelligent," and enable users to delegate more responsibility, the metaphor of the interface as *agent* (considered radical in the early 1980s) will become more commonplace for tasks that require delegation.

Agent-style interfaces need to have not only expertise in a particular task domain but also a general ability to communicate with users. Such communication is necessary to convey information about complex situations, to win users' confidence that the system agent is acting appropriately in their behalf, and to appropriately distribute responsibility between the users and the system. Although tool-based direct manipulation interfaces embody a theory of communication, communication in other kinds of interfaces is typically handled in an ad hoc manner. We have proposed several ways in which the grounding process can be systematically supported in agent-style interfaces, particularly when the currency of interaction is speech or language (Brennan & Hulteen, 1995; Cahn & Brennan, 1997). With an architecture that supports grounding in human–machine dialog, language-based interfaces could become as easy for the average user as direct manipulation ones.

The theoretical framework proposed by Clark and his colleagues (Brennan, 1990a; Clark, 1996; Clark & Brennan, 1991; Clark & Schaefer, 1989; Clark & Wilkes-Gibbs, 1986; Isaacs & Clark, 1987; Schober & Clark, 1989) provides a systematic way in which to model communication between two communicating agents, whether they are human or machine (Brennan & Hulteen, 1995). In everyday conversation, partners seek and provide both positive and negative evidence about beliefs, intentions, and interpretations, in order to make portions of their mental states converge (Brennan, 1990a). Many language-based interfaces provide ample *negative* evidence in the form of error messages but only minimal *positive* evidence; they also act as if most of their responses will be acceptable to users by not seeking evidence of acceptance from users and not providing any way to initiate clarification subdialogs. If language-based interfaces are to support mixed initiative dialogs (in which either user or system can flexibly take the initiative), then they need to support the systematic exchange of both positive and negative evidence.

The Synergy Between Psycholinguistics and Human–Computer Interaction

Finally, the domain of human–computer interaction is a particularly relevant application for cognitive and social psychologists who study psycholinguistics, for two reasons. First, experimental research has illuminated general principles about processing, representation, and interaction that can be applied directly to explaining, predicting, and improving human–computer interaction. Without such underlying principles, progress in interface design will be ad hoc at best, especially for multimodal, "intelligent" systems that use speech and language. At the same time, human–computer interaction provides an ideal testbed for demonstrating and testing models and principles such as the contribution model (Clark & Schaefer, 1987, 1989), the principle of least collaborative effort (Clark & Wilkes-Gibbs, 1986), and the costs and tradeoffs of grounding in different media (Clark & Brennan, 1991). Transporting models from social and cognitive psychology to electronic communication and embodying such models in software has the potential to bring additional clarity and pragmatism to these fields.

ACKNOWLEDGMENTS

I thank my collaborators: Heather Bortfeld, Janet Cahn, Herbert Clark, Eric Hulteen, Gregory Lee, Justina Ohaeri, Pamela Stellmann Reis, Claire Rubman, and especially, Michael Schober, who also provided valuable comments on this chapter. I am also grateful to the very patient editors of this volume, Susan Fussell and Roger Kreuz. This material is based upon work supported by the National Science Foundation under Grants IRI9202458 and IRI9402167 and by Apple Computer, Inc. Any opinions, findings, and conclusions or recommendations expressed in this material are those of the author and do not necessarily reflect the views of the National Science Foundation or of Apple Computer, Inc.

REFERENCES

Bortfeld, H., & Brennan, S. E. (1997). Use and acquisition of idiomatic expressions in referring by native and non-native speakers. *Discourse Processes, 23,* 119-147.

Brennan, S. E. (1988). The multimedia articulation of answers in a natural language database query system. In *Proceedings, Second Conference on Applied Natural Language Processing* (pp. 1–8). Austin, TX: Association for Computational Linguistics.

Brennan, S. E. (1990a). *Seeking and providing evidence for mutual understanding.* Unpublished doctoral dissertation, Stanford University, Stanford, CA.

Brennan, S. E. (1990b). Conversation as direct manipulation: An iconoclastic view. In B. K. Laurel (Ed.), *The art of human–computer interface design* (pp. 393–404). Reading, MA: Addison-Wesley.

Brennan, S. E. (1991). Conversation with and through computers. *User Modeling and User-Adapted Interaction, 1,* 67–86.

Brennan, S. E. (1996, October). Lexical entrainment in spontaneous dialog. In *Proceedings, ISSD 96, International Symposium on Spoken Dialog* (pp. 41–44). Philadelphia, PA: Acoustical Society of Japan.

Brennan, S. E. (in press). The vocabulary problem in spoken dialog systems. In S. Luperfoy (Ed.), *Automated Spoken Dialog Systems.* Cambridge, MA: MIT Press.

Brennan, S. E., & Clark, H. H. (1996). Lexical choice and conceptual pacts in conversation. *Journal of Experimental Psychology: Learning, Memory, and Cognition, 22,* 1482–1493.

Brennan, S. E., & Hulteen, E. (1995). Interaction and feedback in a spoken language system: A theoretical framework. *Knowledge-Based Systems, 8,* 143–151.

Brennan, S. E., & Ohaeri, J. O. (1994). Effects of message style on user's attributions toward agents. In *Conference Companion, CHI '94, Human Factors in Computing Systems* (pp. 281–282). Boston, MA: ACM Press.

Brennan, S. E., & Williams, M. (1995). The feeling of another's knowing: Prosody and filled pauses as cues to listeners about the metacognitive states of speakers. *Journal of Memory and Language, 34,* 383–398.

Brown, P., & Levinson, S. C. (1987). *Politeness: Some universals in language usage.* Cambridge, England: Cambridge University Press.

Cahn, J. E., & Brennan, S. E. (1997). *A computational architecture for the progression of mutual understanding in dialog.* Manuscript submitted for publication.

Clark, H. H. (1996). *Using language.* Cambridge, England: Cambridge University Press.

Clark, H. H., & Brennan, S. E. (1991). Grounding in communication. In L. B. Resnick, J. Levine, & S. D. Behrend (Eds.), *Perspectives on socially shared cognition* (pp. 127–149). Washington, DC: American Psychological Association.

Clark, H. H., & Marshall, C. R. (1981). Definite reference and mutual knowledge. In A. K. Joshi, B. Webber, & I. A. Sag (Eds.), *Elements of discourse understanding* (pp. 10–63). Cambridge, England: Cambridge University Press.

Clark, H. H., & Schaefer, E. F. (1987). Collaborating on contributions to conversations. *Language and Cognitive Processes, 2,* 19–41.

Clark, H. H., & Schaefer, E. F. (1989). Contributing to discourse. *Cognitive Science, 13,* 259–294.

Clark, H. H., & Wilkes-Gibbs, D. (1986). Referring as a collaborative process. *Cognition, 22,* 1–39.

Cohen, P. R. (1984). The pragmatics of referring and the modality of communication. *Computational Linguistics, 10,* 97–146.

Draper, S. W. (1986). Display managers as the basis for user–machine communication. In D. A. Norman & S. W. Draper (Eds.), *User centered system design* (pp. 339–352). Hillsdale, NJ: Lawrence Erlbaum Associates.

Gibson, J. J. (1977). The theory of affordances. In R. E. Shaw & J. Bransford (Eds.), *Perceiving, acting, and knowing.* Hillsdale, NJ: Lawrence Erlbaum Associates.

Holtgraves, T. M. (1998). Interpersonal foundations of conversational indirectness. In S. R. Fussell & R. J. Kreuz, (Eds.), *Social and cognitive approaches to interpersonal communication.* Hillsdale, NJ: Lawrence Erlbaum Associates

Hutchins, E. L., Hollan, J. D., & Norman, D. A. (1986). Direct manipulation interfaces. In D. A. Norman & S. W. Draper (Eds.), *User centered system design* (pp. 87–124). Hillsdale, NJ: Lawrence Erlbaum Associates.

Isaacs, E. & Clark, H. H. (1987). Reference in conversation between experts and novices. *Journal of Experimental Psychology: General, 116,* 26–37.

Jefferson, G. (1972). Side sequences. In D. Sudnow (Ed.), *Studies in social interaction* (pp. 294–338). New York: Free Press.

Krauss, R. M. & Weinheimer, S. (1966). Concurrent feedback, confirmation, and the encoding of referents in verbal communication. *Journal of Personality and Social Psychology, 4,* 343–346.

Laurel, B. (1990). Interface agents: Metaphors with character. In B. Laurel (Ed.), *The art of human–computer interface design* (pp. 355–366). Reading, MA: Addison-Wesley.

Lewis, C., & Norman, D. A. (1986). Designing for error. In D. A. Norman & S. W. Draper (Eds.), *User centered system design* (pp. 411–432). Hillsdale, NJ: Lawrence Erlbaum Associates.

Luperfoy, S. & Duff, D. (1996). A centralized troubleshooting mechanism for a spoken dialogue interface to a simulation application. *Proceedings, ISSD 96, International Symposium on Spoken Dialog* (pp. 77–80). Philadelphia, PA: Acoustical Society of Japan.

Moore, J. D. (1989). Responding to "Huh?": Answering vaguely articulated follow-up questions. *Proceedings, CHI '89, Human Factors in Computing Systems.* (pp. 91–96). Austin, TX: ACM Press.

Moore, J. D. (1995). *Participating in explanatory dialogues*. Cambridge, MA: MIT Press.

Norman, Donald A. (1990). *The Design of Everyday Things*. New York: Doubleday.

Ochsman, R. B. & Chapanis, A. (1974). The effects of 10 communication modes on the behavior of teams during cooperative problem-solving. *International Journal of Man–Machine Studies, 6*, 579–619.

Reichman, R. (1986). Communication paradigms for a window system. In D. A. Norman & S. W. Draper (Eds.), *User centered system design* (pp. 285–313). Hillsdale, NJ: Lawrence Erlbaum Associates.

Rheingold, H. (1985). *Tools for thought: The people and ideas behind the next computer revolution*. New York: Simon & Schuster.

Schmandt, C., Arons, B., & Simmons, C. (1985). Voice interaction in an integrated office and telecommunications environment. In *Proceedings, 1985 AVIOS, American Voice I/O Society* (pp. 51–57). San Jose, CA: American Voice I/O Society.

Shneiderman, B. (1982). The future of interactive systems and the emergence of direct manipulation. *Behavior and Information Technology, 1*, 237–256.

Shneiderman, B. (1983). Direct manipulation: A step beyond programming languages. *IEEE Computer, 16*, 57–69.

Shneiderman, B. (1986). *Designing the user interface: Strategies for effective human–computer interaction* (1st ed.). Reading, MA: Addison-Wesley.

Shneiderman, B. (1992). *Designing the user interface: Strategies for effective human–computer interaction* (2nd ed.). Reading, MA: Addison-Wesley.

Shneiderman, B. (1993, January). Beyond intelligent machines: Just do it! *IEEE Software*, 100–103.

Schober, M. F., & Clark, H. H. (1989). Understanding by addressees and overhearers. *Cognitive Psychology, 21*, 211–232.

Smith, V. L. & Clark, H. H. (1993). On the course of answering questions. *Journal of Memory and Language, 32*, 25–38.

Sutherland, I. E. (1963). *Sketchpad: A man–machine graphical communication system*. MIT. Lincoln Laboratory Technical Report (No. 296) Lexington, MA: MIT Lincoln Laboratory.

Whittaker, S. J., Brennan, S. E., & Clark, H. H. (1991). Coordinating activity: An analysis of interaction in computer-supported cooperative work. In *Proceedings, CHI '91, Human Factors in Computing Systems* (pp. 361–367). New Orleans, LA: Addison-Wesley.

Wilkes-Gibbs, D. (1986). *Collaborative processes of language use in conversation*. Unpublished doctoral dissertation, Stanford University, Stanford, CA.

Wilkes-Gibbs, D., & Clark, H. H. (1992). Coordinating beliefs in conversation. *Journal of Memory and Language, 31*, 183–194.

Yngve, V. H. (1970). On getting a word in edgewise. In *Papers from the sixth regional meeting of the Chicago Linguistic Society* (pp. 567–578). Chicago: Chicago Linguistic Institute.

PART IV

Cognition, Language, and Social Interaction

— 10 —

Cognition, Language, and Communication

Gün R. Semin

Kurt Lewin Institute, Free University Amsterdam

We live in a world where words have taken over from physical or nonverbal forms of communication. With words, information about human interaction and other events is communicated and stored. Words have become the currency of an information culture that has grown increasingly incapable of dealing with nonverbal action. Indeed, humanity was on the way toward losing its reliance on nonverbal communication the moment that it realized that words could capture more complex forms of reality and abstract these forms in a more economical manner. With words, people engage in social interaction, and through a better understanding of words and their use people can begin to appreciate communication as joint action. Many actions essentially involve communication and are produced by using language. It is therefore not unreasonable to expect that the study of language and its use can contribute to an informative appreciation of not only the *communicative processes* that drive joint action or symbolic communication but also of the *psychological processes* (cognitive, motivational, emotional). The present chapter is intended as an attempt and a contribution to elucidate the interface between symbolic communication as mediated by language and cognition.

Social behavior and interaction are enabled by means of symbolic communication. This insight is certainly not recent; it is one of the main contributions of G. H. Mead (e.g., 1934). In the Median tradition of social psychology, forms of language are treated not merely as mediators of social interaction but also of cognition, consciousness, and, inevitably, of the self (cf. Rock, 1979). This broader perspective is also central to socio-cultural theory and semiotic mediation (cf. Wertsch, 1991, 1994; Wertsch & Rupert, 1993). Communication is seen as a joint activity that is mediated by the use of a variety of *tools*. The most significant of these tools is undoubtedly language. The idea that human action is mediated by tools is also a central theme of Vygotsky's work and of the sociocultural approach that attempts to examine human action in terms of its cultural, institutional and historical embeddedness (cf. Wertsch, 1991). As Vygotsky (1978) noted, the introduction of culture through language affects the nature of interpersonal functions. "It does this by determining the structure of a new instrumental act just as a technical tool alters

the process of natural adaptation by determining the form of labor operations"
(Vygotsky, 1981, p. 137). He further points out: "As soon as speech and the
use of signs are incorporated into any action, the action becomes transformed and
organized along entirely new lines" (Vygotsky, 1978, p. 28).

In the following, I first outline the theoretical framework that has informed
my work on the language, cognition, and communication interface. This
theoretical framework is in large part, although by no means entirely, inspired
by Vygotsky's socio-cultural approach. Central to this framework is the analytic
distinction between language and language use as tool and tool use respectively.
The second section is designed to exemplify the feasibility of such a theoretical
framework by furnishing an integrated series of empirical programs that have as
their aims: (a) the investigation of tools as the medium of communication, and
(b) the investigation of how messages are conveyed by strategic tool use in two
situated communicative contexts. These analytically and empirically separable
programs constitute part of a broad research strategy that is being developed to
illustrate experimentally not only the relationship between a medium and a
message in a communication but also the interfacing role of intrapsychological
processes (e.g., cognition). The concluding section draws the implications of
this research strategy for issues such as the interface between language, culture,
communication, and cognition. Additionally, I suggest the methodological
implications of the conceptual framework and the ensuing research strategies:
These implications suggest the possibility of advancing practicable strategies
that complement the methodological individualism prevailing in psychology.

SYMBOLIC COMMUNICATION AS STRATEGIC TOOL USE: THE ANALYTIC FRAMEWORK AND ITS IMPLICATIONS

The Tool and Tool Use Model

The idea or metaphor that language is a tool on which knowledge is mapped is
critical to the development of the perspective that I advance here (Semin, 1995,
1996). I adopt the tool analogy expressly to invite thinking about linguistic
devices such as verbs, adjectives, and nouns in very much the way in which a
person would think about hammers, saws, and pliers. These tools, which are
feats of centuries of engineering, are not only the *products* of collective
experience and knowledge,[1] they also *represent* this knowledge. These special
tools contain the distilled knowledge about the relation between a task and the
best fit between a task or goal and human propensities (in particular, physical

---

[1]This knowledge is *unauthored* but authorized.

propensities like movement, handling, and vision). A person can split a piece of wood with a hammer, but a saw is a more sophisticated tool engineered for this purpose. Indeed, a person can push a nail into wood with the end of a saw, but a hammer is a more appropriate tool. Yet, people can do other things with hammers, which are suitable for extracting nails and so on. Similarly, words are communication tools that are culturally engineered for specific ranges of purposes similar to the ranges of purposes that saws, hammers, and pliers have been engineered for. Like carpenters' tools, words also contain distilled knowledge about the relationship between a particular communicative intent and its reception.

Tools have *properties* that have been engineered to optimize their use in a variety of contexts or practical domains. For instance, in the case of hammers, the tool has a shaft and a peen, a hard, solid head at a right angle to the handle; depending upon their functions, hammers can display other properties. One such property is a claw on the head for extracting nails, which typically appears on carpenters' hammers. A tool's properties are distinct from its *affordances*—the variety of things that people can do with it, or its uses. Thus, although a hammer has a limited number of properties, the uses that it can be put to are unlimited. A hammer can be used to smash a window, kill a person, beat a drum, or drive a nail into wood. A hammer's many uses are its *affordances*, to use Gibsonian terminology (Gibson, 1966/1977, 1979).[2] Such affordances are possible only to the extent that there are human beings who have the *capacity* to use a tool. Hence, *usability as a hammer,* as an affordance, is relational and manifested pragmatically only in the interfaces between tool and tool user. The relational conditions that are necessary for the manifestation of such tool affordances should not detract from the fact that it is possible to investigate the properties of such tools (or their affordances) analytically and in empirical contexts (e.g., experimentally). Thus, although affordances have a relational aspect, properties do not. Further, although the properties of a tool, like a hammer or a linguistic tool, are *determinate* and *finite*, the affordances of a tool are *indeterminate*. Thus, it is possible to list the properties of a hammer but the uses that it can be put to are indeterminate (e.g., extracting and inserting a nail, smashing a window, or killing somebody).

The indeterminacy of tool affordances has several important consequences. Tools, in the hands of one master, can create a chair, a table, or a chalet, but in a different cultural context or with a different master, the same tools can result in

---

[2]The important difference between hammers and so on as tools and language as tools is that whereas the former are designed for human interaction with the object world with the sole purpose of transforming the object world, the latter (language) is designed for interhuman interaction. Thus, the "dialogue" that tools are intended for inevitably influences their features, namely, the type of knowledge that is mapped on them.

different functional products like a pagoda, a Chinese bridal cabinet, and so on. Even in the same culture, the same tools can yield different outcomes and different products as a function of the intentions, desires, wishes and goals of the person using them.

Just as the same physical tools can yield many unique outcomes, so too can the strategic use of language as a tool. The same social event can be represented in many different ways—through the use of different tools in a communicative act—as a function of the intentions, desires and wishes of the person who is doing the reporting and, inevitably, as a function of the characteristics of the interlocutor to the communicative act (e.g., Higgins, 1981; McCann & Higgins, 1992). Bakhtin (1994) drew attention to this issue, and the following passage dovetails nicely with the distinction made here between tool (type of tool and its properties, or the reiterative aspect of language) and tool use (the affordances of tools, or the nonreiterative aspects of language use), as well as with the relationship between the two. Bakhtin (1994, pp. 283–284) wrote that:

> Every text presupposes a system of signs understandable to everybody (that is, conventional, valid within the limits of a given collectivity), a "language." . . . To this system belong all the elements of the text that are repeated and reproduced, reiterative and reproducible . . . At the same time, however, every text (by virtue of constituting an utterance) represents something individual, unique, nonreiterative, and therein lies all its meaning (its intention, the reasons why it has been created) . . . In relation to this aspect, all that is reiterative and reproducible turns out to be raw material and means [tool properties, in the context of this chapter]. To that extent, this second aspect, or pole goes beyond the boundaries of linguistics and philology. It is inherent to the text, but becomes manifest only in concrete situations and within sequences of texts (within verbal communication in a given realm). This pole is not tied to the (reiterative) elements of the system of language (that is, to signs), but to other (nonreiterative) texts by particular relations of a dialogical nature.

To the extent that language is a condition for speech, discourse, text or communication, it is also reproduced in any speech event. As Giddens (1976, pp. 121–122, emphasis in the original) points out:

> Language exists as a "structure", syntactical and semantic, only in so far as there are some kind of traceable consistencies in what people say, in the speech acts which they perform. From this aspect to refer to rules of syntax, for example, is to refer to the reproduction of "like elements"; on the other hand, such rules *generate* the totality of speech acts which is the spoken language. It is this dual aspect of structure, as both inferred from observations of human doings, and yet as also operating as a medium

whereby these doings are made possible, that has to be grasped through the notions of structuration and reproduction.

Thus, any communicative act does two things at the same time: It enables the communication of the intentions, goals, desires, and wishes of the participants and also reproduces "language." Thus, the very *production* of verbal communication always entails the *reproduction* of language. Otherwise, every communicative act would be entirely contextualized and variable. Inevitably, such an entirely contextualized approach would not be able to deal with the fact that people communicate in the first place. Furthermore, such an approach could not deal with the fact that intersubjectivity is an ontological precondition to subjectivity (e.g., Berger, 1966; Vygotsky, 1979) and a "fundamental limiting condition" to relativity (Semin & Manstead, 1983) .

These considerations lead to the conclusion suggested already by Riceour (1955; see also Semin & Fiedler, 1991, pp. 2–3) that language can be considered as a "structure," a "complex skill," and as a "practical activity." In the first instance (i.e., structure), language constitutes an abstract property of a linguistic community and can be conceived of as an abstract set of rules that are "virtual and outside of time" (Ricoeur, 1955. pp. 534). Giddens (1976) referred to this notion as structure; the idea is related to Bakhtin's notion of the reproduced or reiterative elements of the text. These are what I refer to here as the tools that are employed in communication. These tools and their properties are not intended. Language as a structure or institution that is reproduced or reiterated is not the intended product of any one subject or oriented toward another. Although language is (re)produced by individuals as historically located agents, they do not do so by their own choosing.[3] Thus, Riceour refers to language as "virtual and outside of time." This analytic perspective toward language corresponds to the one that I refer to here as the "tool" with its attendant "properties."

The production of a series of speech acts by speakers is a process comparable to a master carpenter's producing, for instance, a Chinese bridal cabinet. In this context, language becomes a *complex skill* that belongs to masters who are members of a linguistic community. This skill is analogous to a person's mastery of a saw, a hammer, a screwdriver, and so on. In fact, in this analytic context it is probably better to speak about a toolbox that is available to a particular linguistic community rather than about tools.

---

[3]The fact that language as an institution is the unintended product of individuals who are historically located has important implications for the unconscious manipulation of linguistic behavior in communicative contexts. Attention is drawn here to the question-answer paradigm (cf. Semin & de Poot, 1997), but less subtle instances of such effects exist in the linguistic manipulation of presuppositions, as in the eyewitness research introduced by Loftus and her colleagues (e.g., Loftus, 1975; Loftus & Palmer, 1974, inter alia).

Finally, the third analytic incision introduced by Ricoeur (1955) suggests regarding language as a medium for practical activity, namely, *speech*. Speech refers to the situated doings of subjects with regard to their intended consequences. The comparable reference here is to Bakhtin's notion of the "individual, unique, nonreiterative," noted earlier. In this final context, language is seen as the medium facilitating intended communication. Language both facilitates communicative intention and is the intended medium. The distinctive features of speech are its presupposing a subject and its being dialogical. Thus, the analysis of speech in the context of the approach advanced here becomes the systematic analysis of the types of tools that people use strategically in the pursuit of their intentions, goals, wishes and desires.

The Tool and Tool Use Research Agenda

The analytic distinction between tools and tool use suggests the need to develop a systematic model of the tools of communication and their properties as well as their affordances (Gibson, 1966/1977). The following four considerations must be addressed: (a) the types of tools that mediate communication; (b) the particular jobs for which such tools have been tailored; (c) the ways such tools are put to use in specific communicative contexts; and, finally, (d) the interface between cognition, tool, and tool use in communicative contexts. These considerations address analytic or conceptual distinctions or aspects of a unitary process that simultaneously entails cognition, languag, and communication among others. These considerations are not independent of each other. Nevertheless, it is possible to develop research strategies that maximize the investigative accentuation of one aspect over another. The current methodological commitment in psychology has maximized an accentuation of cognition and cognitive processes at the expense of other aspects.

The first consideration invites classification—identifying types of tools. In the case of tools such as hammers, saws, and pliers, people can identify tool types more readily because they have more discernible features. The domain is that of manual tools, along with specific categories in this domain such as saws and hammers. Domain specification and within-domain classifications are more readily identifiable in this case, as the match between tool, task, and movement is more discernible than in the case of linguistic tools. Linguistic tools are not so transparent, because language, in most of its facets (apart from its surface semantics), constitutes what Polanyi (1967) termed *tacit knowledge*. Its properties are implicit. Nevertheless, linguistic categorization is possible and is discussed in the first part of the following section.

The second consideration, namely the jobs that the tools have been tailored for, is a research question that invites a focus on the properties of these tools.

Such tools have not one but multiple properties (cf. Semin & Marsman, 1994). The specific question thus becomes an identification of the properties that are relevant and this task is inevitably influenced by the type of classificatory cut introduced in the first consideration because classification also sets the level of generality at which the properties of the respective categories have to be defined. This issue constitutes the second part of thefollowing section.

The third consideration, tool use in specific communicative contexts, is the subject of the third part of the next section. The research paradigms discussed here present the systematic use of different tools in question–answer and stereotype-transmission contexts. The aim here is not only to illustrate the broad range of applications that a systematic analysis of tools and their properties can be put to (namely their affordances), but also to address the more central fourth consideration: the interface between cognition, language and communication in these illustrative communicative contexts.

The broad research agenda described above is illustrated by a specific application of the type of analytic framework inherent in a tool and tool use approach to the domain of interpersonal language and symbolic communication about interpersonal events.

TOOLS OF INTERPERSONAL LANGUAGE: THE LINGUISTIC CATEGORY MODEL

The example I will be using for classifying the types of tools used in communication comes from the domain of interpersonal relations. This domain is fairly central in the communication about persons, their relationships, and their characteristics, and spans a broad spectrum of research issues in social psychology, from attributional phenomena to social cognition in general as well as intergroup relations inter alia. I begin by providing an overview of the *Linguistic Category Model* (LCM; Semin & Fiedler, 1988,1991; Semin & Greenslade, 1985), a taxonomy of the linguistic tools people use in the description of persons, relationships, and interpersonal events. After the classification, I present the properties of the tools in this domain—the features of social interaction and the properties of persons as these are systematically marked in such language. My presentation of the tool classification and tool properties will be brief for two reasons. First, extensive sources for the tool classification (e.g., Semin & Fiedler, 1991, 1992a) and tool properties (e.g., Semin & Marsman, 1994) already exists. Second, one of my emphases here is the methodological accentuation of empirically investigating tool properties, which, as I argue in the concluding section, involves a reversal of the common methodological commitment in psychology (cf. Semin, 1996).

The Classification Model and its Criteria

The LCM is a classificatory approach to the domain of interpersonal terms; it consists of interpersonal (transitive) verbs that are tools used to describe actions (help, push, cheat, surprise), psychological states (love, hate, abhor), and adjectives. that are employed to describe people's characteristics (e.g., extroverted, helpful, religious). The analytic cut at which the LCM is offered is at a level beyond particular semantic domains (such as presumed responsibility, Fillenbaum & Rapaport, 1971; Fillmore, 1971a, b) or the relationships between terms in specific semantic domains such as trait terms (adjectives, cf. Semin, 1989).

Many classifications of interpersonal verbs in the literature have a certain degree of convergence between them (e.g., Abelson & Kanouse, 1966; Brown, 1986; Brown & Fish, 1983; Gilson & Abelson, 1965; McArthur, 1972; Semin & Greenslade, 1985). The classification furnished by the LCM does not necessarily contradict or conflict with previous classifications. It is nevertheless more differentiated on one level and less so on another level. In principle, it starts with a simple observation and a criterion that have previously been presented in the literature (e.g., Gilson & Abelson, 1965), namely between interpersonal terms referring to *observable* events (verbs of action) and those referring to *unobservable* events (verbs of state). Although the distinction between observable and unobservable events is critical for identifying the properties of interpersonal verbs, a subdivision of the observable category into subgroups (see below) and the addition of an adjective category introduces a more differentiated level. This more differentiated level is necessary to the extent that it marks distinct gradations of the inferential properties of action verbs. The distinction between the four verb categories is obtained on the basis of conventional grammatical tests and semantic contrasts (cf. Miller & Johnson-Laird, 1976).

The main reason to proceed with criteria that are independent of these tools' properties is to avoid circularity in establishing a category system. One problem of classificatory approaches in psychology is that they often invite circularity. That is, the defining features of categories are often not independent of the properties that such categories are supposed to have. If the defining feature of a category is identical to the critical property of that category, this is a typical instance of circularity. An illustration of this circularity can be found in the prototype approaches to the classification of the trait domain (e.g., Hampson, Goldberg & John, 1987; Hampson, John & Goldberg, 1986; John, Hampson & Goldberg, 1991), whereby category breadth versus narrowness is defined by the range of behaviors encompassed by a trait. Thus, *reliable* is regarded as a broad trait because it encompasses a broad range of behaviors whereas *punctual* refers to a more specific domain of behavior and so on. The critical defining feature of the category is precisely the variable in which the differences are also observed.

In the case of the LCM, identifying a number of convergent linguistic criteria makes it possible to systematically differentiate between different types of interpersonal verbs and adjectives (cf. Bendix, 1966; Brown & Fish, 1983; Miller & Johnson-Laird, 1976). As Table 10.1 shows, the LCM classification system distinguishes between four interpersonal verb categories: *Descriptive Action Verbs* (DAV), *Interpretative Action Verbs* (IAV), *State Action Verbs* (SAV), *State Verbs* (SV) and *Adjectives* (ADJ) (cf. Semin & Fiedler, 1991, 1992a). The LCM distinguishes between SVs and the three action verbs on the basis of two separate criteria. It is difficult to use the imperative unrestrictively in the case of SVs (e.g., "Please admire me!" or "Need money!"). Additionally, SVs resist taking the progressive form (e.g., "John is liking Mary"). Whereas both SVs and SAVs refer to psychological states in contrast to IAVs and DAVs, it is possible to distinguish between SAVs and SVs by means of the *but* test (cf. Bendix, 1966; Johnson-Laird & Oatley, 1989, p. 98–99). SAVs refer to states caused by the observable action of one person and describe the emotional consequences of this action upon another person (e.g., *surprise, bore, thrill*). In contrast, SVs refer to unobservable states (e.g., *love, hate, despise*). Whereas a person can say "I like Mary, but I do not know why," it is awkward to say "Mary entertained me, but I do not know why." The reason is mainly because SAVs "signify a feeling that has a cause known to the individual experiencing it" (Johnson-Laird & Oatley, 1989, p. 99).

The distinction between DAVs and IAVs from SAVs and SVs is self-evident. The latter refer to psychological states; the former do not. Finally, DAVs are distinct from IAVs in that they refer to an invariant physical feature of action, as in the case of *kick* or *kiss*. In contrast, IAVs serve as frames for many actions that can be described by the same verb. Thus, *to help* may refer to a variety of distinct and different actions such as mouth-to-mouth resuscitating or aiding an elderly lady to cross the street.

The Properties of Interpersonal Language

The inferences mediated by interpersonal verbs constituted the main research agenda in this field, rather than the systematic classification of the interpersonal domain—however important such classifications may be. This situation was undoubtedly due to the fact that interpersonal verbs presented systematic and fascinating phenomena that asked for explanations. Indeed, the unusual properties of interpersonal verbs have drawn people to them. For instance, the very first studies that reported the remarkable properties of interpersonal verbs were originally designed to investigate inductive logic (Gilson & Abelson,

TABLE 10.1

Classification and Classification Criteria for Linguistic Terms
in the Interpersonal Domain: The Linguistic Category Model.

Category	Examples	Characteristic Features
Descriptive action verbs (DAV)	to call to meet to kick to kiss	Reference to single behavioral event. Reference to specific object and situation. Context essential for sentence comprehension. Objective description of observable events.

Classification criteria: Refer to one particular activity and to a physically invariant feature of the action; action has clear beginning and end; in general do not have positive or negative semantic valence.

Interpretive action verbs (IAV)	to cheat to imitate to help to inhibit	Reference to single behavioral event. Reference to specific object and situation. Autonomous sentence comprehension. Interpretation beyond description.

Classification criteria: Refer to general class of behaviors; have defined action with a clear beginning and end; have positive or negative semantic valence.

State action verbs (SAV)	to surprise to amaze to anger to excite	Like IAV, refer to states evoked in object of sentence by unspecified action but no reference to concrete action frames.

Classification criteria: As with IAV, no reference to concrete action frames but to states evoked in object of sentence by unspecified action. *But-test* to distinguish from SVs (cf. Bendix, 1966).

State verbs (SV)	to admire to hate to abhor to like	Enduring states, abstracted from single events. Reference to a social object, not situation. No context reference preserved. Interpretation beyond mere description.

Classification criteria: Refer to mental and emotional states; no clear definition of beginning and end; do not take the progressive form; not freely used in imperatives.

Adjectives (ADJ)	honest impulsive reliable helpful	Highly abstract person disposition. No object or situation reference. No context reference; highly interpretive. Detached from specific behaviors.

Note: Adapted from G. R. Semin and K. Fiedler, "Properties of interpersonal language and attribution." In G. R. Semin and K. Fiedler, Eds., *Language, Interaction, and Social Cognition,* (p. 60). Newbury Park, CA: Sage. Copyright 1992 by G. R. Semin and K. Fiedler. Adapted with permission.

1965). What these authors discovered "as a surprise" (Gilson & Abelson, 1965, p. 304) was the powerful and systematic influence that interpersonal verbs exert on generalizations.

This research program on the rules of generalization processes as a function of the types of interpersonal verbs flourished well into the early 1970s under the guidance of Abelson (e.g. Abelson & Kanouse, 1966; Kanouse, 1972; McArthur, 1972). Independently in linguistics, there has been a brief interest in the causal properties of transitive verbs which complemented the work done in psychology (e.g., Caramazza, Grober, Garvey, & Yates, 1977; Garvey, Caramazza, & Yates, 1976). More recently, there has been a renewed interest in this subject since Brown and Fish (1983) revived the interest in the causality implicit in interpersonal verbs. These authors were able to demonstrate a phenomenon: Verbs of action (e.g., *help*, *cheat*, *kick*) and verbs of state (e.g., *like*, *adore*, *abhor*) systematically mediate inferences about who initiates an event.

Indeed, this finding is probably the most widely researched aspect of interpersonal verbs (e.g., Au, 1986; Brown & Fish, 1983; Fiedler & Semin, 1988; Semin & Marsman, 1994). When asked to identify who initiated an event described in a simple subject–verb–object sentence that is constructed with an action verb (e.g., "John helped David"), participants predominantly identify the sentence subject (John) as the initiator. In contrast, for sentences with state verbs (e.g., "John likes David"), participants identify the sentence object (David) as the initiator. This inference pattern about event initiation is better known as "the causality implicit in interpersonal verbs" (cf. Brown & Fish, 1983), and research into the cognitive processes mediating this phenomenon has been relatively prolific, as there is no obvious linguistic explanation (cf. Brown & Fish, 1983; Fiedler & Semin, 1988; Hoffman & Tchir, 1990; Lee & Kasoff, 1992; Semin & Marsman, 1994). The so-called "causality implicit in interpersonal verbs" is but one of the systematic inferences mediated by interpersonal verbs.

As can be seen in Table 10.2, numerous other inferences are mediated systematically by interpersonal verbs. For instance, Au (1986) and subsequently Fiedler and Semin (1988; see also Franco & Arcuri, 1990) were able to demonstrate that participants, when asked to generate the event preceding or following a stimulus sentence (e.g., "John helped David"), displayed systematic inferences as a function of whether the stimulus sentence contained a verb of action (*help*) or state (*like*). In sentences created to describe the event preceding the stimulus sentence, participants made more frequent reference to the stimulus sentence subject (John) in the case of action verbs but to the stimulus sentence object (David) in the case of state verbs.

This pattern was reversed for the sentences participants generated describing what happened after the stimulus sentence occurred (consequent events): In this case, stimulus sentences with action verbs elicited more frequent references to the stimulus object whereas sentences with state verbs elicited more frequent consequent references to the sentence subject. The data in support of this pattern of antecedent and consequent event inferences is reasonable but not entirely convincing, particularly for the consequences of action verbs and the antecedents of state verbs (cf. Semin & Fiedler, 1992a, p. 64).

Another proposed correlational property of verbs of action and state is volitional control. According to Gilovich and Regan (1986), actions are under the volitional control of agents, and experiences (states) are under the control of stimuli. Alternatively, Kasoff and Lee (1993) showed that the salience of sentence subject and object is mediated by interpersonal verbs. Thus, the sentence subject is more salient for sentences with verbs of action and the

TABLE 10.2

Some Properties and Systematic Inferences Mediated by Interpersonal Verbs.

Type Of Inference	Verbs Of Action (DAV/IAV/SAV)	Verbs Of State (SV)
Causal inference	Subject	Object
Antecedent context inference	Subject	Object
Consequent context inference	Object	Subject
Salience	Subject	Object
Statement verifiability	Easy	Difficult
Event imaginability	Easy	Difficult
Dispositional inference	Subject (strong)	Subject (weak)
Event initiation	Subject	Object
Repetition likelihood	Low	High
Event duration	Short	Long
Affect/state	Subject	Subject
Number of behaviors referred to	Low	High

Note: Adapted from Fiedler & Semin, 1988; Maass, Salvi, Arcuri & Semin, 1989; Semin & Fiedler, 1988, 1991; Semin & Marsman, 1994.

sentence object is more salient for sentences with verbs of state. Semin and Fiedler (1988, 1992a) have shown that verbs of action and state lead to systematically different inferences about how verifiable a sentence is, how easy or difficult it is to imagine an event, the perceived duration of an event, and the number of behaviors an event refers to (see Table 10.2 for details). Further, it has been shown that the likelihood of an event recurring is systematically affected by verb type (Maass, Salvi, Arcuri, & Semin, 1989), as are dispositional inferences and event initiation inferences (Semin & Marsman, 1994). Inevitably, there have been numerous attempts to explain these consistent and systematic effects, some of which have been shown to be stable across a great many linguistic communities such as English, German, Dutch, Greek, Spanish, Turkish, Chinese and Japanese. I do not review the different explanations that have been advanced to account for the observed phenomena aside from making some general remarks about the nature of these explanations; then I focus on the specific types of shortcomings that these explanations display. These shortcomings become apparent in the context of the *Tool and Tool Use Model* (TATUM) advanced here. In the following section, I first identify the general features and the characteristic shortcomings of the explanations advanced in this field. Then, I advance an explanatory framework that can be generated by using TATUM.

VERB-MEDIATED INFERENCE PROCESSES: A RECONCEPTUALIZATION FROM A TOOL–TOOL USE FRAMEWORK

Features and Shortcomings of Explanatory Models for Verb-Mediated Inferences

Since the influential contribution by Brown and his colleagues (Brown & Fish, 1983; Brown & Van Kleeck, 1989; Van Kleeck, Hilliger, & Brown, 1988), research on verb-mediated inferences has taken the implicit causality inferences mediated by interpersonal verbs as the pivotal phenomenon requiring explanation. This explanatory focus may seem surprising in a distanced assessment of the entire set of findings to date. The causal inferences may be valued in everyday life because explanations of events are of critical importance in general. Nevertheless, the inference pattern observed with causal inferences is only one of many; there are no particular a priori theoretical or empirical reasons to privilege this inference pattern over the others although there is a historical reason for why this may be the case—the prominence of attribution theory and the centrality that causality has had within attribution theory (e.g., Kelley, 1973). Attribution theory informed and influenced Brown and his colleagues' explanatory attempts. Thus, the mediating cognitive schemata they postulated to explain implicit causality inferences were coupled with the attribution-theoretical principles of consensus and distinctiveness (e.g., Kelley, 1973). Not surprisingly, there emerged a privileged focus on implicit causality, which turns out to be conceptually and empirically problematic not only in this research (Semin & Marsman, 1994) but in general (cf. Hamilton, 1988, 1992; Hewstone, 1989).

The diverse explanations of implicit causality include a dual schema model (Brown & Fish, 1983), a linguistic relativity account (Hoffman & Tchir, 1990) a sentence context model (Fiedler & Semin, 1988), and a salience framework (Kasoff & Lee, 1993). These explanations share at least two substantial logical shortcomings. First is the postulated relationship between a verb and the dimension of the so-called inference process (e.g., implicit quantifiers, Abelson & Kanouse, 1966; dual schema hypothesis, Brown & Fish, 1983; implicit salience theory, Kasoff & Lee, 1993; morphological hypothesis, Hoffman & Tchir, 1990). All these theoretical approaches rely on the assumption that the sentence verb evokes, elicits, activates, or triggers a particular inference process or dimension in some manner or another. According to each explanation, a specific cognitive process is elicited or activated by a particular type of interpersonal verb. Each approaches assumes a determinate relationship between verb type and a cognitive process.[4] All the theoretical models in this field can be described as single dimension or single feature activation models: They all assume that an interpersonal verb activates an inference process. This observation leads to the first substantial logical incoherence inherent in the research in this field so far.

In the previous section, I showed that interpersonal verbs mediate not one but a number of systematic inferences, not all of which are correlated. Some inference dimensions have been shown to be orthogonal to each other (cf. Semin & Fiedler, 1992a; Semin & Marsman, 1994). The fact that systematic inferences are possible on multiple dimensions or features (some of which are orthogonal) with the same set of verb types must mean that every account resorting to a theoretical explanation with a single inference dimension is by definition incorrect. Consequently, all explanations using a single dimension or feature activation model can be regarded as logically inappropriate to deal with the data obtained to date.

---

[4]As pointed out in a recent paper (Semin & Marsman, 1994), each of these approaches adopts a form of linguistic relativism when the approach postulates a one-to-one correspondence between the type of interpersonal verb and the activated inference process. Some theories do so explicitly (e.g., Hoffman & Tchir, 1990). Others approaches maintain that they are doing exactly the opposite and are investigating a universal thought process (e.g., Brown, 1986), although they rely on the same one-to-one correspondence between verbs and the thought processes they trigger.

The second logical incoherence is also based on the observation that there are many possible inference sets from interpersonal verbs. There are no a priori theoretical or empirical reasons to privilege, for instance, implicit causality over any other properties of interpersonal verbs (e.g., salience, event-recurrence). As I mentioned in the previous section, there is a potential historical explanation for why this may be have been the case—namely the prominence of attribution theory during the emergence of the notion of the causality implicit in interpersonal verbs—but because there are many different inference sets (Table 10.2), the inevitable conclusion must be that *interpersonal verbs in their own right do not elicit, or cue in or activate any particular inference process.* By implication, no particular inference pattern is privileged over another, at least not until the primacy of a specific inference pattern over other inference patterns can be convincingly argued for . So far, no such argument has been advanced.[5]

If these two conclusions are correct, then by definition all the explanations advanced to date have missed something about the phenomenon. I do not suggest that there is no phenomenon and do not deny the empirical outcomes demonstrated so far. I only suggest that a proper explanation has been somewhat elusive. The obvious question is: What is the phenomenon in the first place? The phenomenon may have been incorrectly identified to begin with; that is, it is incorrect to identify or locate the phenomenon of verb-mediated inferences as a cognitive process. It is to this argument that I now turn.

The Tool and Tool Use Model and Verb-Mediated Inferences

As discussed earlier, the distinctive flavor of TATUM is that it makes an analytic distinction between the *properties* of linguistic *tools* (e.g., interpersonal verbs) that can be studied in the abstract and *tool use* (affordances of tools). As I argue below, taking this distinction seriously leads to strong conclusions about the relationship among language, cognition, and communication.

From a TATUM perspective, interpersonal verbs are a set of tools with a variety of properties (Semin & Marsman, 1994). These different properties can be manifested only in pragmatic contexts in the hands of skilled or capable tool users. The range of empirical studies to date thus constitutes a series of investigations that have constructed systematic pragmatic-use contexts or controlled and situated contexts to investigate different affordances of interpersonal verbs by demonstrating them contextually. This phenomenon is like providing a participant with a nail, a block of wood, a hammer, and a saw;

---

[5]Nevertheless, it is possible to envisage the theoretical option of advancing such an argument by anchoring the primacy of particular inference dimensions over others in a cultural context. *Why* questions may be asked more frequently in some naturally occurring situations in an individualistic community than in comparable situations in collectivistic communities.

posing the experimental question, "Which of these three can you use together?";
repeatedly observing that the saw is excluded; and observing the affordance of
hammering-a-nail-into-a-block-of-wood.

To illustrate what is meant by a contextual realization (affordance) of a
property of interpersonal verbs, I use a simplified representation of an
experimental condition–dependent variable (DV) constellation as an instance of a
controlled and situated context. My example is a simplified implicit causality
instance that can be derived from the instructions originally employed by Brown
and Fish (1983):

(1a) *Stimulus*: David *likes* classical music concerts.

    DV1: To what extent is this due to something about David?
    DV2: To what extent is this due to something about classical music
        concerts?
    DV3: To what extent is this due to other factors?

(1b) *Stimulus*: David *goes* to classical music concerts.

    DV1: To what extent is this due to something about David?
    DV2: To what extent is this due to something about classical music
        concerts?
    DV3: To what extent is this due to other factors?

The critical variables are DV1 and DV2. The difference between these two
variables gives an idea of the direction in which implicit causality is ascribed.
The general finding is that when DV1 and DV2 responses are compared, in the
case of 1a, DV1 < DV2, and in the case of 1b it is the reverse, namely: DV1 >
DV2. This experimental realization is regarded as a translation of what occurs in
the course of a normal conversational context in everyday life. Thus, 1a and 1b
can respectively be translated into:

(2a) Why do you think that David likes classical music concerts?
(2b) Why do you think that David goes to classical music concerts?

Questions 2a and 2b, formulated in a conventional conversational form, are
inquiries about the reasons or causes of the appeal that *concerts* have for David
(2a) or the reasons or causes behind *David's* concertgoing behavior (2b). The
inquirer's particular choice of verb in posing this question is strategic. The
goals pursued by 2a and 2b are different. In the case of 2a, the inquirer is
directing or focusing the answer upon the question object (classical music
concerts) whereas in the case of 2b, the inquirer is directing or focusing the

answer upon the question subject (David). Thus, by judicious positioning of sentence subject and object positions, and verb type, the inquirer can use interpersonal verbs as tools deployed to give implicit instructions about how the respondent is expected to shape the answers.

This example is a particular contextual realization (or affordance) of one property of interpersonal verbs. Similar examples can be furnished for the list of properties noted in Table 10.2. This example illustrates the argument, emerging from a TATUM-driven reanalysis of the research on interpersonal verbs, that research to date has incorrectly identified or located interpersonal verbs as being responsible in driving cognitive inference processes. Interpersonal verbs in their own right do not drive any cognitive processes at all: Interpersonal verbs on their own or in the form of simple subject–verb–object sentences do not convey any information. Only in communicative contexts or in settings with the addition of intended conversational goals do they acquire specific or contextualized meanings.

Examples 1 and 2 are two possible affordances of the property of implicit causality. Thus, the property of implicit causality may be used in many contexts for many purposes (e.g., Semin & Poot, 1997a, 1997b). The range of possibilities in which interpersonal verbs can be used to direct the communicative intent or goal of who caused what is, in principle and practice, unlimited. This property of interpersonal verbs can thus be used in various contexts to subtly or indirectly indicate who initiated an event. These contexts include legal (e.g., interrogations), clinical interview, survey , opinion, and attitudinal contexts. This property of interpersonal verbs facilitates many subtle affordances for competent language users.

Interpersonal verbs are thus used as tools in the service of constructing a message (or a speech act—Austin 1962; Searle, 1969) in a communicative context. In such a message construction process, interpersonal verbs, as well as other devices, are employed as tools in the pursuit of realizing communicative goals or intentions. Thus, a person' goals are given expression in the form of an utterance or a symbolic communication. This symbolic communication consists of strategically composing each sentence by emphasizing specific affordances of some tools by the use of other linguistic tools, such as the *why* question form that provides a situated context to the question. These constructions serve the purpose of directing the course of the symbolic communication. An instructive example of such strategic deployment of tool use is the following:

[C]onsider a situation where a vice-squad officer is interviewing a rape victim. The officer wants to know the answer to how the evening prior to the critical event unfolded and wants to probe with an action verb. The officer has at least two options. The victim can be asked as to whether she danced with the perpetrator or alternatively whether the perpetrator danced with her. Given the fact that the two did dance at the party, the answer must be yes in both cases. However, if the victim is in the sentence subject position in the question then she is more likely to be perceived as the causal origin of the event. Yet, if the victim is in the sentence object position, then it is more likely that the officer will form the opinion that she is the victim." (Semin & De Poot, 1997, p. 98).

We were able to show in this research that when a person simulating a vice-squad officer in an experimental situation is confronted with a choice between a series of such questions that imply either victim or perpetrator causation of the event, the previous expectations about the victim's trustworthiness or lack thereof that the person brings into the situation guides his or her question choice in a systematic, significant manner. In this research, we have been able to show that when participants enacting vice-squad officers regarded the victim as untrustworthy, they predominantly chose questions implying victim causation, and vice versa. Thus, the choice of tools in such situations is driven by the goals that people pursue and these goals in turn are driven by people's expectations about the subject of their symbolic communication.

Indeed, the further contribution of TATUM is to be found in the informed entry into the psychological processes (cognitive or motivational) driving people's communications. This idea is precisely the mirror image of my previous argument, which was that the goals that a person pursues influences the tools he or she chooses to realize these goals. The mirror image of this argument is: If a person knows the properties of the tools used then he or she can uncover the goals being pursued by analyzing the discourse. The principle is simple: Once a person knows the properties of tools and therefore their varied contextualized realizations, then he or she can select many communication contexts and analyze them with regard to the psychological processes that could have given rise to the specific communication objectives observed in the communicative act aside from the surface message. These communication objectives (or goals) are manifested in terms of the strategic composition of tools in the communicative act. Thus, by analyzing the types of tools that a person uses in a communicative act, it is possible to infer the cognitive and motivational principles that drive such goals in communication contexts.

Numerous research examples have attempted to do precisely this. A widely researched example of this type of approach pertains to the analysis of the types of tools used in the transmission and communication of stereotypes. This work, initiated by Maass and her colleagues (e.g., Maass, Salvi, Arcuri & Semin, 1989; Maass, Milesi, Zabbini, & Stahlberg, 1995), analyzes the tools used in different communicative messages to infer which of a set of alternative theoretical models (cognitive or motivational) about the psychological processes behind stereotype transmission is in operation. The tool model they employ is the

LCM described earlier in this chapter. Thus, it is possible to investigate psychological processes by the analysis of symbolic communication whereby communicative acts are treated as messages designed to carry a communicative goal. Further applications of this type of analysis can be found in legal contexts (e.g., Catellani, Pajardi, Galardi, & Semin, 1996; Schmidt & Fiedler, in press), and interview situations (e.g., Semin, Rubini, & Fiedler, 1995) among others.

In the concluding section I pull these considerations together by drawing the implications of TATUM for the relationships among language, cognition, and communication as well as the type of methodological orientation inherent to this model.

CONCLUSIONS AND FUTURE DIRECTIONS: IMPLICATIONS OF THE TOOL AND TOOL USE MODEL

I now summarize what TATUM entails and why it was conceived. TATUM is based on the general assumption that people should treat language as a tool with a set of properties. A systematically worked out example of this is the LCM, a programmatic investigation of the language used in the interpersonal domain. Obviously, this tool domain is one of many. In addition, TATUM suggests that once the properties of language are known, researchers can examine its situated use in a variety of constructed or naturally occurring communicative contexts. TATUM does not prescribe what these contexts are or what the psychological processes (cognitive or motivational) driving these communicative acts are. TATUM does not provide a particular psychological explanation or process model; rather, it states a set of paradigmatic assumptions that are important to consider in investigating the relationships among psychological processes, symbolic communication processes, and the medium for symbolic communication.

TATUM provides a framework that makes an explicit distinction between the different types and levels of analysis entailed in cognition, language and communication. The framework makes an analytic separation between the psychological processes manifested by specific tool use strategies (realized affordances) and the tool and its properties. This distinction is also of practical importace. It draws attention to the methodological separation of different sources of variation in communication processes and the identification of these sources. Thus, TATUM suggests a clear distinction between (a) systematic properties of language as a tool (not to be confused with psychological processes) and (b) psychological processes that entail using specific tools with different properties in particular ways to maximize (deliberately or automatically) the realization of specific plans, intentions, or goals. Thus, TATUM is not a model of psychological processes or of the ways such processes are manifested. It consists merely of a set of analytic assumptions about the relationship among language, cognition, and communication. Nevertheless, it provides a framework that guides the development of psychological process models by separating the properties of the medium by which they are expressed from the way that the message is packaged or composed.

The Link Between Cognition, Language, and Communication

The approach advanced by TATUM introduces a different way of looking at the relationship among language, cognition ,and communication. It does so primarily by analytically identifying and separating the type and level of analysis entailed by a focus on the tools of communication from an analysis that focuses on tool use. In other words, tool and tool use are constructs that analytically and contrastively distinguish between two aspects of a relation found in the medium–message interface. The medium is the carrier of the message, the intersubjective means by which the subjective message can be communicated from one person to another. The medium is the intersubjective that enables the communicability of the idiosyncratic or the subjective: The message is the subjective. As Vygotsky (1985, p. 51) pointed out:

> In order to transmit some experience or content of consciousness to another person, there is no other path than to ascribe the content to a known class, to a known group of phenomena, and as we know this necessarily involves generalization. Thus, it turns out that social interaction necessarily presupposes generalization and the development of word meaning, i.e. generalization becomes possible in the presence of the development of social interaction.

This consideration of the relationships between tool and tool use, medium and message, and subjective and intersubjective gives rise to a possible view on the relationships among cognition, language and communication. This point emerges only when considering the relationship between cognition and language in the context of symbolic communication. Vygotsky referred to this issue as a relationship between subjectivity and intersubjectivity. In his view, "The social dimension of consciousness is primary in time and in fact. The individual dimension of consciousness is derivative and secondary" (Vygotsky, 1979, p. 30). Similar views are found, for instance, in Berger's (1966) writings about the relationship between what he referred to as psychological realities and social structure, where he noted that intersubjectivity is the precondition for and precedes subjectivity.

Thus, tools exist as means for giving expression to particular goals. They have properties and in this sense they have cognitive properties (Semin, 1995, 1996), which are realized only in communicative contexts. Psychological factors (cognitive or motivational) are the processes that drive the generation of communicative goals and that find expression in symbolic communication. The two facets of psychological factors—or better, intra-psychological factors[6]—are the formation of communicative goals and the strategic use of tools in the composition of messages. This fact was illustrated earlier with the type of question choice that a suspicious vice-squad officer manifests or the type of message a person displays when she or he wishes to communicate a stereotypic vision of an in- or outgroup to another person. To the extent that the tools used in a communicative context also issue instructions to a listener to act in one particular way, they shape the type of communicative message that they have to produce. The example I used in a previous section was how a question constitutes an instruction to focus on the sentence subject ("Why do you read *The New York Times?*") or the sentence object ("Why do you like *The New York Times?*"). It has been shown that such instructions systematically structure a respondent's answer but do not influence their cognitions or cognitive representations of the event or object in question (cf. Semin & De Poot, 1997b, in press, for further implications of this relationship).

This way of contextualizing the relationships among cognition, language, and communication leads to a reconceptualization of specific domains of research, such as the work to date on the types of phenomena demonstrated with interpersonal verbs. As I have argued, the research in this field can be seen as a series of systematic investigations of the affordances of these verbs. In other words, the findings so far can be regarded as consisting of a series of contextualized specifications of the metasemantic properties of interpersonal verbs, some of which have been listed in Table 10.2. Each semantic domain is defined by surface relationships as in the case of verbs of change of possession (e.g., Croft, 1985; Fillmore, 1971a), terms of presumed responsibility (Fillenbaum & Rapaport, 1971; Fillmore, 1971a), and verbs of judgment (Austin, 1962), among others (cf. Levin, 1993). The metasemantic properties go beyond specific domains and describe distinct patterns of use with respect to specific dimensions, such as causation, time, and relationship, across a broad range of interpersonal verbs. The phenomena observed to date can thus be defined as a mapping of a taxonomy of the metasemantic properties of interpersonal verbs, in other words, the affordances of the tools that are available in the interpersonal domain.

Recent research (Semin & De Poot, 1997b) has also demonstrated the operation of such metasemantic properties. A written message or a narrative is assumed to consist of words that, in connection with larger contexts (linguistic or nonlinguistic), establish relationships (e.g., referential, descriptive,

---

[6]Intrapsychological, because joint action, within which communication is manifested, also has a psychological reality that can be called the interpsychological reality in Vygotskian terms.

denotative, extensional, factual) to extralinguistic entities, events, or states of affairs. Communication of meaning is apparently highly sensitive to the content of what is written down or spoken. This recent research, however, has shown that metasemantic features of narratives are independent of any particular content.

In these studies, participants generated narratives by writing down many events unique to them. It is highly unlikely that any two events were described with the same words. These descriptions were generated by a question formulated with either an action verb or a state verb (e.g.., "Why do you read *The New York Times*?" versus "Why do you like *The New York Times*?"). As I argued, these two types of questions provide instructions to focus in the answers on either the question–sentence–object or the question–sentence–subject as the focal event requiring explanation. These verb choices structure the answers of respondents systematically and significantly.

When third parties read these diverse descriptions about uniquely personal events, they find systematic and reliable differences as a function of the verb type that generated the narrative. Events described in responses to questions containing action verbs were viewed as being shorter and caused by the narrator, whereas events described in responses to questions with state verb questions were viewed as having lasted longer and having been caused by people or factors outside of the narrator. It is not the surface semantics that drive these systematic inferences, but the properties of interpersonal language that go beyond the surface semantic level and have been identified by the LCM (Semin & Fiedler, 1988, 1991, 1992a; Semin & Marsman, 1994). These metasemantic properties, which cut across narrative domains, have a strong, systematic influence on central inferences of third parties, such as time, causation, and qualities of the interpersonal relationship, such as its stability.

A general conclusion from such research is the need to be attentive to the metasemantic properties of communication. These metasemantic properties play an important role in influencing answers when they are systematically used in question formulation, and the manner in which they systematically convey messages to third parties is of critical importance. As this research shows, although the structure of the message is influenced by the tool a person uses in constructing an answer, and is perceived to be so many unique descriptions, this instructional tool use does not influence a respondent's perception of the event as such. In this sense, the use of a tool establishes a convention for answering, but not a psychological reality by modifying the represention of the event.

Shift in Methodological Commitment

A consequence of modeling the relationship among cognition, language, and communication in TATUM is that modeling invites reconsidering this relationship in terms of a methodological angle different from that commonly adopted in psychological research. In mainstream psychological research, the primary methodological commitment is to the processes or properties that are distinctive of individual agents. In other words, the methodological commitment in psychology privileges processes and properties at the individual level (cf. Semin, 1996).

The earlier critique of the research and theoretical modeling of the causality implicit in interpersonal verbs illustrates both the potential and actual logical fallacy of a privileged analysis at the individual processes level. Analyzing language or tools (linguistic devices) with a view to mapping their underlying cognitive properties at the individual level of functioning turns out to be a misunderstanding for many reasons. Because language has multiple inference-inviting properties (Semin & Marsman, 1994) and because any one (or more) of these properties is primarily reproduced in joint action entailing symbolic communication for the purpose of mediating a message, it is impossible to speak of cognitive properties or processes that a tool elicits or activates. The analytic approach adopted here privileges a methodological commitment that introduces a focus on the analysis of the properties of tools, not only that of individuals. This approach means a shift to the properties of the tools by which communication is enabled. Obviously, a tool can display properties only by virtue of the fact that an individual has the capability to use it (e.g., Noble, 1991). However, the possibility of focusing on one metasemantic property of interpersonal terms, such as implicit causality, means not focusing on an analysis of individual functioning but rather on the properties of the tool. By experimentally bracketing out the context (affordance) as well as the participant, researchers simply make the properties of a tool the object of empirical investigation. The lack of a clear vision of the methodological subject was can be held responsible for potential confusion about the relationship between language and cognitive (or motivational) processes.

By shifting the methodological commitment to the tool and by bracketing the subject, it is possible to explain sources of variance that are due to tool properties in idealized contexts (e.g., implicit causality studies). Because tools have affordances, it is possible to separate systematic effects in a communicative setting caused by tool properties (e.g., instructional variations), by intra-psychological processes (e.g., cognitive or motivational), and by situated demands (contexts). A more detailed example of this type of research can be found in a recent report by Marsman and Semin (in press), in which the contributions of linguistic factors to spontaneous trait inferences (cf. Uleman, 1987; Uleman, Newman, & Winter, 1992) are highlighted. This research did not attempt to identify intrapsychological processes as such but rather the types of instructional demands created by particular verb classes and their mnemonic implications.

The advantage of privileging a methodological commitment to the tool in simple, practical terms is that a major source of variation which has hitherto either gone unnoticed in investigations or has been confused with other sources such as intrapsychological processes becomes identified and separated. Thus, the contribution of different interpersonal verbs to spontaneous trait inferences (cf. Uleman, 1987) identifies a source of variance in this research which has hitherto gone unnoticed; nobody considered the possibility that the composition of stimulus sentences and the verbs that are used in such sentences can exert an influence on trait inference processes (cf. Marsman & Semin, in press; Semin, 1995). Using a TATUM framework sensitizes people to the sources of variation caused by psychological processes as well as the sources of variance caused by tool properties. The privileging of a methodological commitment to the tool is not to be understood as a commitment away from the processes and properties of individual agents. Rather, this privileging should be seen as increasing attention to the interfacing sources of variation, a clear identification of the sources that contribute to observed regularities, or a reduction of what may have simply gone unnoticed as error variance.

In conclusion, TATUM can be regarded as a general framework that attempts to redress the imbalance between an individual-centered methodology and a tool-centered methodology. The systematic models of tool properties (e.g., LCM, Semin & Fiedler, 1991) and tool use (e.g., Maass et al., 1989, 1995; Semin et al., 1995) are detailed, contextualized models of how specific tools are used at the service of specific psychological processes or goals. In this sense, TATUM constitutes a general orientation toward investigating the interfaces among language, cognition and communication.

Culture, Cognition, Language, and Communication

A final implication of TATUM pertains to the role that culturecan play with regard to the interfaces among cognition, language, and communication. In the introductory section of this chapter I showed that it is possible to realize different projects with the same tools. In other words, when exploring the possibilities of variation and generality across cultural communities, it is possible to find both by realizing that although the tools are identical and display generality, their differential and culturally contextualized use gives rise to variation. Some evidence emerging from the domain of interpersonal verbs and their properties would seem to support the contention of generality in variation.

There is evidence that the properties (in particular, the causal inferences) of interpersonal verbs are identical across a wide range of diverging linguistic communities. There is also substantial independent evidence of variations in social cognitive processes of individualistic and collectivistic cultural communities. Whereas individualistic communities are more likely to use person-centered explanations for social events, collectivistic communities are more likely to use situationalist ones. This research is has been based in large part on content analyses of narratives generated by the respective samples of respondents. Such narratives use interpersonal verbs and adjectives that are also the mediators of the content analyses conducted by the investigators.

In a recent study, Semin and Zwier (1997) have shown that two cultural communities differing significantly in terms of their cultural orientation (collectivistic versus individualistic) nevertheless have interpersonal verbs with the same tool properties. These authors also showed that the same tools are used in systematically different ways by respondents from two cultural communities. Whereas respondents from a collectivistic community are more likely to use interpersonal verbs to mark the significance of situational or external factors and to move away from the focal person in the social event, respondents from an individualistic community are more likely to use these verbs to focus on the reasons for the event or on the central figure in the narrative. The TATUM approach thus facilitates the separation of the sources that contribute to generality and variation by focusing attention on the diverse ways that social events can be represented with strategic use of, in this case, culturally driven strategic differences in the use of the same tools.

Thus, TATUM provides an avenue to identify generality in variation. It does so by drawing the path for mapping tool properties and by separating this path from its use as a manifestation of psychological and cultural sources of variation. TATUM achieves this result by emphasizing tool properties and individual processes as both conceptually and methodologically critical distinctions that should be equally emphasized theoretically and practically.

ACKNOWLEDGMENTS

The writing of this chapter was facilitated in part by a Netherlands Organization for Scientific Research Pionier Grant, No. PGS 56–381. I would like to express my thanks for the helpful comments extended by the Pionier group (Carien Görts, Toon Taris, Wolanda Werkman, Daniel Wiegboldus, and Sandra Zwier) on an earlier draft of this chapter. In particular, I would like to thank Roger J. Kreuz for his most attentive reading of my chapter, and Sue Fussell, who has drawn my attention to some tricky conceptual problems and has certainly contributed to the clarification of one of the chapter's central distinctions. I hope that the text has improved as a function of her input. Please address correspondence to Gün R. Semin, Kurt Lewin Institute, Department of Social Psychology, v. d. Boechorststr. 1, 1081 BT Amsterdam.
Email: GR.Semin@psy.vu.nl

REFERENCES

Abelson, R. P., & Kanouse, D. E. (1966). Subjective acceptance of verbal generalizations. In S. Feldman (Ed.), *Cognitive consistency: Motivational antecedents and behavioral consequences* (pp. 171–197). New York: Academic Press.

Au, T. K. (1986). A verb is worth a thousand words: The causes and consequences of interpersonal events implicit in language. *Journal of Memory and Language, 25,* 104–122.

Austin, J. L. (1962). *How to do things with words.* Oxford, England: Oxford University Press.

Bakhtin, M. M. (1994). *Estetika slovesnogotvorchestva* [The aesthetics of verbal creativity]. In Wertsch J. V., The primacy of mediated action in socio-cultural studies. *Mind, Culture, and Activity, 1,* 202–288.

Bendix, E. H. (1966). Componential analysis of general vocabulary: The semantic structure of a set of verbs in English, Hindu and Japanese. The Hague, Netherlands: Mouton.

Berger, P. (1966). Identity as a problem in the sociology of knowledge. *Archives Européennes de Sociologie, 7,* 105–115.

Brown, R. (1986). Linguistic relativity. In S. H. Hulse & B. F. Green (Eds.), *One hundred years of psychological research in America: G. Stanley Hall and the John Hopkins tradition* (pp. 241–276). Baltimore: Johns Hopkins University Press.

Brown, R., & Fish, D. (1983). The psychological causality implicit in language. *Cognition, 14,* 237–273.

Brown, R., & Van Kleeck, M. H. (1989). Enough said: three principles of explanation. *Journal of Personality and Social Psychology, 75,* 590–604.

Caramazza, A., Grober, E., Garvey, C., & Yates, L. (1977). Comprehension of anaphoric pronouns. *Journal of Verbal Learning and Verbal Behavior, 16,* 601–609.

Catellani, P., Pajardi, D., Galardi, A. & Semin, G. R. (1996) *Implicit attributions in question–answer exchanges: Analyzing language in court.* Manuscript submitted for publication.

Croft, W. A. (1985). Indirect object "lowering." *BLS, 11,* 39–51.

Fiedler, K., & Semin, G. R. (1988). On the causal information conveyed by different interpersonal verbs: The role of implicit sentence context. *Social Cognition, 6,* 21–39.

Fillenbaum, S., & Rapaport, A. (1971). *Structures in the subjective lexicon.* New York: Academic Press.

Fillmore, C. J. (1971a). Topics in lexical semantics. In R. W. Cole (Ed.), *Current issues in linguistic theory* (pp. 76–138). Bloomington: Indiana University Press.

Fillmore, C. J. (1971b). Verbs of judging: An exercise in semantic description. In C. J. Fillmore & D. T. Langendoen (Eds.), *Studies in linguistic semantics* (pp. 273–296). New York: Holt, Rinehart & Winston.

Franco, F., & Arcuri, L. (1990). Effect of semantic valence on implicit causality of verbs. *British Journal of Social Psychology, 29,* 161–170.

Garvey, C., Caramazza, A., & Yates, J. (1976). Factors influencing assignment of noun antecedents. *Cognition, 3,* 227–243.

Gibson, J. J. (1977). The theory of affordances. In R. Shaw and J. Bransford (Eds.), *Perceiving, acting and knowing; Toward an ecological psychology* (pp. 67–82). Hillsdale, NJ: Lawrence Erlbaum Associates. (Original work published 1966)

Gibson, J. J. (1979). *The ecological approach to visual perception.* Boston: Mifflin.

Giddens, A. (1976). *New rules of sociological method.* London: Hutchinson.

Gilovich, T., & Regan, D. (1986). The actor and the experiencer: Divergent patterns of causal attribution. *Social Cognition, 4,* 342–352.

Gilson, C., & Abelson, R. P. (1965). The subjective use of inductive evidence. *Journal of Personality and Social Psychology, 2,* 301–310.

Hamilton, D. L. (1988). Causal attribution viewed from an information processing perspective. In D. Bar-Tal & A. W. Kruglanski (Eds.), *The social psychology of knowledge.* (pp. 359–387). Cambridge, England: Cambridge University Press.

Hamilton, D. L. (1992, July). *Dispositional and attributional inferences: Similarities and differences.* Paper presented at the joint meeting of the European Association of Experimental Social Psychology and the Society of Experimental Social Psychology, Louvain, Belgium.

Hampson, S. E., Goldberg, L. R., and John, O. P. (1987). Category breadth and social desirability values for 573 personality terms. *European Journal of Personality, 1,* 241–258.

Hampson, S. E., John, O. P., & Goldberg, L. R. (1986). Category breadth and hierarchical structure in personality: Studies of asymmetries in judgments of trait implications. *Journal of Personality and Social Psychology, 51,* 37–54.

Hewstone, M. (1989). *Causal attribution: From cognitive processes to collective beliefs.* Oxford, England: Blackwell.

Higgins, E. T. (1981). The "communication game": Implications for social cognition and persuasion. In E. T. Higgins, M. P. Zanna, and C. P. Hermans (Eds.), *Social cognition: The Ontario symposium* (Vol. 1, pp. 343–392). Hillsdale, NJ: Lawrence Erlbaum Associates.

Hoffman, C., & Tchir, M. A. (1990). Interpersonal verbs and dispositional adjectives: The psychology of causality embodied in language. *Journal of Personality and Social Psychology, 58,* 765–778.

John, O. P., Hampson, S. E., & Goldberg, L. R. (1991). The basic level in personality-trait hierarchies: Studies of trait use and accessibility in different contexts. *Journal of Personality and Social Psychology, 60,* 348–361.

Johnson-Laird, P. N. & Oatley, K. (1989). The language of emotions: An analysis of the semantic field. *Cognition and Emotion, 3,* 81–123.

Kanouse, D. E. (1972). Language, labeling, and attribution. In E. E. Jones, D. E. Kanouse, H. H. Kelley, R. E. Nisbett, S. Valins, & B. Weiner (Eds.), *Attribution: Perceiving the causes of behavior* (pp. 121–134). New York: General Learning Press.

Kasoff, J., & Lee, J. Y. (1993). Implicit causality as implicit salience. *Journal of Personality and Social Psychology, 65,* 877–891.

Kelley, H. H. (1973). The processes of causal attribution. *American Psychologist, 28,* 107–128.

Lee, J. Y., & Kasoff, J. (1992). Interpersonal verbs and interpersonal experiences. *Journal of Social Psychology, 132,* 731–740.

Levin, B. (1993). *English verb classes and alternations.* Chicago: University of Chicago Press.

Loftus, E. F. (1975). Leading questions and the eyewitness report. *Cognitive Psychology, 7,* 560–572.

Loftus, E. F., & Palmer, J. C. (1974). Reconstruction of automobile destruction: An example of the interaction between language and memory. *Journal of Verbal Learning and Verbal Behavior, 13,* 585–589.

Maass, A., Milesi, A., Zabbini, S., & Stahlberg, D. (1995). The linguistic intergroup bias: Differential expectancies or in-group–protection? *Journal of Personality and Social Psychology, 68,* 116–126.

Maass, A., Salvi, D., Arcuri, L., & Semin, G. R. (1989). Language use in intergroup contexts: The linguistic intergroup bias. *Journal of Personality and Social Psychology, 57,* 981–993.

Marsman, G. J., & Semin, G. R. (in press). The mnemonic functions of interpersonal verbs: Spontaneous trait inferences. *Social Cognition.*

McArthur, L. (1972). The how and what of why: Some determinants and consequences of attribution. *Journal of Personality and Social Psychology, 22,* 171–193.

McCann, C. D., & Higgins, E. T. (1992). Personal and contextual factors in communication: A review of the "communication game." In G. R. Semin & K. Fiedler (Eds.), *Language, interaction and social cognition* (pp. 144–172). Newbury Park, CA: Sage.

Mead, G. H. (1934). *The social psychology of George Herbert Mead.* Chicago: University of Chicago Press.

Miller, G. A., & Johnson-Laird, P. (1976). *Language and perception.* Cambridge, England: Cambridge University Press.

Noble, W. (1991). Ecological realism and the fallacy of "objectification." In A. Still & A. Costall (Eds.) *Against cognitivism* (pp. 199–224). London: Harvester Wheatsheaf.

Polanyi, M. (1967). *The tacit dimension.* London: Routledge.

Ricoeur, P. (1955). The model of the text: Meaningful action considered as text. *Social Research, 38,* 530–547.

Rock, P. (1979) *The making of symbolic interactionism.* London: Macmillan.

Schmidt, J., & Fiedler, K. (in press). Language and implicit attributions in the Nuremberg trials: Analyzing prosecutors' and defense attorneys' final speeches. *Human Communication Research*

Searle, J. R. (1969). *Speech acts.* Cambridge, England: Cambridge University Press.

Semin, G. R. (1989). Impressions of personality revisited: The contribution of linguistic factors to attribute inferences. *European Journal of Social Psychology, 19,* 85–101.

Semin, G. R. (1995). Interfacing language and social cognition. *Journal of Language and Social Psychology, 14,* 182–196.

Semin, G. R. (1996). The relevance of language for social psychology. In C. McGarty & A. Haslam (Eds.), *The message of social psychology: Perspectives on mind and society* (pp. 291–304). Oxford, England: Blackwell.

Semin, G. R., & De Poot, C. J, (1997a). Bringing partiality to light: Question wording and choice as indicators of bias. *Social Cognition, 15,* 91–106.

Semin, G. R., & De Poot, C. J. De (1997b). The question–answer paradigm: You might regret not noticing how a question is worded. *Journal of Personality and Social Psychology, 73,*

Semin, G. R., and Fiedler, K. (1988). The cognitive functions of linguistic categories in describing persons: Social cognition and language. *Journal of Personality and Social Psychology, 54,* 558–568.

Semin, G. R., & Fiedler, K. (1991). The linguistic category model, its bases, applications and range. In W. Stroebe, and M. Hewstone (Eds.), *European Review of Social Psychology*, (Vol. 2., pp. 1–30) Chichester, England: Wiley.

Semin G. R., & Fiedler, K. (1992a).The configuration of social interaction in interpersonal terms. In G. R. Semin and K. Fiedler (Eds.) *Language, interaction and social cognition* (pp. 58–78). Newbury Park, CA: Sage.

Semin, G. R., & Fiedler, K. (1992b). Language, interaction and social cognition. In G. R. Semin and K. Fiedler (Eds.) *Language, interaction and social cognition* (pp.1–10). Newbury Park, CA: Sage.

Semin, G. R., & Greenslade, L. (1985). Differential contributions of linguistic factors to memory based ratings: Systematizing the systematic distortion hypothesis. *Journal of Personality and Social Psychology, 49,* 1713–1723

Semin, G. R., & Manstead, A. S. R. (1983). *The accountability of conduct.* New York: Academic Press.

Semin, G. R., & Marsman, G. (1994) On the information mediated by interpersonal verbs: Event precipitation, dispositional inference and implicit causality. *Journal of Personality and Social Psychology, 67,* 836–849.

Semin, G. R., Rubini, M. & Fiedler, K. (1995). The answer is in the question: The effect of verb causality upon locus of explanation. *Personality and Social Psychology Bulletin, 21,* 834–842.

Semin, G. R., & Zwier, S. (1997). *Tools and tool use in cultural perspective: The case of variation and generality in social cognition.* Manuscript in preparation, Kurt Lewin Institute, Free University Amsterdam.

Van Kleeck, M. H., Hilliger, L. A., & Brown, R. (1988). Pitting verbal schemas against information variables in attribution. *Social Cognition, 6,* 89–106.

Vygotsky, L. S. (1985). Izbrannye psikhologicheskie issledovania [Selected psychological research]. In J. V. Wertsch (Ed.). *Culture, communication and cognition: Vygotskian perspectives.* Cambridge, England: Cambridge University Press. (Original work published1956.)

Vygotsky, L. S. (1956/1987). *The collected works of L. S. Vygotsky: Vol. 1, Problems of general psychology.* New York: Plenum Press.

Vygotsky, L. S. (1978). *Mind in society. The development of higher psychological processes.* Cambridge, MA: Harvard University Press.

Vygotsky, L. S. (1979). Consciousness as a problem in the psychology of behavior. *Soviet Psychology, 17,* 3–35.

Vygotsky, L. S. (1981). The instrumental method in psychology. In J. V. Wertsch (Ed.), *The concept of activity in Soviet psychology* (pp. 196–227. Armonk, NY: M. E. Sharpe.

Wertsch, J. V. (1991). *Voices of the mind.* London: Harvester Wheatsheaf.

Wertsch J. V. (1994). The primacy of mediated action in socio-cultural studies. *Mind, Culture, and Activity, 1,* 202–208.

Wertsch, , J. V., & Rupert, L. J. (1993). The authority of cultural tools in a socio-cultural approach to mediated agency. *Cognition and Instruction, 11,* 227–239.

— 11 —

Some Cognitive Consequences
of Communication

Chi-yue Chiu, [*] **Robert M. Krauss,** [**] **and Ivy Y-M. Lau** [*]

[*]*University of Hong Kong and* [**]*Columbia University*

Although psychologists agree that people use language to categorize and describe their experience, there is considerably less agreement about whether the language people use also affects the way they come to know and represent this experience. Study of the relation of language and cognition has had a long and somewhat checkered history in psychology (Brown, 1976; Glucksberg, 1988; Hunt & Agnoli, 1991). Perhaps the most controversial view is incorporated in what has come to be known as the linguistic relativity, or Sapir–Whorf, hypothesis, which holds that the grammatical structures of markedly different languages cause their speakers to experience and mentally represent the world in markedly different ways. As Whorf (1956, pp. 213–214) put it:

> The world is presented in a kaleidoscopic flux of impressions which has to be organized by our minds—and this means largely by the linguistic systems in our minds. We cut nature up, organize it into concepts, and ascribe significances as we do, largely because we are parties to an agreement to organize it in this way—an agreement that holds throughout our speech community and is codified in the patterns of our language. The agreement is, of course, an implicit and unstated one, but its terms are absolutely obligatory; we cannot talk at all except by subscribing to the organization and classification of data which the agreement decrees.

The Sapir–Whorf hypothesis has generated a substantial body of empirical research in color memory (e.g., Brown & Lenneberg, 1954; Heider, 1972; Heider & Olivier, 1972; Kay & Kempton, 1984; Lantz & Stefflre, 1964; Lucy & Shweder, 1979, 1988), categorization (e.g., Carroll & Casagrande, 1958), person perception (e.g., Hoffman, Lau, & Johnson, 1986; Lau & Hoffman, in press), and counterfactual reasoning (e.g., Au, 1983, 1984; Bloom, 1981). Yet, despite psychologists' early enthusiasm for the hypothesis, recent reviews of the empirical literature (Brown, 1976; Glucksberg, 1988; Pinker, 1994; Rosch, 1987) find little support for it. Pinker finds "no scientific evidence that languages dramatically shape their speakers' ways of thinking" (Pinker, 1994, p. 12). The lack of unequivocal empirical evidence, coupled with a shift within linguistics from an emphasis on linguistic diversity to an overriding concern with language universals, has contributed to the waning of interest in the Sapir–Whorf hypothesis. Many cognitive scientists now appear to favor the view that mental representations are independent of their linguistic instantiations. For example, Chomsky (1992) argues that "The computational system of language that determines the forms and relations of linguistic expressions may indeed be invariant; in this sense, there is only one human language, as a rational Martian observing humans would have assumed" (p. 50). Pursuing a similar theme, Pinker concludes that "a visiting Martian scientist would surely conclude that aside from their mutually unintelligible vocabularies, Earthlings speak a single language" (1994, p. 232).

Rejection of the Sapir–Whorf hypothesis has been interpreted by some as support for the proposition that language has no cognitive consequences. In part, this belief may result from a semantic confusion. The word *language* has both a generic sense (as in "*Language* permits humans to communicate with a degree of flexibility that is unmatched by other species") and a specific sense (as in "Hopi and English are two *languages* with markedly different grammars"). The two senses are related but not synonymous. The Sapir–Whorf hypothesis is concerned with the second sense, and the balance of evidence seems to support the conclusion that speakers of structurally different languages do not represent their experience in markedly different ways. Even if structural differences among languages do not affect cognition, however, language (in its generic sense) could still have important cognitive consequences.

In this chapter we describe an alternative approach to conceptualizing the relation between language and cognition, a relation deriving from a consideration of language use in communication. There is considerable evidence that *using* language can affect a variety of cognitive processes. For instance, habitual ways of reading in a language can influence preferences in directional scanning (Braine, 1968; Chen & Chen, 1988; Hoosain, 1991; Kugelmass & Lieblich, 1970); phonological properties of language used to rehearse stimulus materials can affect performance on verbal memory (Ellis & Hennelly, 1980; Hoosain & Salili, 1987; Neveh-Benjamin & Ayres, 1986); labeling of visual stimuli can affect memory of their visual form (Carmichael, Hogan, & Walter, 1932; Daniel, 1972); verbal framing of a decision problem can affect the way the problem is represented and subsequent decision-making (Kahneman & Tversky, 1984; Levin, Schnittjer, & Thee, 1988; Northcraft & Neale, 1986); and the way a problem is presented verbally can affect performance on problem-solving tasks (Glucksberg & Weisberg, 1963). What is distinctive about these cognitive effects is that all involve the *use* of language in mental operations.

Our proposal is that describing or referring to a state of affairs can create or activate a corresponding verbal representation (Paivio, 1986), which conflicts with other representations in memory. As a result, when the state of affairs is later recalled, its representation in memory may be affected by information contained in the description (e.g., Fallshore & Schooler, in press; Schooler & Engstler-Schooler, 1990). One implication of this view is that, because extralinguistic contextual factors can affect how a state of affairs is characterized in communication, the same factors can also influence subsequent mental representations of that state of affairs. In the next two sections, we review evidence bearing on this proposal.

COGNITIVE EFFECTS OF LANGUAGE USE

The Verbal Overshadowing Effect

It is well-established that articulating or comprehending an utterance can result in at least three different (though related) mental representations. They are: (a) *the surface form*: a superficial representation of the utterance's syntactic, semantic, and pragmatic properties; (b) *the propositional text base*: a representation of the utterance's meaning in the form of an interconnected network of ideas; and (c) *the situation model*: a representation of how the speaker experiences the situation described in the utterance (van Dijk & Kintsch, 1983). For example, *We elected a new mayor* and *A new mayor was elected* have the same propositional representation but different surface forms. The situational representation of *The incumbent mayor lost his seat* is different from those of the previous two sentences, although their propositional representations may be similar. There is good evidence that memory for the surface form tends to be most short-lived, whereas memory for the situation model tends to be most enduring (see Fletcher, 1994).

Because the situational experience of many stimuli described in an utterance could easily be represented in a network of propositions, describing such stimuli may evoke a propositional representation similar to the situational representation that the description has created. Moreover, for a stimulus that is readily describable, the resulting propositional and situational representation may be similar to other nonverbal representations of that stimulus. Under such circumstances, verbalization of visual stimuli can enhance memory for them (Ellis & Daniel, 1971; Klatzky, Martin, & Kane, 1982; Paivio, 1986).

By the same mechanism, verbalization can *reduce* the accuracy of visual memory for stimuli that are difficult to characterize verbally. For example, Schooler and Engstler-Schooler (1990) found that describing a target person's face not only failed to enhance participants' memory of the face, it actually resulted in nontransient memory impairments. To explain this result, Schooler and Engstler-Schooler proposed that using language to describe, characterize, or label a state of affairs creates or activates verbal representations of that state of affairs. Later, when the state of affairs is retrieved from memory, such verbal representations may compete with or "overshadow" other nonverbal representations in memory. According to this *verbal overshadowing hypothesis,* "verbalizing a visual memory may produce a verbally-biased memory representation that can interfere with the application of the original visual memory" (Schooler & Engstler-Schooler, 1990, p. 36). Thus, verbal recoding of a visual memory can result in a nonveridical, verbally biased representation that overshadows the visual encoding. Schooler and Engstler-Schooler found that limiting participants' response time to 5 seconds (presumably long enough to activate the visual code but not its verbal counterpart) ameliorated the negative consequences of verbalization on recognition memory.

In addition, most states of affairs can be described in more than one way. These different descriptions can evoke different verbal representations that affect memory by interfering with one another (Mani & Johnson-Laird, 1982; Morrow, Greenspan, & Bower, 1987; Perrig & Kintsch, 1985). Perrig and Kintsch (1985) had participants read a description of a town from either an aerial perspective (e.g., "North of the highway just east of the river is a gas station.") or from the perspective of a motorist driving through (e.g., "On your left just after you cross the river you see a gas station.") When later asked to draw a map of the town and recall the description, participants in the aerial perspective condition found it easier to draw the map but more difficult to recall the description than did participants in the driver perspective condition. Perrig and Kintsch argued that the aerial perspective description facilitates the construction of a spatial-situational representation of the town, which makes drawing the map easier. However, the situational representation may interfere with the propositional representation of the text and make recall of the propositional text base difficult.

Although these experiments are concerned primarily with effects of discourse comprehension on memory, analogous effects have been found for communicative use of language. For example, Wilkes-Gibbs and Kim (1991) presented participants with a set of ambiguous graphic designs that could be referred to by one of two alternate expressions (e.g., "Viking ship" vs. "person swimming"), inducing them to encode the drawings by one or the other set of expressions, and then had them communicate about the figures in a referential communication task. Subsequently, participants' memories for the stimuli were biased in the direction of the label they used.

Analogous effects have been found using attitudinal objects and social information as stimulus materials. It often is the case that different linguistic expressions for the same state of affairs have different evaluative connotations. The social category once referred to as *crippled* or *handicapped* is currently often referred to as *disabled* or *physically challenged*. Although the expressions denote the same social category, evaluatively they connote somewhat different things. The verbal overshadowing hypothesis suggests that use of evaluatively-charged words can affect speakers' attitudes by evoking mental representations that are consistent with the terms' evaluative connotations. A series of experiments by Eiser and his colleagues provide evidence consistent with this view. For example, Eiser and Ross (1977) and Eiser and Pancer (1979) had participants write essays reflecting their views on capital punishment. Some were instructed to employ words that were pro-capital punishment and negative in connotation (e.g., *irresponsible, indecisive, romanticizing*) and others to employ words that were anti-capital punishment and negative in connotation (e.g., *barbaric, uncivilized*). Subsequently, participants' attitudes toward capital punishment changed in the direction of the words they had included in their essays.

Such effects of language use on attitude change tend to be relatively short-lived. Within 6 days, the changed attitudes of Eiser and Pancer's participants had reverted substantially in the direction of their original attitudes. The fleeting effect of language use on attitude change is analogous to the transient attitudinal effects of heuristically-processed information. For example, attitudinal influences induced by a credible source subside over time if the arguments presented by the source are weak, a phenomenon often referred to as the *sleeper effect* (Hovland & Weiss, 1951). Although verbalization may lead to attitude changes, the changed attitudes are difficult to sustain in the absence of new supporting evidence.

Codability Effects

Referent codability refers to the availability of a linguistic form that will allow its referent to be denoted easily, rapidly, concisely, and consistently. For example, there are words that make it easy to refer to certain shapes (triangles, trapezoids, etc.), but there are no convenient ways of referring to others. Similarly, there are names for certain person categories *(yuppies, intellectuals,* etc.), but not for others. Chinese has a term, *shì gù,* that refers to a person who is worldly, experienced, socially skilled, devoted to family, and somewhat reserved—a category for which there is no term in English.

One factor that can influence how a complex, multidimensional state of affairs will be characterized is how readily its different aspects can be represented verbally. For example, people often have multiple reasons for making a decision or for liking or disliking an attitudinal object, but not all of these reasons may be equally codable or readily characterized. When asked to explain why they held a particular attitude or made a particular decision, other things being equal, people are more likely to give the reasons that are easy to express verbally, and despite the fact that these reasons may not have been the ones that determined the original choice, they may come to dominate speakers' decisions and overshadow initial preferences. Consistent with this view, Wilson and his colleagues found that providing reasons for decisions can produce judgmental biases (e.g., Wilson, Dunn, Kraft, & Lisle, 1989; Wilson et al., 1993; Wilson

& Schooler, 1991). Participants who were asked to give reasons for their choices of one of several strawberry jams and college courses tended to make choices that were suboptimal, compared to participants who did not verbalize the reasons (Wilson et al., 1993).

The effects of referent codability on preferences in a communication context is illustrated in a just-completed experiment by Wong and Chiu in which blindfolded participants haptically explored textured ceramic floor tiles and, on the basis of this tactile information, evaluated each tile's suitability for either a sitting room or a storeroom. Participants in an articulation condition described and later rated the tiles' suitability for one or the other room. People have relatively little experience describing tactile experience, and such sensations were expected to be generally low in codability. However, some aspects of tactile stimulation are more describable than others. For example, a tile's roughness or smoothness can be readily and uniformly described, and participants' descriptions in *both* the sitting room and storeroom conditions tended to focus on such qualities. By contrast, a tile's expressive qualities (i.e., features that express the users' personality, values, and aesthetic preferences) seldom appeared in participants' descriptions, and when they did, the descriptions (e.g., "feel like a tile for an orderly person") were quite variable across participants. In a control condition, participants rated the tiles' suitability, but did not describe them.

Pilot studies revealed that people choosing floor tiles for a storeroom tended to focus on the more codable functional properties of the tiles (e.g., roughness), whereas people choosing floor tiles for a sitting room tended to focus on the tiles' less codable expressive qualities.

In the control conditions, preferences for sitting room and storeroom tiles were negatively correlated ($r = -.61$): A tile judged suitable for a sitting room tended to be judged unsuitable for a storeroom, and vice versa. However, these preferences were *positively* correlated ($r = .76$) in the articulation condition. Because the tactile information relevant to the tiles' suitability for a sitting room was difficult to express verbally, participants instead used the relatively more codable linguistic terms for characterizing the tiles' suitability for a storeroom. If participants' descriptions in the sitting room condition overshadowed their preference judgments, there should be a lack of correspondence between judgments of the tiles' suitability for a sitting room in the articulation and control conditions, and this is what was found. In the sitting room conditions, the correlation between the preference ratings of the tiles in the no articulation and control conditions was 0, whereas the corresponding correlation in the storeroom conditions was close to 1 ($r = .93$).

These findings are of particular interest when considered in the historical context of the linguistic relativity debate. Brown and Lenneberg's (1954) finding of a positive correlation between color codability and color memory was seen as strong support for the linguistic relativity hypothesis. Subsequently, psychologists' confidence in the hypothesis was greatly undermined by the findings that cross-language differences in color codability did not predict differences in color memory for speakers of different languages and that both color codability and color memory derived from universal sensory and perceptual processes. However, although cross-language differences in referent codability may have little cognitive consequence, codability may have nontrivial cognitive effects (e.g., on attitudes and preferences) when speakers must refer to innominate (i.e., uncodable) attributes of an attitudinal object. We believe that such linguistic properties as referent codability must be activated by language use in order for them to affect cognition. A similar conclusion was reached by Kay and Kempton (1984), who found that color codability affected color perceptions only when the relevant color terms were used to encode the colors.

The Role of Language Use

We have described several phenomena that demonstrate cognitive effects of language use. Our central assumption is that actually using language to encode thought or to describe a state of affairs is critical for producing these cognitive effects. This hypothesis is illustrated in an experiment by Wilson, Hodges, and LaFleur (1995), in which participants read behavioral descriptions of a target person that contained both positive and negative elements and then articulated reasons for liking or disliking the target. Immediately before they verbalized their reasons, either the positive or the negative behavioral information was made cognitively accessible. This accessibility manipulation affected subsequent impressions of the target: participants liked the target more when positive (rather than negative) behavioral information had been made accessible. In a control condition in which participants memorized the behavioral descriptions instead of verbalizing the reasons for their attitudes toward the person, the accessibility manipulation did not affect subsequent impressions of the person. Such evidence suggests that language use is necessary for such biasing effects to occur.

To examine the role of language use in attitude change, Cheung and Chiu had participants indicate their agreement or disagreement with a social belief (e.g., collective interests are more important than individual freedom) embedded in a set of other items. Some participants were asked to articulate the reasons for or against their own acceptance of the belief, and others were asked to think about reasons that supported or opposed it. Their responses to the items were again assessed after the manipulation. When participants introspected or articulated reasons that supported their belief, no attitude change was observed, possibly because these reasons were already highly accessible to the participants. Articulating reasons against their initial belief, however, increased the accessibility of counter-attitudinal cognitions and produced attitude change in the direction away from participants' initial positions, while introspecting about counter-attitudinal reasons had no effect on attitudes. The results underscore the critical role of language use on cognition.

The differential effects of introspection and language use can be understood in terms of the representational model introduced earlier. Like verbalizing an attitude object, introspection can activate propositional representations related to the attitude object. Unlike verbalization, however, introspection does not facilitate the construction of a situation model that relates the attitude object to the speaker's experience of it. There is evidence that compared to propositional representations, situation models can be more readily retrieved from memory (Schmalhofer & Glavanov, 1986) and have more enduring effects on subsequent cognitions (Kintsch, Welsch, Schmalhofer, & Zimny, 1990).

CONTEXT OF COMMUNICATION

Thus far, we have argued that the way a state of affairs is described, characterized, or labeled can affect the representation of that state of affairs in memory. Obviously, features of the state of affairs will be important determinants of how it is referred to. However, the specific form of the referring expression also will be affected by a number of extra-linguistic factors. The substance of our argument is that these factors, through their influence on language use, may also activate or create language-biased memory representations and by so doing have far-reaching cognitive effects.

The Referential Context

In communication, language use is grounded in a context, and how an object or event is described depends in part on the context in which it is set. For example, in referential communication, participants share a physical/perceptual environment that includes both the referent (the state of affairs being referred to) and nonreferents that are co-present with the referent.[1] The nonreferents may share common features with the referent, and the referring expressions may incorporate redundant information about the common features. Felicitous referring expressions, however, must contain discriminating information— information about features that are distinctive for the referent.

Several studies have shown that the form of referring expressions is affected by the nonreferent context (Hupet, Seron, & Chartraine, 1991; Krauss & Weinheimer, 1966; see Krauss & Fussell, 1996, for a review of this literature). In an experiment by Chiu and Hong, participants took part in a referential

---

[1] Frequently the referential context is implicit or projected. In describing someone to be met at the airport, the describer must imagine the features that are likely to distinguish the target person from others who will be present, and incorporate those features into the description.

communication task in which half saw the concentric circles shown in Figure 11.1 as Set 1 and described the referent (B) so that a listener could select it from the co-present nonreferents, A, C, and D. The remaining participants saw the same B in Set 2 with nonreferents E, F, and G and described the referent to a listener.

In the *Pattern Description* condition, participants described the brightness pattern of the referent. With Set 1 as the context, they typically described the referent as consisting of two concentric circles (redundant information), with the outer circle being the darkest and inner circle being the brightest (discriminating information). Participants using Set 2 tended to describe B as consisting of two concentric circles, with the outer circle being the brightest and the inner circle being the darkest. In the *Position Description* condition, participants described the position of the referent in the stimulus array.

A day later, participants were shown all of the nonreferents (A, C, D, E, F, and G) and asked to rate their confidence that each was the stimulus they had described the day before. As expected, memory for the referent was systematically distorted to be consistent with the descriptions only for participants in the Pattern Description condition: Compared to participants

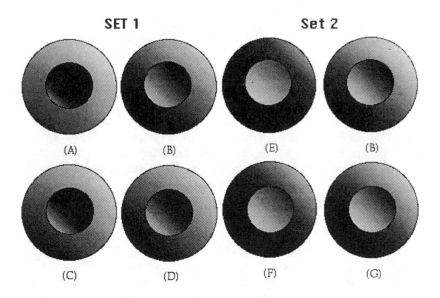

FIG. 11.1: Stimulus sets 1 (A, B, C and D) and 2 (E, B, F and G) used in Chiu and Hong's experiment.

given Set 2, those given Set 1 were more confident that a nonreferent with a brighter inner circle and a darker outer circle was the "referent" they had described. The effect was not found for participants in the Position Description condition.

Audience Design

As Krauss and Fussell (1996) have argued, communication is more than an orderly sequence of encoding and decoding, in part because language is not a one-to-one mapping system in which a single, unambiguous meaning is associated with each message. To "understand" a message is to reconstruct the communicative intention that underlies it, and to accomplish this a listener must engage in a process of inference. In formulating a message, a speaker must try to anticipate the information a listener will need to infer the intended meaning. Specifically, speakers must make assumptions about the common ground they share with their listeners and must formulate their message in a manner consistent with what is mutually known (Clark & Marshall, 1981; Clark & Murphy, 1982; Clark, Schreuder, & Buttrick, 1983). For example, a person talking with a stranger will avoid idiosyncratic expressions that are unlikely to be part of their common ground (Fussell & Krauss, 1989a, b). Someone referring to city landmarks is more likely to call them by name when talking to people who are familiar with the city than to people who are not (Isaacs & Clark, 1987). In successive references to the same referents, speakers keep track of and utilize the mutual knowledge that has accumulated over the course of communication (Clark & Wilkes-Gibbs, 1986; Krauss & Glucksberg, 1977; Krauss & Weinheimer, 1966).

Audience design is the term used to describe the process by which speakers adapt messages to specific listeners. Research on this topic has generally focused on how the process is manifested in message formulation and the extent to which it facilitates message comprehension. Our contention is that speakers' efforts to formulate messages that are comprehensible to their listeners may have unintended consequences for the speakers' own cognitions.

The effects of audience design on a speaker's cognitions were tested in an experiment by Chiu et al. (in press) in which University of Hong Kong undergraduates described the shapes of 10 states of the United States either to a grade school child or to a college student. As expected, the descriptions were formulated in accordance with the audience's perceived characteristics. Four decoders then decoded the descriptions from each condition by matching the state to each description. Errors in matching the descriptions were used to construct a similarity matrix of the states for each condition, and the resulting similarity matrices were subject to separate multidimensional scaling. Participants were also presented with an incidental memory task for the states' shapes in which they were given the names of the 45 possible states pairs and asked to judge each pair's similarity from memory. Multidimensional scalings were performed on the memory-based similarity judgments from the two audience conditions. Multidimensional structure derived from the recall measure of participants in the grade school description conditions agreed highly with structures derived from those descriptions, but not with a structure derived from descriptions in the college student description condition. These results suggested that designing a message to communicate to a particular audience can affect subsequent representations of a referent in a speaker's memory.

Audience design can enhance the accessibility of cognitions that otherwise might be relatively inaccessible and by so doing can increase the influence of those cognitions. Ying and Lau obtained University of Hong Kong undergraduates' private evaluations of their school. Almost unanimously, students ranked the university as the best in Hong Kong, suggesting that negative cognitions about the school were relatively inaccessible in this population. Other undergraduates evaluated the school after having described their impressions of the school to themselves, to a student from another university, or to a reporter from a student publication notorious for its criticism of university policies. After describing their impression of the school to themselves or to a student from another university, participants' evaluations were highly positive. However, evaluations were markedly less positive after participants had conveyed their impressions to the reporter—on average, they ranked their school as the second best in Hong Kong. Communicating to a listener who was critical of the school appears to have activated participants' less accessible negative thoughts about the school and thereby lowered their evaluation of it. As in the Eiser experiments (Eiser & Pancer, 1979; Eiser & Ross, 1977), these induced changes were relatively short-lived. Asked to give their evaluations of the school one day later, participants in all experimental conditions gave highly positive evaluations.

Perlocutionary Intentions

Language is used communicatively to convey information, but it also is used to accomplish a number of additional purposes, among them the promoting intimacy and effecting a positive self-presentation (Higgins, 1981; Higgins, McCann, & Fondacaro, 1982). As Austin (1962) noted, in addition to their illocutionary force, utterances also have perlocutionary force (i.e., an effect on a listener). Typically, utterances are produced for the purpose of achieving such effects. As Krauss and Fussell (1996) have noted:

> Speakers formulate their utterances in order to accomplish particular ends, and the way an utterance is formulated will be very much a consequence

of the end it is intended to accomplish. ...[T]he communicative intention that underlies an utterance is itself a product of a more general goal toward which the speaker's behavior is oriented. It makes sense to think of a *perlocutionary intention* (an intention to accomplish some specific result by an act of speaking) as underlying the speaker's communicative intention (pp. 673).

The relation between message formulation and its perlocutionary significance is suggested by a series of studies by Maass, Semin, and their associates (Fiedler, Semin, & Finkenauer, 1993; Maass, Milesi, Zabbini & Stahlberg, 1995; Maass, Salvi, Arcuri, and Semin, 1989; Rubini & Semin, 1994), who asked participants to describe behavior of ingroup and outgroup members. Previous research had shown that people tend to see positive ingroup and negative outgroup behavior as caused by group members' dispositional qualities; conversely, they tend to perceive situational inducement as the cause of negative ingroup and positive outgroup behavior. These perceptual biases are reflected in the tendency to use more abstract verbtypes in describing undesirable outgroup and desirable ingroup behavior and more concrete verb types in describing desirable outgroup and undesirable ingroup behavior. Any particular instance of interpersonal behavior can typically be characterized in a variety of ways. As Semin, Fiedler, and associates have shown, describing concrete behavior using abstract linguistic categories attenuates the perceived causal contribution of situational factors and enhances the perceived causal contribution of dispositional factors (Semin & Fiedler, 1988; Semin & Greenslade, 1985).

Obviously, speakers try to formulate messages in a way that is consistent with their perlocutionary intentions. In a series of studies, Higgins and associates (e.g., Higgins & Rholes, 1978; McCann, Higgins, & Fondacaro, 1991) demonstrated how descriptions of a person varied with a listener's attitude towards that person. Participants in these experiments were provided with evaluatively ambiguous behavioral descriptions of a fictitious person named *Donald* and asked to convey their impression to a listener who either liked or disliked Donald. Not surprisingly, messages were biased to be evaluatively consistent with the listener's attitudes toward Donald. But shaping the message to accord with the listener's attitude also had cognitive consequences for the speaker. The speaker's subsequent recall of Donald's characteristics was distorted in the direction of the previously distorted message. It is important to note that participants had to verbalize their message for memory distortion to occur. The recall of participants who were prepared to verbalize their impressions but did not actually write a summary of them showed no such bias, suggesting that it is the actual *use* of language, not the *intention* to verbalize or communicate, that has cognitive consequences.

CONCLUSION

Research on communication has traditionally focused on how a listener is affected by a communicator's message. Such an approach conceptualizes communication as a process in which information is transferred from speakers to listeners through the medium of messages. Because the flow of information is unidirectional, so are its consequences.

Communication is, however, as Higgins (1981) puts it, a "purposeful social interaction occurring within a socially defined context, involving interdependent social roles and conventional rules, stratagems, and tactics for making decisions and obtaining various goals" (p. 346). In line with this view, we have discussed findings illustrating that speakers often take their listeners' perspectives, the nonreferent context, and their own perlocutionary intentions into consideration when formulating messages and that these factors, through their effects on message formulation, can create language-biased memory representations of the referent in a speaker. Not only can communication influence the informational environment of a listener, it also can modify a speaker's representation of the referent within and beyond the immediate communication situation.

The linguistic relativity hypothesis has been shrouded in controversy since it was initially proposed in the 1930s. Unfortunately, neither Benjamin Lee Whorf nor his mentor Edward Sapir attempted to describe the psychological mechanisms by which language influenced thought. Thus, research on this topic has traditionally fallen into one of two conceptual camps: One view, *linguistic determinism,* holds that the language one speaks determines one's perception of the world and a variety of cognitive processes (e.g., Hunt & Agnoli, 1991). The opposing position, *linguistic universalism,* contends that these cognitive processes are unaffected by language and invariant across speakers of different languages (e.g., Rosch, 1987). Yet, these two positions do not exhaust the possibilities for the relations of language and cognition, and we propose that a more productive approach would be to focus on the circumstances under which language has cognitive consequences.

Recently, investigators have begun to address the issue of *how* language could affect cognition (Hoosain, 1991; Hunt & Agnoli, 1991; Hunt & Banaji, 1988; Lau & Hoffman, in press; Semin, 1998). With a few exceptions (e.g., Semin, 1998), most of this research has focused on language as a medium of thought. The approach we have described in this chapter emphasizes another important function of language—its use for interpersonal communication—and attempts to explicate the effects of the communicative use of language on users' cognitive processes. We have examined three contextual constraints on language use (nonreferent context, audience design, and a speaker's perlocutionary intentions) and have considered how these factors can affect a speaker's subsequent cognitions via their influences on language use.

As speakers take their listeners' cognitions (knowledge, beliefs, attitudes, etc.) into consideration in an effort to produce messages that are relevant, appropriate, and comprehensible, the messages they formulate may create or evoke linguistic representations that differ from their private cognitions. The evidence seems clear that such representations can affect the way speakers later recall, think, and feel about the state of affairs under discussion. It is customary to regard communication as an orderly set of message exchanges through which participants come to affect how other participants think. In this chapter we have attempted to describe another way that participants are affected by communication—that is, by the consequences of producing messages. In an influential early essay on perspective-taking, Ragnar Rommetveit argued that even the simplest communicative act rests upon the participants' mutual commitment to "a temporarily shared social world" (1974, p. 29). The evidence we have reviewed suggests that a possible consequence of sharing another's social world, even temporarily, may be to change the nature of one's own world. It has frequently been noted (e.g., Krauss, 1968) that one function of language use is to make the contents of speakers' minds accessible to the minds of their listeners. The burden of the proposal presented in this chapter is that the lines of influence are not unidirectional: Using language to make the contents of speakers' minds accessible to others may force speakers to incorporate all or part of others' points of view into their own.

REFERENCES

Au, T. (1983). Chinese and English counterfactuals: The Sapir–Whorf hypothesis revisited. *Cognition, 15,* 155–187.

Au, T. (1984). Counterfactuals: In reply to Alfred Bloom. *Cognition, 17,* 289–302.

Austin, J. L. (1962). *How to do things with words.* Oxford, England: Oxford University Press.

Bloom, A. H. (1981). *The linguistic shaping of thought: A study in the impact of language on thinking in China and the West.* Hillsdale, NJ: Lawrence Erlbaum Associates.

Braine, L. G. (1968). Asymmetries of pattern perception observed in Israelis. *Neuropsychologia, 6,* 73–88.

Brown, R. (1976). Reference: In memorial tribute to Eric Lenneberg. *Cognition, 4,* 125–153.

Brown, R., & Lenneberg, E. (1954). A study in language and cognition. *Journal of Abnormal and Social Psychology, 49,* 454–462.

Carmichael, L., Hogan, H. P., & Walter, A. A. (1932). An experimental study of the effect of language on the reproduction of visually perceived form. *Journal of Experimental Psychology, 15,* 73–86.

Carroll, J. B., & Casagrande, J. B. (1958). The function of language classification in behavior. In E. E. Maccoby, T. R. Newcomb, & E. L. Hartley (Eds.), *Readings in social psychology* (3rd ed.). New York: Holt, Rinehart & Winston.

Chen, H. C., & Chen, M. J. (1988). Directional scanning in Chinese reading. In I. M. Liu, H. C. Chen, & M. J. Chen (Eds.), *Cognitive aspects of the Chinese language* (pp. 15–26). Hong Kong: Asian Research Service.

Chomsky, N. (1992). *Language and thought*. Wakefield, RI: Moyer Bell.

Clark, H. H., & Marshall, C. E. (1981). Definite reference and mutual knowledge. In A. K. Joshi, I. Sag, & B. Webber (Eds.), *Elements of discourse understanding*, (pp. 10–63). Cambridge, England: Cambridge University Press.

Clark, H. H., & Murphy, G. L. (1982). Audience design in meaning and reference. In J.-F. L. Ny & W. Kintsch (Eds.), *Language and comprehension*. New York: North Holland.

Clark, H. H., Schreuder, R., & Buttrick, S. (1983). Common ground and the understanding of demonstrative reference. *Journal of Verbal Learning and Verbal Behavior, 22,* 245–259.

Clark, H. H., & Wilkes-Gibbs, D. (1986). Referring as a collaborative process. *Cognition, 22,* 1–39.

Daniel, T. C. (1972). Nature of the effect of verbal labels on recognition memory for form. *Journal of Experimental Psychology, 96,* 152–157.

Eiser, J. R., & Pancer, S. M. (1979). Attitudinal effects of the use of evaluatively biased language. *European Journal of Social Psychology, 9,* 39–47.

Eiser, J. R., & Ross, M. (1977). Partisan language, immediacy, and attitude change. *European Journal of Social Psychology, 7,* 477–489.

Ellis, H. C., & Daniel, T. C. (1971). Verbal processes in long-term stimulus-recognition memory. *Journal of Experimental Psychology, 90,* 18–26.

Ellis, N. C., & Hennelly, R. A. (1980). A bilingual word-length effect: Implications for intelligence testing and the relative ease of mental calculation in Welsh and English. *British Journal of Psychology, 71,* 43–51.

Fallshore, M., & Schooler, J. W. (in press). The verbal vulnerability of perceptual expertise. *Journal of Experimental Psychology: Learning, Memory and Cognition.*

Fiedler, K., Semin, G. R., & Finkenauer, C. (1993). The battle of words between gender groups: A language-based approach to intergroup processes. *Human Communication Research, 19,* 409–441.

Fletcher, C. R. (1994). Levels of representation in memory for discourse. In M. A. Gernsbacher (Ed.), *Handbook of psycholinguistics* (pp. 589–607). New York: Academic Press.

Fussell, S. R., & Krauss, R. M. (1989a). The effects of intended audience on message production and comprehension: Reference in a common ground framework. *Journal of Experimental Social Psychology, 25,* 203–219.

Fussell, S., & Krauss, R. M. (1989b). Understanding friends and strangers: The effects of audience design on message comprehension. *European Journal of Social Psychology, 19,* 509–525.

Glucksberg, S. (1988). Language and thought. In R. S. Sternberg & E. E. Smith (Eds.), *The psychology of human thought*, (pp. 214–241). New York: Cambridge University Press.

Glucksberg, S., & Weisberg, R. W. (1963). Verbal behavior and problem solving: Some effects of labeling in a functional fixedness problem. *Journal of Experimental Psychology, 71,* 659–664.

Heider, E. R. (1972). Universals in color naming and memory. *Journal of Experimental Psychology, 93,* 10–20.

Heider, E. R., & Olivier, D. C. (1972). The structure of the color space in naming and memory for two languages. *Cognitive Psychology, 3,* 337–354.

Higgins, E., T. (1981). The "communication game": Implications for social cognition and communication. In E. T. Higgins, C. P. Herman, & M. P. Zanna (Eds.), *Social cognition: The Ontario symposium.* Hillsdale, NJ: Lawrence Erlbaum Associates.

Higgins, E. T., McCann, C. D., & Fondacaro, R. A. (1982). The "communication game": Goal-directed encoding and cognitive consequences. *Social Cognition, 1,* 21–37.

Higgins, E. T., & Rholes, W. S. (1978). "Saying is believing": Effects of message modification on memory and liking for the person described. *Journal of Experimental Social Psychology, 14,* 363–378.

Hoffman, C., Lau, I., & Johnson, D. R. (1986). The linguistic relativity of person cognition: An English-Chinese comparison. *Journal of Personality and Social Psychology, 51,* 1097–1105.

Hoosain, R. (1991). *Psycholinguistic implications for linguistic relativity: A case study of Chinese.* Hillsdale, NJ: Lawrence Erlbaum Associates.

Hoosain, R., & Salili, F. (1987). Language differences in pronunciation speed for numbers, digit span, and mathematical ability. *Psychologia, 30,* 34–38.

Hovland, C. I., & Weiss, W. (1951). The influence of source-credibility on communication effectiveness. *Public Opinion Quarterly, 15,* 635–650.

Hunt, E., & Agnoli, F. (1991). The Whorfian hypothesis: A cognitive psychology perspective. *Psychological Review, 98,* 377–389.

Hunt, E., & Banaji, M. R. (1988). The Whorfian hypothesis revisited: A cognitive science view of linguistic and cultural effects on thought. In J. W. Berry, S. H. Irvine, & E. B. Hunt (Eds.), *Indigenous cognition: Functioning in cultural context,* (pp. 57–84). Dordrecht, Netherlands: Martinus Nijhoff.

Hupet, M., Seron, X., & Chartraine, Y. (1991). The effects of the codability and discriminability of the referents on the collaborative referring process. *British Journal of Psychology, 82,* 449–462.

Isaacs, E. A., & Clark, H. H. (1987). References in conversation between experts and novices. *Journal of Experimental Psychology: General, 116,* 26–37.

Kahneman, D., & Tversky, A. (1984). Choices, values, and frames. *American Psychologist, 39,* 341–350.

Kay, P., & Kempton, W. (1984). What is the Sapir–Whorf hypothesis? *American Anthropologist, 86,* 65–79.

Kintsch, W., Welsch, D., Schmalhofer, F., & Zimny, S. (1990). Sentence recognition: A theoretical analysis. *Journal of Memory and Language, 29,* 133–159.

Klatzky, R. L., Martin, G. L., Kane, R. A. (1982). Semantic interpretation effects on memory for faces. *Memory and Cognition, 10,* 195–206.

Krauss, R. M. (1968). Language as a symbolic process in communication. *American Scientist, 56,* 265–278.

Krauss, R. M., & Fussell, S. R. (1996). Social psychological models of interpersonal communication. In E. T. Higgins & A. Kruglanski (Eds.), *Social psychology: Handbook of basic principles* (pp. 655–701). New York: Guilford.

Krauss, R. M., & Glucksberg, S. (1977). Social and nonsocial speech. *Scientific American, 236,* 100–105.

Krauss, R. M., & Weinheimer, S. (1966). Concurrent feedback, confirmation and the encoding of referents in verbal communication. *Journal of Personality and Social Psychology, 4,* 343–346.

Kugelmass, S., & Lieblich, A. (1970). Perceptual exploration in Israeli children. *Child Development, 41,* 1125–1131.

Lantz, D., & Stefflre, V. (1964). Language and cognition revisited. *Journal of Abnormal and Social Psychology, 69,* 472–481.

Lau, I., & Hoffman, C. (in press). Accountability, cognitive busyness, and the linguistic relativity hypothesis: Attentional and motivational effects on the linguistic shaping of thought. *Social Cognition.*

Levin, I. P., Schnittjer, S. K., & Thee, S. L. (1988). Information framing effects in social and personal decisions. *Journal of Experimental Social Psychology, 24,* 520–529.

Lucy, J. A., & Shweder, R. A. (1979). Whorf and his critics: Linguistic and nonlinguistic influences on color memory. *American Anthropologist, 81,* 581–615.

Lucy, J. A., & Shweder, R. A. (1988). The effect of incidental conversation on memory for focal colors. *American Anthropologist, 90,* 923–931.

Maass, A., Milesi, A., Zabbini, S., & Stahlberg, D. (1995). Linguistic intergroup bias: Differential expectancies or in-group protection? *Journal of Personality and Social Psychology, 68,* 116–126.

Maass, A., Salvi, D., Arcuri, L., & Semin, G. R. (1989). Language use in intergroup contexts: The linguistic intergroup bias. *Journal of Personality and Social Psychology, 38,* 689–703.

Mani, K., & Johnson-Laird, P. N. (1982). The mental representation of spatial descriptions. *Memory and Cognition, 10,* 181–187.

McCann, C. D., Higgins, E. T., & Fondacaro, R. A. (1991). Primacy and recency in communication and self-persuasion: How successive audiences and multiple encodings influence subsequent judgments. *Social Cognition, 9,* 47–66.

Morrow, D. G., Greenspan, S. L., & Bower, G. H. (1987). Accessibility and situation models in narrative comprehension. *Journal of Memory and Language, 26,* 165–187.

Naveh-Benjamin, M., & Ayres, T. J. (1986). Digit span, reading rate, and linguistic relativity. *Quarterly Journal of Experimental Psychology, 38A,* 739–751.

Northcraft, G. B., & Neale, M. A. (1986). Opportunity costs and the framing of resource allocation decisions. *Organizational Behavior and Human Decision Processes, 37,* 348–356.

Paivio, A. (1986). *Mental representations: A dual coding approach.* Oxford, England: Oxford University Press.

Perrig, W., & Kintsch, W. (1985). Propositional and situational representation of text. *Journal of Memory and Language, 24,* 503–518.

Pinker, S. (1994). *The language instinct.* New York: Morrow.

Rommetveit, R. (1974). *On message structure: A framework for the study of language and communication.* New York: Wiley.

Rosch, E. (1987). Linguistic relativity. *Et cetera, 44,* 254–279.

Rubini, M., & Semin, G. R. (1994). Language use in the context of congruent and incongruent in-group behaviors. *British Journal of Social Psychology, 33,* 355–362.

Schooler, J. W., & Engstler-Schooler, T. Y. (1990). Visual overshadowing of visual memories: Some things are better left unsaid. *Cognitive Psychology, 22,* 36–71.

Schmalhofer, F., & Glavanov, D. (1986). Three components of understanding a programmer's manual: Verbatim, propositional, and situational representations. *Journal of Memory and Language, 25,* 279–294.

Semin, G. R. (1998). Cognition, Language, and Communication. In S. R. Fussell & R. J. Kreuz (Eds.), *Social and cognitive approaches to interpersonal communication.* Mahwah, NJ: Lawrence Erlbaum Associates.

Semin, G. R., & Fiedler, K. (1988). The cognitive functions of linguistic categories in describing persons: Social cognition and language. *Journal of Personality and Social Psychology, 54,* 558–568.

Semin, G. R., & Greenslade, L. (1985). Differential contributions of linguistic factors to memory-based ratings: Systematizing the systematic distortion hypothesis. *Journal of Personality and Social Psychology, 49,* 1713–1723.

Van Dijk, T., & Kintsch, W. (1983*). Strategies of discourse comprehension.* New York: Academic Press.

Whorf, B. L. (1956). *Language, thought, and reality: Selected writings of Benjamin Lee Whorf.* New York: Wiley.

Wilkes-Gibbs, D., & Kim, P. H. (1991*). Discourse influences on memory for visual forms.* Paper presented at the meeting of The Psychonomic Society, San Francisco, CA.

Wilson, T. D., Dunn, D. S., Kraft, D., & Lisle, D. J. (1989). Introspection, attitude change, and attitude-behavior consistency: The disruptive effects of explaining why we feel the way we do. *Advances in Experimental Social Psychology, 222,* 287 343.

Wilson, T. D., Hodges, S. D., & LaFleur, S. J. (1995). Effects of introspecting about reasons: Inferring attitudes from accessible thoughts. *Journal of Personality and Social Psychology, 69,* 16–28.

Wilson, T. D., Lisle, D. J., Schooler, J. W., Hodges, S. D., Klaaren, K. J., &LaFleur, S. J. (1993). Introspecting about reasons can reduce post-choice satisfaction. *Personality and Social Psychology Bulletin, 19,* 331–339.

Wilson, T. D.., & Schooler, J. W. (1991). Thinking too much: Introspection can reduce the quality of preferences and decisions. *Journal of Personality and Social Psychology, 60,* 181–192.

AUTHOR INDEX

SUBJECT INDEX

—A—

Adjacency pairs, 78
Adjectives, 12, 123, 192–193, 236–238, 253
Affect, *See Emotion*
Affordance theory, 12, 203, 231–232, 234–235, 243–245, 247, 249, 251
Anger, communication of, 35, 116–118, 120, 123–125, 127, 129, 134, 238
Attitudes, 13, 21, 94, 107, 150, 152, 245, 263, 265
  effects of language on, 270
  effects on message production, 270
  expression in surveys, 45–46, 56,
  verbalization of, 266
Audience, 30, 41, 153, 191, 197
  effect on communication, 21, 268, 271–272

—B—

Background knowledge, 10–11, 152, 154
Behavior, 39, 49–51, 60, 62, 115, 130, 135, 171, 176, 180, 208, 233, 238, 240, 244
Biases, 39, 43–44, 53, 55–56, 60–61, 271

—C—

Clarifications, requests for, 39, 42–43, 45, 47, 78, 94, 118, 121, 128, 193, 214, 222

Clinical, 114, 124, 245
Codability, effects on memory and cognition, 263–264
Cognition, 39, 58, 66, 113, 115–118, 126, 135, 152, 177, 187, 193–194, 227,
  relationship between language and, 3, 229–230, 238, 243, 245–246, 248, 259, 265, 270–271
Cognitive processes, 239, 251
  in TATUM, 247
  in verb-mediated inferences, 243
Collaboration, 26, 73, 120–121, 130, 160, 163–165, 192, 194, 202
Collaborative Theory of communication, 7, 11, 193
Collectivism, 84–85
Common ground, 24, 25, 41–43, 56, 109, 154, 158, 165, 180, 193–195, 201–202, 210, 215, 220, 268, *See also Mutual Knowledge*
  between author and reader, 29
  grounding processes, 11, 42, 202–209, 212, 214, 219, 221
  in human–computer interaction, 202
Communication, 39, 55, 61, 71–72, 79, 91, 98, 104, 109, 113–114, 118, 120–121, 124, 128, 132–134, 146, 176, 179–180, 184, 186, 188–189, 202, 220, 230, 233–234, 243, 245–246, 249
  as collaborative action, 202
  as goal-directed activity, 6
  effects of audience on, 21, 30, 34, 41, 153, 191, 197, 268, 269, 271